UNDERSTANDING

B
2
B

MATTHEW FRIEDMAN AND MARLENE BLANSHAY

Senior Acquisitions Editor: Jean Iversen Cook
Senior Managing Editor: Jack Kiburz
Cover design: Sputnik Art + Design Inc.
Interior design and layout: Kyle Gell Design

Published by Dearborn Trade, a Kaplan Professional Company.

Printed in Canada

01 02 03 10 9 8 7 6 5 4 3 2 1

Library of Congress Cataloging-in-Publication Data

Friedman, Matthew.
    Understanding B2B / Matthew Friedman and Marlene Blanshay.
        p. cm.
Includes index.
ISBN 0-7931-4489-2 (6x9 hardcover)
1. Electronic commerce. I. Title.
HF5548.32 .F74 2001
658.8'4 — dc21   2001000044

Change begets change. Nothing propagates so fast.
—Charles Dickens

Men are only as good as their
technical development allows them to be.
—George Orwell

I always begin at the left with the opening word of the sentence
and read toward the right and I recommend this method.
—James Thurber

CONTENTS

ACKNOWLEDGMENTS

This book began with a short e-mail message in the spring of 2000. It snowballed into several months of intense, often frustrating, but always rewarding work. We would like to acknowledge the help we received from the editorial staff at Macmillan Canada and from the Electronic Commerce Group at Queen's University's School of Business. Above all, we want to thank Andrew Winton, whose e-mail got the book started and whose guidance and support kept it going.

FOREWORD

I like this book. I like it because it blends vision and practicality, bits and atoms, business and technology, the past and the future. Plus—it's fun to read.

The e-business PR machine has raged in high gear, and many books reflect the hype—in fact, they amplify it. Now, I'm as much of a believer in the vision of e-business as the next person—but, I also expect that we are but five years into a fifteen-year transition. And now that the dot-com bubble has burst, we can settle down to the practical realities of making e-business happen with the help of books like this one. Matthew Friedman and Marlene Blanshay show us both the possible—the vision—*and* the practical realities of achieving an e-business vision.

Chapter 4 is introduced by the wonderful observation, "You don't tend to think of locomotives and Web servers in the same sentence..." At some point, e-commerce has to make the change from moving bits around the Internet to moving atoms around physical geography. Many dot-coms faltered on this transition, and it is one area in which traditional "brick" organizations have shown the "click" organizations a thing or two. I appreciate the authors' foray into Logistics—managing the movement of physical goods around the world—as a vital part of e-commerce.

Pick one: Business will never be the same; Business is just business. Caught up in the euphoria of the "New Economy," quite a few pundits have explained how business will never be the same and how executives must relearn everything. Conversely, many critics of the New Economy attempt to derail the juggernaut by decrying it as technological mumbo-jumbo and insisting that the fundamentals of business haven't changed. The authors provide keen insight into both sides of this issue, with examples of how both statements are true and how they are false, and therein help us steer through the morass of conflicting advice.

The New Economy didn't spring miraculously from the ether when IBM coined the word "e-business" in 1997. I've always enjoyed history— it provides a context in which to interpret the present and envision the future. I therefore like the way the authors mix historical perspectives and current topics. The supply chain discussion, for example, provides perspective on the current hot topic of XML by first delving into the history of EDI—and how EDI will continue to be important even as the transition to XML occurs. The authors suggest that success in the New Economy will not come from excising all memories prior to 1997, but from blending a sense of history and the best of the New Economy into a powerful vision for the future.

Finally, and maybe most importantly, I like this book because it's fun to read. I can't even count the number of well-publicized e-business books relegated to my "started-but-not-finished" pile because they are just terminally boring. Not this book. Read it to find out about "fecund rabbits," the Burgess Shale, or the relationship between B2B commerce and Western line-dancing. The authors blend facts and stories, big pictures and details, people and events—and a little humor—in such a way that you are drawn into reading further.

Understanding B2B will provide some common ground to help CEOs, CIOs (and quite a few people who work for them), as they forge ahead into the New Economy quagmire.

Jim Highsmith, Director, E-Project Management Practice; Fellow, Cutter Technology Council, Cutter Consortium and author of *Adaptive Software Development: A Collaborative Approach to Managing Complex Systems*

February 2001, Salt Lake City, UT

INTRODUCTION

Tom Bruce had a message for the Internet cognoscenti who gathered in May 1994 for a conference called "The Electronic Superhighway: The Shape of Technology and Law to Come." The Net, he said, was about to undergo a profound transformation. "No one here wants to admit it, but the Internet is going to go commercial," Bruce said, "and pretty soon." The high-tech guru at Cornell University's on-line Legal Information Institute, and creator of Cello, the first graphical Web browser for the PC, Bruce had been watching the growing popularity of all things Internet with a combination of fascination and relish. But there was also a vague sense of alarm. "It's happening because the Internet is going to the dogs."

"Going to the dogs" was a new shorthand for the transformation the Internet was undergoing. Just a few months earlier, *The New Yorker* ran its celebrated cartoon featuring a pair of precocious canines at a computer. "On the Internet," one says to the other, "nobody knows you're a dog." That cartoon, more than anything else, marks the exact moment that the Internet penetrated the North American public consciousness. In his presentation to the conference, Bruce noted that the Internet community, at least the old guard from the universities, research facilities, and high-technology campuses of North America, had begun to refer to the golden age of the Net — a mythical, heroic epoch when the Internet was free, anarchic, and not yet commercialized — as the time "before the dogs." Even in 1994, some hoped to hold back the tide of common canines who knew nothing of the Internet's 25-year history. But Bruce said it was inevitable, and with the arrival of the dogs, the Internet itself, now referred to in the media as the "Information Superhighway," would change. "The [media] focus on the information superhighway means that the number of people sharing the same dataspace is going to increase exponentially," Bruce said. "And that means that the dataspace itself will change."

Looking back, it's hard to imagine a time when the Internet *wasn't* a commercial medium. At the beginning of the 21st century, it has not only become, as Bruce expected, a place where people do business, it is becoming *the* place where they do business. The old guard's legendary distaste for the term "Information Superhighway" — it seemed, at the time, to be little more than government PR hot air — seems somehow appropriate today. The Internet has become less a highway than the world's virtual Wall Street, Bay Street, and Main Street. Every advertisement, billboard, and beer label bears a URL; Internet banking and online shopping have become commonplace; soon-to-be-married couples and expectant parents can even register their preferences at any of a dozen on-line gift registries.

It's abundantly clear that we're in the middle of an electronic commerce revolution, surging forward on the crest of the Internet wave, and the consumer side is only part, a relatively minor part, of it. The real news isn't how much easier it is to buy books or CDs on the Internet, but how the Net and electronic commerce have begun to revolutionize the relationships between companies. Local businesses have gone global, regional distributors are shipping to resellers on the other side of the world, manufacturers are turning out products built to their customers' exact specifications — updated in real time over secure network connections. All the old financial, logistical, and managerial assumptions of traditional business have been swept aside by the new realities of something called "e-business."

Indeed, along with its new capabilities, economies, and advantages, the electronic commerce revolution has brought uncertainty and confusion. Fully 75 percent of the corporate chief executives surveyed for the A.T. Kearney study *Strategic Information Technology and the CEO Agenda,* released in August 2000, said that they expect e-business to have an "impact" on their products, and almost all of them said that they expect information technologies to play a "significant role in the future success of their business."[1] The problem is that the *expectations* of e-business are not quite matched with the executives' understanding of how to *use* all that technology. In fact, no less than 43 percent of the sample group conceded that they had yet to integrate their e-business strategies with their companies' overall business plans. In effect, everyone knows this stuff is important, but almost half don't know where to go from there.

That's not surprising. It's all happening so quickly, and the pace of technological change is so accelerated, that even technology specialists have trouble keeping up. Decisions have foundered on innovation, its constant companion obsolescence, and a constant and changing stream of jargon and acronyms. What's *really* important, CRM, EIPs, ERP, or XML? (Don't worry about the alphabet soup, we'll explain all those acronyms throughout the book.) How do you do business in the information age when you haven't quite figured out the distinction between e-business and business-to-business electronic commerce? And is it even about *business* at all anymore?

In fact, the only differences between e-business and business-to-business electronic commerce are arbitrary and academic. It's pointless to talk about business at all without discussing the relationships between partners and suppliers. It's just as absurd to describe how those relationships have been enabled, accelerated, and amplified by computers, software, and networks without talking about the impact of those technologies *within* the enterprise. In fact, the bottom line is that e-business, or B2B, or whatever you choose to call it, isn't really about technology at all. It's about business — in fact, it's *only* about business. For all of the excitement over the Internet and the hype surrounding every succeeding technological innovation, electronic commerce is commerce, pure and simple. Enabling a well-run, competitive business with electronic commerce technologies makes it a world-beater; enabling a poorly run, uncompetitive business with the same technologies will probably make it fail more quickly, and on a global scale. "Either every business model boils down to the same one that my great-grandfather used in his dry goods store in

Brooklyn, or they don't hold water at all," observed Peter Fader of the University of Pennsylvania's Wharton School of Business. "And that idea is: bring in visitors, have them buy, have them come back and buy again, and have them buy more stuff. And that's the way to do things."

Having said that, commerce in the age of the Internet, instant global communications, artificial intelligence, and automated production lines is something new — and it's inescapable. Even the gritty world of low-tech business, like logging and fishing, has found its way onto the Internet. E-business has fundamentally transformed all business; it's a whole new ball game. Your partners, as well as your competitors, may be at the end of a global supply chain, on another continent. You may never actually *speak* to your customers. Even the distinction between big business and small business has begun to crumble, as a virtual corporation with a few dozen employees can have tens of millions of dollars of annual sales and command influence beyond the wildest dreams of the erstwhile captains of industry.

The present book may not be the definitive work on doing e-business in the information age; it can't be. *That* book will never be written. Electronic commerce can no more be summed up in a few hundred, or even a thousand, pages than can commerce itself. Neither is this book a how-to manual, taking you step-by-step through the process of setting up an e-business. What we hope is that this book will provide a guide to the central issues of business-to-business electronic commerce, and perhaps an answer to the question "What does this all mean to me?" Our goal is to put the technologies into the context of business strategy, to provide a foundation for what so many of the executives surveyed in the A.T. Kearney report found lacking — an integration of the *expectations* of electronic commerce with the hard-nosed realities of business strategy in the real world.

In other words, this book is *about* understanding B2B.

To achieve that goal — ambitious as it is — we have sought out the freshest research and the informed opinions and observations of the leading minds and top players in the world of electronic commerce.

Moreover, we have drawn on the experience and expertise of a panel of some of North America's top electronic commerce theorists, strategists, and scholars, ranging from solutions providers to academics and analysts, to focus on and profile the key strategic questions and issues raised in the main section of this book. They are Sandy Jap of MIT's Sloan School of Management, Anindya Datta of the iXL Center for E-Commerce at the Georgia Institute of Technology, author and legal expert Sunny Handa, Robert Thibadeau of Carnegie Mellon University's eCommerce Institute, Piyush Bhatnagar and Colin Davies of Accenture, Gary Allen of Cap Gemini Ernst & Young, Marco Argenti of Microforum, and Wharton's Dr. Fader. They have helped us put the issues of business-to-business electronic commerce in their proper context.

Finally, in *Understanding B2B,* we have endeavored to keep our focus global, rather than settling for the comfortable familiarity of local markets and local experience. Today, in the early years of the 21st century, we are doing business in the first truly global economy in human history, and electronic commerce is, almost by definition, a global phenomenon; what happens in North America — or in the European community or the Pacific Rim — inevitably has a profound effect on electronic commerce everywhere. Understanding that is the first step to understanding B2B. As Tom Bruce observed in 1994, "The Internet is everywhere, or it will be soon. That, alone, could be a big attraction to business. It means I can do business anywhere from anywhere — and we're only seeing the very beginning."

REAL BUSINESS IN
VIRTUAL SPACE

FIRST STEPS

"If you're not an active Internet citizen by the mid-1990s," wrote analyst and Internet evangelist Patricia Seybold in 1994, "you're likely to be out of business by the turn of the century."[1] It was both a promise and a threat. It was a challenge to North American business to catch the coming technological tsunami and, as self-evident as her words seem today, the whole idea that the Internet would soon be the single most important medium for North American commerce was vaguely preposterous in 1994.

Seybold observed at the time that corporate managers were frankly afraid of the Internet — and for good reason. "It looks like an undisciplined universe of hackers just waiting to besiege their corporate systems and waste their employees' time."[2] Indeed, the Internet was still a peripheral network, populated mainly by university researchers, computer geeks, and graduate students. It may have been well known and used by engineers in defense-oriented industries, but the Internet was far from a business priority. It was far-fetched to talk about using the

Internet for anything aside from e-mail at the time, let alone electronic commerce, and to suggest that its use might someday be the sine qua non of business success was vaguely absurd.

Yet, even before 1994, things had begun to change. In 1986, even before the word "Internet" had become a household word, the National Science Foundation deployed its then-blazingly fast 56 kbps backbone. By the following year, there was sufficient — though still marginal — interest for Rick Adams and Mike O'Dell to offer commercial access to Usenet, a public discussion system carried on the Internet. The World, the first commercial Internet access provider, opened the floodgates in Boston in 1990. In 1991, Tim Berners-Lee developed the World Wide Web for CERN, the European nuclear physics research organization. The Web was originally intended as a medium for physicists to publish and exchange research notes, but then the National Center for Supercomputing Applications released the Mosaic Web browser in 1993. Internet users could now "surf" — a term coined in 1992 — using a simple point-and-click graphical interface. The Internet became easy to use, and its explosive growth took off.

As Seybold observed, and as Cornell's Tom Bruce suspected, 1994 was the year the Internet got real. The best measure of how real was the way, in the following 12 months, business began to stake out its claim to virtual real estate. The Bank of First Virtual opened, providing a credit card proxy service for the expected surge of Internet-based commerce. Users would register their credit cards with the "bank," which would then charge their account for purchases made at participating Web sites. The "bank" never caught on, but the surge came anyway, and before the year was out, you could buy everything from pizzas at an on-line Pizza Hut to Pinot Blanc at Virtual Vineyard.

Before "the dogs," Internet users had been a relatively small, often anarchic community generally hostile to the merest whiff of commercialism. Writing of the etiquette — or netiquette — of posting public messages to Usenet, Brendan Kehoe in *Zen and the Art of the Internet* observed in 1992, "There is a Usenet custom of keeping commercial traffic to a minimum. If such commercial traffic is generally considered worth carrying, then it may be grudgingly tolerated."[3] That tolerance was sorely tested in April 1994 when the Arizona law firm Canter & Siegel flooded all 5,000 Usenet forums with messages promoting its immigration and green card services. Within hours, outraged Internet users fired back with 35,000 flames — angry messages — to the firm's single e-mail address. In 1994, commercial advertising on the Internet was still a touchy subject.

It shouldn't be surprising, then, that the first successful commercial ventures on the Internet were focused directly on the consumer market and on products near and dear to the average Internet user's heart. Indeed, in the same year that Canter & Siegel were flamed, the first company set up shop on the Web. Maybe because of the then-typical Internet user's insatiable appetite for science fiction and fantasy literature, Palo Alto's Future Fantasy Bookstore fared much better in its first tentative foray into electronic commerce. "I didn't know anything about it and I didn't expect anything," recalled owner Jean Schroeder. "Electronic commerce certainly wasn't what it is now. Someone said, 'Do you want to do this?' and I said, 'Sure.' It's not like I had a lot to lose."

But she had everything to gain. Future Fantasy's on-line store was quiet at first; it took about a month for the word to get around to the small Internet community. "Then it took off," Schroeder said. "Within two or three months, it was about one-third of our business. There were all of these people who wanted to shop here, but couldn't get to where we were geographically located."

In fact, the first commercial steps onto the Internet were more full of promise than any expectation of immediate market gain. But entrepreneurs — particularly small-business people — were definitely attracted by the promise. The Net allowed them to think locally and operate globally. Merchants in out-of-the-way places like Nome, Alaska, or Halifax, Canada, could sell in any market served by the Internet. In any event, that was the theory. At the time, Roswell James, a Halifax-based bookseller, marveled at the fact that he could sell across the border into the

United States, and he liked to talk about a customer in Oslo who ordered books from his store.

One of the first e-commerce superstars was Virtual Vineyards (now Wine.com). Co-founder Peter Granoff recalled that, in the mid-1990s, the promise of Internet commerce was just too tempting to ignore. "Things were converging," he said. "My brother-in-law [co-founder Robert Olson] was a software engineer, and he was convinced that the Internet was a great business opportunity. The problem was that he had no idea what he might sell. He had no idea he was going into the wine business."

Nevertheless, as with science fiction books, the Internet was, in Granoff's opinion, a fertile market for fine wine. "It made sense that the people who had computers were professionals or they had disposable income," he said. "Those are the kind of people who buy wine." More importantly, the Internet offered a means of getting around the ossified and moribund distribution channels of the traditional wine industry. Granoff had built a career as a wine buyer in northern California, and he had become concerned that the old way of doing things simply didn't work. He wanted a new way. "I had been watching distribution problems multiplying in the wine industry," he said. "I saw the Internet as an opportunity to get around them, and a way to do something new."

The first on-line offerings were typically crude efforts that employed the text-based Gopher interface and e-mail, and relatively simplistic Web sites. They most certainly didn't employ real-time transaction processing. Michael Strangelove, the publisher of the *Internet Business Journal,* one of the first e-business newsletters, may have been a little over-enthusiastic about the immediate prospects of Internet commerce. Merchants like Roswell James were set to take on the world, he said at the time. "Internet users don't need glossy come-ons to be attracted to a product or an idea," he said. "What they need is a good product marketed by a responsive company that'll be there on the Net if they ever have any questions or need support."

As naïve as that seems today, Strangelove nevertheless hit on one of the fundamental truths of the new, then-emerging electronic commerce paradigm. Even as the electronic commerce revolution was just beginning, the business imperative to explore the new medium was already reaching a pitch. The commercial benefits may not have been immediately apparent, but it was already essential for companies "to create an on-line profile, and get involved in the day-to-day activities of the Internet community," Strangelove said in 1994. "There's little doubt now that astute and imaginative business people will be able to market to hundreds of millions of people on the Net by the end of the decade."

In Business and On-line

In the years since Seybold's challenge, the Internet has, indeed, become the sine qua non of business success. At the dawn of the 21st century, it would actually be possible to make the case that, if you're not on the Internet, and if you're not at least exploring electronic commerce, you're probably not serious about being successful. Electronic commerce may not be a wholly new idea — one that sprang full-grown from the head of Zeus in 1994 — but, coupled with the Internet, it has achieved a momentum that promises to fundamentally transform business.

The Internet has changed everything, providing a cheap and effective medium for vendors to reach markets anywhere in the world and giving buyers — whether they're businesses or consumers — access to a virtual feast of suppliers. The growth of electronic commerce is staggering. According to International Data Corp., the volume of global Internet commerce was expected to rise from $15.4 billion in 1997 to $272 billion in 2000, and $2.6 trillion in 2004. The media stars of electronic commerce, of course, are household names like Amazon.com and Granoff's Wine.com. They're building their fortunes, and their media cachet, on a booming business-to-consumer market. Indeed, according to Giga Information Group, retail electronic commerce is racking up some impressive numbers, growing from $25 billion in 1999 to an expected $233 billion in 2004.

However, retail is just the beginning. The real action is business to business. If only $233 billion of electronic commerce spending will be done by consumers in 2004, who is spending the rest of the $2.6 trillion? The answer, of course, is companies. Business-to-business electronic commerce — the sale of goods and services between companies over data networks — utterly dwarfs business-to-consumer commerce in real and projected spending and growth, and it's light years from where it was in 1994. Internet transactions are fueling the boom by enabling more businesses to get on-line, and by emancipating them from the expense and investment in time required by older electronic commerce technologies like Electronic Data Interchange (EDI). "A few years ago e-commerce was limited to EDI," said Joe Greene, a senior analyst at IDC Research. "Doing electronic commerce over the Net has made it simpler and easier for businesses to use. It's efficient and cheap, and the trend is likely to continue."

As the Internet attracts more businesses on-line, business-to-business electronic commerce is set to grow exponentially. Analysts expect the boom to just keep booming. In March 2000, the Gartner Group said the business-to-business explosion was imminent and predicted the worldwide market would grow from $145 billion in 1999 to $953 billion in 2001 and $2.18 trillion in 2002. The Boston Consulting Group was even more bullish, projecting 33 percent annual growth between 1998 and 2003, reaching $2.8 trillion in transaction value for business-to-business electronic commerce in the United States alone.

The simple fact is that we're poised on the brink of a period of electronic commerce hypergrowth. High-tech industries have been moving ever closer to the center of the U.S. economy since the 1980s. If the beating high-technology stocks took on Wall Street proved anything, it is how dependent our economy has become on software, microchips, and semiconductors. While there's no doubt that the "new economy's" IPO phenoms like Red Hat and Palm Computing are probably overvalued, the collateral impact of their stock market tribulations was stunning proof of how important they have become.

America has both the brains and the technological brawn for a widespread adoption of electronic commerce technologies. According to the Boston-based Gartner Group, America is becoming wired at an almost incredible rate. By the end of 2000, half of all American homes already had access to the Internet, and the number is expected to rise to 75 percent by 2005. At the same time, the Cahners In-Stat Group, an IT market research firm based in Scottsdale, Arizona, found that 70 percent of American workers had access to the Web at work in 2000 and that 85 percent would by 2004. The Internet is becoming a familiar household tool and, as Patricia Seybold predicted, it has become the way businesses do business.

Americans, Canadians, Europeans, Japanese, and Indians are buying more and more software, equipment, and services than ever. According to the Department of Commerce's Bureau of Economic Analysis (BEA), software companies racked up $256 billion in sales in the United States alone in 1999 — a 24 percent increase over 1998 and more than double the amount for 1995. Moreover, it's not just Americans who want to buy the latest and greatest technology. U.S. high-tech exports have grown at a breakneck pace, feeding an increasingly wired and technology-hungry world. According to the BEA, computer and telecommunications-related equipment and accessories accounted for $123 billion in exports from the United States in 1999, up almost 11 percent over the previous year.[4] In 1998, U.S. providers exported almost $4 billion in computer and information services to the rest of the world.[5] And it's a global phenomenon; in the same year, the United States imported more than $8 billion in telecommunications services. The high-tech economies of Europe, Canada, and a recovering Asia are just as hot, mutually fueling technological innovation as the ties that bind the global economy grow tighter.

There's a kind of cascade effect in all this activity. Innovations beget other innovations, new industries beget ancillary industries, high-tech companies give rise to other high-tech companies to complement and supplement their offerings, and where one company succeeds, ten more emerge to get a piece of the action. Moreover, as early adopters deploy the latest and greatest technologies — the successful ones, at any rate — to gain a competitive edge, they force their partners to keep up. Technology adoption ripples from one tier to the next. "Think of it as an ecosystem," IDC's Greene explained. "The large suppliers are forcing their partners to get on-line by effectively saying, 'Do it electronically or not at all.' They're finding it's easier to do it that way and eventually their suppliers and partners move to electronic commerce."

The stage is set for an electronic commerce explosion that Cambridge, Massachusetts-based Forrester Research said will account for 8.6 percent of all global commerce by 2004. North American businesses have led the way in adopting business-to-business electronic commerce technologies. The continent is the heartland of the high-technology revolution, and its highly trained and educated workforce and robust, high-speed telecommunications infrastructure have made it fertile ground for electronic commerce. In a November 2000 study, ActivMedia Research, based in Peterborough, New Hampshire, found that fully half of all American businesses already purchase on the Internet.

Manufacturing, petroleum, cultural and information industries, and utilities are in the vanguard of the business-to-business revolution. "B2B is penetrating all vertical market segments, with manufacturing on the leading edge," said Jim Westcott, senior analyst at IDC Research. "Specifically, process manufacturing, primary resources, and other vertical industries such as transportation and logistics. Primary industries are interested in getting their products to market, and using an integrated supply chain with e-commerce means they can get it there faster." And that means cutting costs. According to Westcott, cutting costs is one of the factors behind the business-to-business boom. "It boils down to saving money and making money," he said. "E-commerce also helps you make money by enabling you to sell on a global basis and reach new marketplaces."

It's an attractive promise, and businesses have been willing to invest the time, resources, and money necessary to see it fulfilled. Electronic commerce is rapidly becoming the main priority of corporate IT spending. AMR Research in Boston predicts that the proportion of IT budgets spent on electronic commerce services and applications will rise from 19 percent in 2000 to 23 percent in 2002. In 1997, U.S. companies spent $2.9 billion on electronic commerce services and products, according to IDC Research, and that total is expected to rise to $2.1 billion by 2002 — almost an eight-fold increase in *five years!* And it's not just a question of throwing money at product vendors, Westcott said. Businesses are using the products they buy more efficiently than they did five years ago, with planned implementations and real strategies for Internet commerce. "Businesses are integrating their front- and back-end, supply chain, inventory, demand, transportation," Westcott said. "They are beginning to see it as a whole, rather than just implementing software and then doing something else, or doing nothing."

It didn't take long for Internet commerce to evolve from something an obscure bookseller did because she had nothing to lose, to become the main mode of global commerce. It might not be an overstatement to observe that, in less than a decade, commerce has *become* electronic commerce, and that business has *become* e-business. Nevertheless, it's a mistake to imagine that the revolution in electronic commerce happened overnight. Indeed, it would not have happened so quickly — and maybe not at all — if there had not already been a firm technological and commercial foundation laid decades before.

THE B2B FOUNDATION

The roots of business-to-business electronic commerce stretch back a long way, but the real foundation was laid with the establishment of the electronic data interchange (EDI) standard and the development of electronic funds transfer (EFT) technology in the 1960s and 1970s. For all the innovations in networking and electronic commerce in the decades since then, EDI and EFT remain the foundation of the electronic business-to-business relationship.

GROUND ZERO

Everything has to begin somewhere. However, in the case of electronic commerce, the starting point is almost impossible to pin down.

A case could be made for its relative antiquity. The first transcontinental telegraph network was deployed in the United States in the 1860s, and it was put to commercial use almost immediately. Within a decade, Western Union was offering financial wire transfers and up-to-the-minute stock ticker information from Wall Street. Of course, no one called it electronic commerce at the time — a "marvel of the modern age" perhaps, but not "electronic commerce." That term didn't enter the business lexicon for more than a century. In that time, trading empires rose and fell, the world economy was transformed from colonial mercantilism to a global market, and the scale and speed of commerce increased incalculably, driven largely by data processing, the emergence of computers, and, finally, the technology of remote networking.

Electronic commerce would not exist at all if the mechanical devices Allied code-breakers used to decipher Nazi secrets hadn't found their way into business immediately after World War II. The line of descent is perfectly straight from the Bletchley Park Colossi — electromechanical calculating machines — to ENIAC and EDSAC, the first digital computers, and then to the UNIVAC and IBM 701, the first computers to make their way into business offices. These early machines could only perform batch functions, like database matching and complex mathematical calculations, but that was enough to make them indispensable business tools. Later generations of more powerful, more affordable systems — mainframes, minicomputers, and PCs — took the technology deeper and deeper into the enterprise. Though a computer was a relatively uncommon sight in a commercial office in 1965, 30 years later few companies could do business without them.

At the same time that computers were first proving their place in the modern office, the world's top computer scientists and engineers were working on ways to get the machines to talk to each other. There were two reasons to do this. One, computers were massive, expensive resources. No one could afford to provide every researcher, engineer, accountant, or employee with his or her own system, so the main vendors — in those days, they were Sperry-Rand, Digital Equipment Corp., and, of course, IBM — came out with time-sharing systems that permitted many people to use the same computer simultaneously. The problem was that the computers were usually in one place, and the users were somewhere else. By the early 1960s, however, the same people who invented time-sharing had developed technologies that permitted users to log in remotely from a "dumb" terminal over a telephone line.

The other main driver for network development is familiar to anyone who has ever tried to integrate a company's core IT processes. More often than not, the data that you really, *really* need is on someone else's computer. While, in many cases, the **sneakernet** — walking over to the other guy's computer and copying the data to a floppy disk — is the easiest way to get that data, it just doesn't work if you're in Atlanta and the other guy's computer is in Seattle. If nothing else, you'd wear out a good pair of shoes.

It didn't take a genius to figure that what worked for remote time-sharing users would work equally well to enable two computers to share data across long distances. Head office in one city could wire proto-type information to the factory in another city; automatic time-card systems could update the personnel payroll system across town; partners could exchange order information. The stage was set for electronic commerce … except for three things. First of all, you could connect only two computers, point-to-point. Second, they had to be the same kind of computers. Finally, you had to use a live telephone line and pay standard long-distance fees to make the connection — and that, in the 1960s, was a very, very expensive proposition.

So maybe the stage wasn't set for electronic commerce after all.

In a 1961 thesis, an MIT graduate student named Leonard Kleinrock came up with one of those ideas that changed the world. The traditional method of telephone communication, **circuit switching,** where the network opens up a direct circuit between callers and keeps it open, whether they're talking or not and until they hang up, was a waste for computers. If you go out for a cup of coffee or to answer the doorbell while the line is open, you're still holding that resource and paying the long-distance bill. In the average telephone conversation, there's silence maybe one-third of the time the line's open, so that's not usually a problem. But it is a problem when you're networking computers. Computer communications are typically **bursty.** They send or request data in bursts and remain silent most — as much as 99.9 percent — of the time.

"The thing that we were solving was the efficiency with which we were using that very expensive communication resource," Kleinrock recalled in 1999. "You've got to 'demand-access' it — only get it when you need it. And that was the important part, to recognize that was the way to do data communications, because data is highly bursty. It comes in spurts and then it's quiet for a while. So the concept of evaluating a resource-sharing or, if you will, demand-access multiplexing scheme was key." The way to do that, Kleinrock concluded, was to employ a technique called **packet switching.** Rather than transmitting data in a continuous stream, it is sent over the network broken up into small message blocks or "packets." Each packet finds its own best route to the destination, where the message is reassembled. Not only does this technique permit a more efficient use of network capacity, but it minimizes the possibility of message loss. If a few packets don't arrive at their intended destination, the recipient's system can request to have them re-sent, using the routes taken by successful packets.[1]

Kleinrock's ideas were put into practice when the U.S. Defense Department's Advanced Research Projects Agency launched **ARPAnet,** the direct ancestor of the Internet, in 1969. The project's original goal was to connect disparate computer systems at research facilities at universities across the United States to share expensive computer resources cheaply and efficiently. Researchers developed applications like file transfer, remote log-in, and electronic mail in short order, and it wasn't long before ARPAnet technology began to trickle into the business world.

The first ventures, like Telenet and a string of abortive offerings from the major telecommunications carriers, were somewhat less than successful. However, throughout the 1970s, the major computer vendors — notably IBM, with its System Network Architecture in 1974 — adopted the ARPAnet technology and later the **Transmission Control Protocol/Internet Protocol (TCP/IP)** that would become the foundation of the Internet for their own purposes. The big telecommunications carriers and system vendors began to offer access to their private **value-added networks (VANs)** and ultimately to the Internet. Computers were multiplying in the business world at a dizzying rate. Automated processes within the enterprise, like computer numerical control (CNC) manufacturing, material requirement planning (MRP), manufacturing resource planning (MRP-II), and computerized accounting, began to create a pressure to connect with companies on the outside. And the network infrastructure was there. All that was needed for electronic commerce was the first inter-enterprise commercial application.

The Electronic Paper Trail

When the leading players in the American transportation industry began meetings to establish a standard for exchanging electronic documents between companies in the mid-1960s, supply chains, trading communities, and business automation were far from their minds. Rather, they were setting out to solve one of the most mundane problems of modern business — paper. In the wake of its vast postwar expansion, the transportation industry was smothering in a tide of dockets, manifests, waybills, and orders. The sheer scale of the paperwork had begun to clog the arteries of inter-state and international shipping. Trucks, trains, and aircraft were routinely delayed while waiting for paper documents such as schedules and manifests.

There had been experiments in computerized shipping and manifest systems and in rudimentary procurement systems in the 1950s and 1960s, and some of these had even been moderately successful. Typically, these involved intermittent dial-in connections that allowed a company's suppliers to download orders. The problems were that these connections were made over the public switched telephone network, with all of the inconveniences that implied, and the message formats — the means by which buyers and suppliers exchanged data — were proprietary. That meant that, if you happened to do business with more than one partner, you were forced to do it according to any number of mutually unintelligible message formats. And in the early days of computers, that often meant devoting a different system to each partner.

In the transportation industry, this technological heterogeneity was, at least to some extent, the legacy of two centuries of industrial consolidation and corporate insularity. Before the war, when the interstate highway system had yet to become the artery of commerce it would become in the 1950s, and when the only market was the local market, regional transport companies tended to do business with themselves. It was only after the exigencies of the wartime economy, and the demographic dispersal that followed, that inter-regional and international trade created pressure on the industry to standardize its paper processes. There was also pressure from the U.S. military, which had already developed a standardized shipping manifest system in order to facilitate the 1948 Berlin airlift. With the widespread adoption of computers in the 1960s and the growing interdependence of transport companies in inter-state and international trade, a standard for inter-enterprise commercial communication had become a necessity.

In 1968, after a few years of informal discussions, the big players in the U.S. rail industry set up the Transportation Data Coordinating Committee (TDCC) to establish a standard for exchanging electronic documents across computer networks. Meanwhile, the retail and automotive industries were coming to grips with similar problems — or at least they were trying to — and were watching the TDCC's efforts closely. "The goals then were the same goals we have now — better, faster, and cheaper," said Sally Fuger, today the Automotive Industry Access Group's (AIAG) program manager for electronic commerce. In the 1970s, however, she was just another IT worker in Rockwell International's automotive division, toiling in the order-entry system. "But it took a while to catch on in our industry. People didn't just jump out and implement it."

By the early 1970s, **electronic data interchange (EDI)**, as the technology became known, was making slow but steady inroads into a number of industries. Third-party, industry-wide proto-EDI systems like the pharmaceutical industry's ORDERNET began operating, tying participants together in a very early version of today's virtual trading communities. However, while early EDI permitted relatively seamless supply chain communications between companies *within* industries, there was no way to bridge the gap *between* industries.

That was a problem. A manufacturer, for example, might have to use one EDI system to exchange order information with its raw material suppliers, another to get its products shipped by the railroads, and yet another to accept purchase orders from retailers and distributors. The natural interdependence of various industries did help to cross-pollinate EDI efforts, but it took time. Rockwell International, for example, was invited to join the AIAG's project, which was, in turn, sharing information with the TDCC. "We had hoped to create something really common throughout industries," Fuger recalled. "That would have been revolutionary. But that's a really complex thing to do. We didn't call it EDI at the time and, the truth is, we were much more concerned about doing something for our industry than in technological revolutions."

The varied industry-specific electronic messaging standards that had emerged in the 1970s gained a measure of uniformity — and inter-intelligibility — at the start of the next decade. Building on the work of the TDCC and the National Association of Credit Management, the American National Standards Institute (ANSI) set up the Accredited Standard Committee to create a uniform EDI standard. Published in 1981, the ANSI **X12** standard established generic message formats across and within industries. "EDI actually became the established moniker for what we were doing when X12 was accredited," said David Barkley, chairman of ANSI's X12 committee and director of industry support at the Federal Home Mortgage and Loan Corporation (Freddie Mac). "The thing that X12 has done so well is go back to the underlying business data and business need and define structures for that."

Though it was intended from the outset to be a common language for electronic business-to-business communications, the X12 standard expanded into a patchwork as industries as diverse as financial services and automobile manufacturers brought their proto-EDI experience to the table. "The mortgage industry came to X12 as an industry, and the insurance and financial services industries found X12 at about the same time," Barkley recalls. "We sent people to see how we could take the best stuff and we found that they didn't have a lot of our business data built into X12. However, we were able to build on best-of-breed, build on the existing procedures, and create our own transaction sets."

The challenge facing X12 and also, to a great extent, the industries that began adopting EDI throughout the 1980s, has been to create consistent business processes and data models. However, the way the standard evolved — one industry at a time — made that extremely difficult to achieve. "All these islands of data and business processes were built, and then we had to connect them," Barkley said. "To enable that, we had to have a certain level of optionality, and that created inconsistencies. We're still living with that reality today, of course, but the really exciting thing about EDI, as it was standardized under X12, is that, despite its inconsistencies, it worked."

PAYING THE PIPER

Almost no one referred to EDI as "electronic commerce" as it was taking its first steps in the 1970s. If you had asked almost anyone to define electronic commerce at the time, you would have heard any number of definitions, none of which had anything to do with EDI, or with what we think of as electronic commerce today. Indeed, the idea of placing orders by computer, over a network like the Internet, and having the funds automatically debited against your credit card or corporate account was as farfetched as the idea of a McDonald's outlet in Red Square. When the *San Diego Union Tribune* announced, "The days of electronic cash have arrived" on September 25, 1986, it wasn't talking about on-line transactions; it was talking about the first time anyone had ever paid for groceries with an ATM card.

Commerce involving real-time transaction processing and on-line payments frankly made no sense in 1986. The idea of conducting disembodied financial transactions in virtual space had been knocking around since banks started using computers in the 1950s, but resistance to the idea, from the business community as much as from the general public, kept it from becoming a reality until the late 1980s. At a time when credit cards and automatic teller machines were still relatively new, yet-to-be fully accepted technologies, businesses still dealt, to a large extent, in paper purchase orders and carbon copies. Even in the 1980s, you could position yourself at a downtown street corner in Toronto, Montreal, Vancouver, and every other Canadian city, at closing time on a Friday afternoon to watch the battalions of business people marching, pouches in hand, to deposit the week's receipts at the local bank. That's the way business was done ... and for more than a few business people, that was the way it always *would* be done.

In these days of digital cash, telephone and Internet banking, on-line brokerages, PalmPilots, and cellular telephones that let you wheel and deal on the stock market while you're stuck in traffic, it's hard to conceive that anyone would object to instantaneous financial transactions. As technologies go, **electronic funds transfer (EFT)** ranks among the most important innovations in the history of electronic commerce. Without it, the process of financial transactions would never have evolved beyond checks and paper bank drafts. EFT is the technological underpinning of most of the advanced banking services, from ATM networks like Interac and Cirrus to point-of-sale debit card systems and Internet electronic commerce. Yet its introduction in the 1970s met with skepticism and intense resistance.

Smaller American banks and independent savings and loans businesses saw EFT as a maneuver by the big banks to put them out of business. They reasoned that because of the expense involved, the big institutions with their big budgets would have an unfair advantage deploying EFT-based services like ATMs. And many small banks saw ATMs as a direct threat to their livelihoods. There was also resistance from the business people who saw in EFT the demise of a time-honored business practice. Check floating — making a payment on the expectation that your account would be able to cover the expense by the time your supplier deposited the check — had become a widespread and generally accepted practice. However, EFT-based payments are instantaneous, so businesses have to have the funds available when they actually *make* the payment. It all seemed unnatural.

The first EFT pilot projects, using the infrastructure set up by the Federal Reserve in the United States in 1975, went smoothly. These were followed by pilot projects in most American states, and James W. Jukes, president of the Kansas Credit Union League — one of the participants in the first EFT pilot — confidently predicted that by 1980 most business would be conducted without the physical transfer of money. The future looked bright for electronic commerce, and then it hit a legislative brick wall. In a dozen states, legislation that prohibited branch banks simply made EFT illegal. The small banks mounted a strong campaign against amending or repealing the branch banking laws. And it was a tough battle. For example, voters in Texas rejected a proposal to amend the state constitution to permit EFT services by 60 percent to 40 percent in 1977 before finally accepting the changes in 1980.

Within a few years, however, the financial foundation of electronic commerce was in place. With EFT, cold, hard cash had been abstracted as data. The next step was to lay the foundation for commercial interactions between companies. That began to happen with the wide deployment of EDI. A revolution was just around the corner.

THE EDI REVOLUTION

EDI was the first electronic revolution in business-to-business commerce. By the early 1990s, before most business people had even heard of the Internet, let alone electronic commerce, EDI had gone a long way toward reducing the commercial paper trail and automating business-to-business transactions. By the early 1990s, it wasn't unusual for EDI-enabled manufacturers, grocery store chains, and transportation companies to send millions — indeed, tens of millions — of messages annually. Yet EDI is really just an electronic message system. What made it revolutionary, and what continues to make it important, is what *kind* of messages it is designed to transmit. For all of the technological innovations of the last half-century, business remains a process of moving discrete packages of organized data from one point to another. What EDI provides is a consistent interface and infrastructure for high-volume messaging.

There is a subset of the ANSI X12 standard for almost every industry. All EDI messages, or transaction sets, in the automotive industry are formatted according to the Automotive Industry Action Group (AIAG) standard; in the grocery industry, it's the Universal Product Code standard (UPC). Though there is some crossover, each industry standard has its own suite of transaction sets, ranging from purchase orders and invoices to manifests and inventory statements. Though trading partners can create customized transaction sets for their specific needs, the standard sets are maintained and overseen by industry EDI councils. It all adds up to a rigidly organized messaging system, but in the case of EDI, in any event, the rigidity has some significant advantages.

For one thing, because all messages of a certain type have exactly the same structure, once your partner knows which transaction set you are using for a particular message, you only need to send the data. In effect, sending an EDI message is like filling out a form and sending the information without the form; your message's recipient can reconstruct the context of the message by simply overlaying the form. In the early days of EDI, this added up to a significant saving in network costs. Even today, when network access is cheap and plentiful, the rigidity of the EDI standard is a major reason for the technology's efficiency and reliability. In essence, to participate in an EDI supply chain, all you need is access to the network, software that will translate your own company's electronic documents — like purchase orders and invoices — into the standard transaction sets, and software that translates into your internal format.

In a typical transaction, for example, the buyer's EDI software translates a purchase order into the appropriate transaction set and sends it over the network to the vendor's EDI mailbox, maintained by the VAN service provider. At the other end of the process, the vendor's system retrieves the document, translates it into its own internal format, and proceeds to fill the order. The process reverses when the vendor sends an electronic invoice back to the buyer. In the earliest days of EDI, the *electronic* part of the transaction would end there and traditional commerce would take over for the transaction's consummation. Once the order was confirmed, the buyer could pay only in the traditional way, by check or credit. With the development of EFT in the 1970s, and its eventual widespread acceptance in the 1980s, the way was cleared for fully electronic transactions. Using the INTER*EDI standard, the buyer could automatically transfer the required funds from his account at his bank, to the vendor's. A transaction that would have taken hours, days, or even weeks using paper documents and telephone calls can be done in minutes through EDI.

Admittedly, that's all old hat to business people who have surfed the succeeding waves of Internet and e-commerce innovation for the last few years. After all, the *whole point* of electronic commerce is to complete complex transactions in no time at all. But EDI was there first. It demonstrated the value and feasibility of an automated supply chain at a time when personal computers were just appearing on office desks and the Internet was still an obscure research project. If anything, the big question is why did it take so long for electronic commerce to take off? Why didn't the revolution start with EDI in the mid-1980s? All the ingredients were certainly in place ...

Yet traditional EDI has some serious shortcomings. To put it mildly, the standards rule with an iron fist. EDI expects everyone in the supply chain to be playing by the same rules — even a minuscule deviation from the standard will create messaging chaos. Furthermore, the high compliance required by traditional EDI comes at a price. It is rarely as simple as slapping translation software onto a computer and plugging into the network. It's both much more difficult and much more expensive than that. The total cost of implementing an EDI solution, integrating it, selecting transaction sets, and, finally, testing for standards compliance can be daunting, particularly for smaller players. "It hits a brick wall after the first tier of suppliers," Fuger said about the automotive industry. "There was quite a bit of resistance, particularly at the beginning. The first-tier companies tend to be very large and sophisticated. Not far beyond that though — if you call a company and ask for the IT department, you'll just get the receptionist. A lot of suppliers in the outer tiers said, 'This is just another way that our customers will push costs off on us'."

To make matters worse, there were soon two standards to worry about. While ANSI was establishing the X12 standard in the United States, the rest of the world was going its own way. As soon as North American companies tried to set up EDI links with their overseas trading partners, they ran into a wall of incompatible standards. Indeed, standards heterogeneity is a continuing theme in the story of international networking and electronic commerce. Though the United States is the heartland of computer technology and networking, there have been parallel developments elsewhere in the world. American and European video formats are incompatible; network providers in the United States deploy services on ANSI's networking standards, while those in Europe use the International Telecommunications Union's. It was perhaps inevitable that North American EDI standards would conflict with the rest of the world's.

The United Nations set up a special committee to unravel the standards issue and propose a common, international set of EDI standards in 1988. Electronic Data Interchange for Administration, Commerce and Trade, or UN/EDIFACT, was supposed to be the lingua franca of international electronic commerce. In the early 1990s, for example, the EDI Council of Canada selected UN/EDIFACT as the national EDI standard in Canada. In Europe and Asia, the new standard *did* have the beneficial effect of smoothing out a chaotic EDI landscape, but in the United States, it only added another layer of complexity to an already complex situation. Few American companies abandoned ANSI X12, and because Canadian companies do the bulk of their business in the United States, there was no compelling reason for UN/EDIFACT to be adopted north of the border, even if it was the national EDI standard.

Ironically, UN/EDIFACT's immediate impact was to aggravate the standards confusion it was supposed to redress. Many Canadian companies put off their EDI implementations until after a standards conversion that never happened. The emergence of effective and economical translation solutions, and the fact that North American business remains committed to X12, ultimately removed most of the edge from the confusion, and EDI continued to be a viable, if not essential business-to-business medium. However, problems with high compliance and the confusion surrounding the various subsets of X12 and UN/EDIFACT were a large factor in many companies' decision to wait until electronic commerce's *next big thing*.

Another, perhaps more important, factor was the basic cost of connecting to an EDI network. Despite the phenomenal growth of Internet use in the 1990s, EDI remained dependent on VANs for network transport, and VANs are both expensive and inefficient. Unlike the Internet, a multi-user, multi-use, multi-node network, VANs are point-to-point networks that users connect to when they need to send or retrieve messages. Because users don't normally maintain a constant connection with a VAN, it is either extremely difficult or extremely costly to use them for a real-time, automated supply chain. Moreover, VANs connect a user to his trading partner's EDI mailbox. Consequently, they are typically single-use connections that can't be used for other applications and services. In effect, users have to pay for their VAN connection, and then pay for whatever other network services they might need.

In a world of Internet video-conferencing, IP telephony, Web sites, e-mail, and instant messaging, traditional EDI over a VAN looks downright wasteful. While it's true that there wasn't any other way to do EDI when it first emerged in the 1970s, the technology's continued reliance on a clearly outmoded and inefficient network transport technology makes it seem archaic and irrelevant to the fast-paced world of modern electronic commerce. For all of its early promise and innovations, EDI might seem ready for the electronic commerce bone yard.

Nothing could be further from the truth.

It's Alive!

The problem for EDI today is not that the technology doesn't work, or even that it doesn't work well. The problem is that, after more than three decades of development, and 25 years of extensive use, it looks quaint and old-fashioned. The revolution in electronic commerce is, after all, about cutting-edge technology, new ways of doing things, the *future* of commerce. EDI has been around for so long that it seems to hearken back to the uncomplicated past of rotary-dial phones and manual typewriters. In the mid-1990s, the smart money was looking for a way to migrate from EDI to a newer, presumably better supply chain technology. Electronic commerce had become a catchphrase and it seemed like everything was moving to the Internet. EDI, with its reliance on VANs and proprietary services, seemed somehow out of step. Writing in *Infoworld* in February 1997, Bob Metcalfe described EDI as "terminally clunky," an opinion shared by many in the high-tech media at the time.

The main complaint was that EDI, based as it is on rigidly defined standards and transaction sets, simply lacked the flexibility to adapt to the new demands of electronic commerce. Moreover, the costs involved in participating in a highly compliant EDI supply chain were exorbitant, effectively keeping smaller players — expected to be the main beneficiaries and drivers of electronic commerce — out of the procurement loop. The stage seemed to be set for something newer, more elegant, and more up to date, like the **Open Buying on the Internet (OBI)** standard. OBI, and technologies like it, were supposed to make EDI obsolete, or at least subsume it in a more flexible and electronic-commerce-friendly way. But it didn't. For all its antiquity EDI remains the key foundation technology of the electronic-commerce supply chain.

Part of that is due to the fact that EDI is already installed and functioning in so many key industries. The automotive, consumer products, transportation, retail, and grocery industries — the industries that pioneered the technology in the 1970s and 1980s — are heavily invested in EDI. Aside from the expense that might be involved in moving to some *other* technology, these EDI users have largely concluded that "if it ain't broke, don't fix it," as Alister Sutherland of IDC Research said. "The fact is that, past a certain size, practically all companies in manufacturing industries are using EDI," he said. "It's legacy, and there's no real incentive to migrate to something else."

But that's only part of the story. EDI has not only held its own but, perhaps surprisingly for a technology that has been dismissed as clunky and given up for dead more than once in the last decade, it has continued to grow. Moreover, a 1999 Giga Information Group study concluded that this growth would continue well into the current century, from $2.7 trillion in EDI transactions in the United States in 1997 to $3.8 trillion in 2002. That's more than 40 percent projected growth over five years — not bad for an "outdated" technology. "There's a growing realization that EDI is an ideal vehicle for highly structured, high-volume transactions," said Ken Vollmer, the Giga Information Group analyst who wrote the EDI study. "And the truth is that it is exactly those kinds of transactions that you find at the backbone of business-to-business electronic commerce."

EDI continues to grow not *despite* the inroads of business-to-business electronic commerce and the growth of the Internet, but precisely *because* of them. As IDC's Sutherland pointed out, the supply chain "has to run on something," and EDI can provide a stable, consistent mechanism at the foundation layer of electronic commerce. That, in fact, is where EDI really shines. "The truth is that, if you scratch the surface of almost any high-volume business-to-business electronic commerce exchange, you'll find EDI," Barkley said. "You'll even find it under the covers of businesses like Amazon.com." If the growth of the Internet has shown anything, it's that technological change is usually evolutionary, building on each previous generation, and not revolutionary. And in that evolution EDI itself has begun to change.

The biggest barrier to participation in the traditional EDI supply chain was the simple cost of network access. However, the Internet has grown to meet the demands of electronic commerce, and with that growth has come a dramatic drop in network connectivity costs. Now that the Internet can provide a cheap alternative to the costly VANs that were once EDI's transport backbone, that barrier has fallen.

It turns out that the Internet isn't killing EDI at all; it's killing VANs. EDI is a message standard, and it doesn't care, one way or another, how it gets from sender to receiver as long as it gets there. Though traditional VANs carried 95 percent of EDI traffic in 1997, the Giga Information Group expects that volume to drop to less than 50 percent by 2002. Though the potential cost saving is an important part of the equation, equally important, if not more significant, is the promise of streamlined operations. There has been a great deal of consolidation in both the EDI and network services markets over the last decade, yet it is not unheard of for a company to find itself locked into one VAN provider, while the customers and vendors it wants to connect with are on another network. Now that the Internet has emerged as the common commercial transport medium, it can liberate EDI users — indeed, the technology itself — from insular, linear supply chains.

EDI had to evolve to do that. The ANSI X12 and UN/EDIFACT standards and their subsets evolved to enable commercial transactions over a certain kind of closed network, and their relative inflexibility reflects both the shortcomings and virtues of that infrastructure. It makes sense to rely on a limited number of rigidly defined transaction sets when you're doing business with a limited (though possibly large) number of trading partners in a closed, tightly controlled network environment like a VAN. Recognizing that, the X12 committee has taken significant steps to redefine the official EDI standard to encompass new Internet-based technologies. "We've passed a resolution that expands the definition," Barkley said. "It's all about expediting the movement of business information; the specifics don't matter."

In effect the medium has historically determined the shape of the EDI message. Consequently, moving EDI to the Internet involves more than just moving messages from a VAN to a more open, electronic commerce supply chain. "It's largely an interface issue, but it's also a question of bringing those huge, vertical data silos that have built up around EDI into a more flexible supply chain," IDC's Sutherland said. "It sounds simple, but a lot of integration has to go on under the surface."

Key Terms

sneakernet

circuit switching

bursty

packet switching

ARPAnet

TCP/IP

value-added networks (VANs)

electronic data interchange (EDI)

X12

electronic funds transfer (EFT)

open buying on the Internet (OBI)

3

THE SUPPLY CHAIN

The supply chain has long been the central business-to-business commercial relationship. However, with the adoption of electronic commerce technologies in manufacturing and distribution, the relationship is rapidly changing. Along with the advantages of shorter cash-to-cash cycles and greater efficiency, e-businesses have to face a whole range of new challenges; supply chains are growing longer, production and distribution cycles are becoming compressed, customers are demanding built-to-order products. The key to success is integration, and though new technologies like XML promise to make that easier, supply chain participants are finding that integration is more than just a question of technology.

PUTTING IT ALL TOGETHER

Celestica Corp. is in a pretty straightforward business. Its customers, high-tech giants like Sun Microsystems, Cisco Systems Corp., and Nortel Networks Corp., tell the electronic components manufacturer what kinds of circuit boards they want, and Celestica builds them. Nothing could be simpler ... well, it's not quite as simple as all that. Celestica's customers are demanding; its products — the electronic guts of some of the most sophisticated computing and networking equipment on the market — are complex and difficult to build. Silicon chips and micro-processors, its raw materials, are both costly and subject to the volatile shifts of supply and price that characterize the semiconductor industry.

However, Celestica is the very model of a modern manufacturer. Keeping the whole sequence of business processes rolling smoothly, from the first point of contact with the customer to the time the finished product ships, requires quick reflexes and delicate choreography. And in the 21st century that means electronic commerce, said Paul Blom, Celestica's vice president for supply chain management. "We make a very high volume of printed-circuit assemblies, as well as complete systems," he said. "Sometimes we'll ship to the **OEM (original equipment manufacturer)**, sometimes directly to customers. The whole process is a delicate balancing act, and we couldn't do it without a carefully managed and integrated supply chain system."

There are few products quite as complex as a state-of-the-art network workstation, and Celestica's role in their manufacture is far more complex than buying parts and building products for high-technology OEMs. Indeed, the company is just one part of the complex chain of partners — vendors, semiconductor manufacturers, and resellers — that collaborate to deliver the essential tools of the information economy. No one link in the chain can do it alone, but by integrating the flow of commercial data between enterprises, they are able to leverage their combined resources and expertise as a single manufacturing organism.

Celestica's participation in the supply chain begins when an OEM delivers its design, conceived and laid out electronically, to the contract manufacturer's **FTP (file transfer protocol)** servers. The designs themselves are a kind of high-tech recipe, typically consisting of a digital computer-assisted design (CAD) schematic of the circuitry and a list of required components. When Celestica retrieves the files, the schematics are fed into its computer-assisted manufacturing (CAM) system, and the parts list is matched with a centralized component database to line up supplies from within the company or to make automated orders from semiconductor suppliers around the world.

This process allows Celestica to take advantage of two significant economies of scale. It aggregates its global spending, procuring components enterprise-wide for manufacturing facilities in North America, Europe, and Asia on a wholesale basis. If it doesn't have the necessary components on hand, it can automatically replenish its inventory, as new orders require. More importantly, however, the centralized information enables an automated supply chain between the company's disparate manufacturing facilities. "Because we have all of this component data in the company, we can turn around quickly if we can't get the right component in the market," Blom said. "We've deployed a database of component sets to all factories. If I have a shortage in one part of the world and a surplus in another, I can cross-network. We might have the right one somewhere else in the company, or we may have a component under a different number that does the same thing. By having the right integration tools, we can move inventory between sites within the company as needed. That makes us fast and flexible."

Speed and flexibility are prerequisites for success in the electronic contract manufacturing business, according to Blom. A surplus of finished products, like Cisco routers or Sun workstations, adds up to wasted resources and wasted money. The two principal goals of Celestica's supply chain management approach are to compress the cash-to-cash cycle and to be able to respond to customer demand as quickly and with as little waste as possible. To meet those goals, Celestica has been able to realize one of the great promises of electronic commerce integration — build to order. Although on the consumer side of electronic commerce, the build-to-order philosophy boils down to giving customers exactly what they want, in the business-to-business supply chain it has a more subtle and profound meaning to the bottom line.

"The other aspect — and this is more important to us — is not committing your components to a finished product until the very last possible moment," Blom said. "If we can postpone the time of building the actual circuit assembly, we can be a bit more flexible with our customers. If one of our customers' sales have an up-tick in Europe and a down-tick in North America, but we've already built for the North American market, then we all end up with a surplus on our hands. That costs us money."

Nevertheless, Celestica's supply chain relationships are about a lot more than maximizing resources and minimizing costs. Its OEM customers are connected directly through the manufacturer and out the other side to the suppliers in — theoretically at least — a single coherent and transparent process. "Where the electronic commerce part of it is particularly valuable is when my customer is connected to me and me to my supplier, so it all works with as little friction as possible," Blom said. "When a customer comes to us and says that they'd like to increase demand by 40 percent, we can simulate that demand to make more educated decisions on resources and production planning. That lets us take up production on a planned schedule, so our customers can plan their sales and deliveries and our suppliers can meet our requirements. Production always involves balancing demand with supplies."

Once that balance is achieved and schedules are synchronized, designs are in the CAD/CAM system, and Celestica's facilities are set up for production, the system runs itself. All that's left is for Celestica's clients — the larger OEMs for now, but soon all of them — to log into the central manufacturing database as if it were their own to check up on the route of their orders through the manufacturing and shipping process. "I won't say the process is completely automated or that it always runs perfectly smoothly," Blom said. "But it works, and it works very well. We really couldn't do what we do any other way today."

SCM TO eSCM

The idea of a commercial or industrial supply chain is nothing new. Since the earliest days of industrial production, companies have relied on some companies to sell them the raw materials they needed to make their products and on others to get those products to market. For example, a steamship built in the swarming shipyards of Boston a century ago required the combined output of dozens of individual companies and hundreds of shipwrights, metal workers, carpenters, and engineers. The iron and steel of its hull may have come from foundries in Pennsylvania, its boilers would have been built in Cleveland, and its vestigial masts would have come from lumber camps as far away as Oregon. The coal that fired its engines would have been mined in West Virginia and the cables that joined its rudder to the bridge wheel might have been contracted from as far away as Liverpool.

Each participant in the chain contributed some small part of the whole vessel that would eventually glide slowly and majestically from its dry dock into the Atlantic Ocean. It was a slow process, moving no faster than the fastest freight train from Chicago or the fleetest transatlantic packet. The shipbuilders, like all businesses of the time, had the luxury of waiting weeks and months for partners to respond to orders dispatched by mail or — in the most urgent circumstances — transmitted by the new technology of telegraphy.

Today, the supply chain remains the essential business relationship in manufacturing and production. Like supply chains of the past, it begins with the customer order and ends with the delivery, encompassing the whole connection from raw material and original component manufacturers to supply, production, distribution, and transportation of finished goods to the customer. But that's where the resemblance ends. The Internet, global markets, and electronic commerce have stepped up pressure on supply chain performance, and the new technologies of on-line business have turned supply chain management into **eSCM (electronic supply chain management)**. Everything from procurement to order tracking, inventory management, and inter-enterprise collaboration is moving to the Web.

The new supply chain is both longer and far more integrated than anything that could have been imagined just a few years ago. "The biggest change for us is that, 10 years ago, we weren't expected to have our own supply chain," said Tim Armstrong, vice president for quality and information systems at Wescast Industries Inc., a tier-one automotive parts supplier to Detroit's Big Three. "We were only participants in someone else's supply chain. But we have our own suppliers, and the supply chain itself is getting longer. We have to use electronic commerce supply chain management [eSCM] technologies to manage it at all."

Whether it's well-founded or not, there's a growing perception that the evolution of SCM (supply chain management) to eSCM — its plugged-in, wired, and integrated descendant — may no longer be a matter of choice. Aberdeen Group research director Katherine Jones, writing in *Manufacturing Systems,* echoed the fears of many managers, alarmed at the thought of being left behind. "The unification of business applications with supply chain data is essential for a competitive position," she wrote. "This requires not smarter people, but smarter processes; processes that can automatically report and capture data from all parts of what traditionally has been called the supply chain."[1]

It's not hard to find reasons for the feeling of pressure. There is no distance on the Internet; one point is equidistant from any other point in virtual space. Customers and partners who may be 200 miles away physically are just next door on the Net. Interactions are immediate, forcing companies to operate 24 hours a day, seven days a week to respond simultaneously to the latest market demands of Berlin and Kuala Lumpur. "The new enterprise is a real time enterprise, which is continuously and immediately adjusting to changing business conditions through information immediacy," observed Donald Tapscott in *The Digital Economy.* "Customer orders arrive electronically and are instantly processed; corresponding invoices are sent electronically and databases are updated."[2]

In the age of electronic commerce, product cycles have been compressed to days and hours, and no one can wait for the next train and remain in business for long. The pressure on enterprises to optimize their supply chain management systems is immense. The imperative to reduce cycle time is driving everything, and companies are desperately nipping and tucking to improve efficiency. "It's an ongoing challenge," said Mike Suman, group vice president of e-business and marketing at Johnson Controls Inc. (JCI), a tier-one automotive supplier in Plymouth, Michigan. "Anyone who hangs on to legacy processes is going to be in trouble." The immediate effect is that the old way of doing things just doesn't cut it anymore. It's almost a vicious circle — products can be produced more quickly, so manufacturers are under pressure to produce more quickly. Production has to be leaner and more efficient, with less waste and more flexibility.

That means integration, at least in theory. Your suppliers' systems and their suppliers' systems work in concert. One company's systems interact directly with the next one down the line, with the whole chain operating like a single precision mechanism. In its purest, most advanced expression, each link joins one company's system to the next, eliminating the inefficient complication of human intervention. However, even in an age of electronic commerce and the Internet, that level of automated perfection is still impossible to attain.

"There's a human management component in there," said Celestica's Blom. "You can't avoid it. Whenever a customer has a design change, for example, we have to make sure our suppliers are synchronized, and the best way to do that is through human management intervention. But once the customer has released the design and we've set up a product, the regular rhythms of planning and producing a product become automated."

Even with human intervention, integration is a tall order, but the potential benefits — reduced lead time, reduced inventory, and a greatly compressed cash-to-cash cycle — can be enormous. With shorter lead times, manufacturers don't have to commit resources to final products too far in advance, making them far more flexible and cutting operational costs. "We don't want to have any more inventory than we absolutely need, because that's cost," Armstrong said. "It doesn't happen so much in our business, but if a buyer suddenly changes his requirements, and we have more than a few days of inventory — that can end up costing us a lot of money."

The inefficiencies of the traditional supply chain can also end up being costly. When Boeing Corp. entered its bid to build a next-generation strike fighter for the U.S. and British military, implementing eSCM was a high priority. To win the contract, Boeing has to do a lot more than design the best supersonic jet fighter in the world, it also has to prove that it can build it on time and within strict budgetary constraints. Tim Ahlberg, senior procurement manager on Boeing's JSF (joint strike fighter) project, knew they couldn't do it the old-fashioned way. "The replacement of paper is a fundamental part of our supply chain process on this project," he said. "In the past, we've defined an aircraft on paper or, more recently, electronically. But even when it was electronic, that was for within the company. The difference today is that we're sharing the design database with our contractors and partners. We're all working in real time with the same data."

The ultimate goal of supply chain integration goes farther than eliminating waste and improving manufacturing and distribution efficiency. It's a kind of inter-enterprise nirvana, where all of the supply chain participants can collaborate in a real-time partnership, rather than as a series of automated transactions. "For many companies, supply chain integration stops at procurement — but we think it's bigger than that," said Ron Schwartz, the partner responsible for e-business and systems integration at PricewaterhouseCoopers (PWC). "It's not just about company A and who it buys from. The real issues are what company A buys from its suppliers and how it makes sure that its suppliers have the right parts on a predictable schedule. The issues are industry optimization and multi-company collaboration."

One of the main aims of Boeing's JSF supply chain system is to ensure that all the parts, from nose cones to tail hooks, are on the assembly line when needed. "Delivering an aircraft on time involves a lot of coordinating of the schedules of a lot of different companies," Ahlberg said. "We used to work out our schedules by passing paper back and forth. We had to understand everyone's schedules and try to translate that information into when we would be able to complete an aircraft. That made it difficult to plan production and we had to commit resources earlier in the process than we wanted to. That's one of the reasons why we never really had much success in multi-service aircraft."

The traditional supply chain was a dimly lit tunnel with bright lights at either end. The location of anything in the process was revealed only when it arrived at the loading dock. However, the integrated supply chain, at its most advanced, illuminates the whole process. That can be essential when you're building the best possible jet fighter at the best possible price. "As a manufacturer buying lots of components, you have better capacity to share forecast info with suppliers," Schwartz said. Manufacturers don't have to guess their future inventory needs anymore. "If you're organized enough to work to a forecast you can help suppliers cut costs."

Manufacturers used to build products to match often-erroneous market expectations, but the integrated electronic commerce supply chain promises to give them the flexibility to respond quickly to customer needs. Changes can be made almost in real time. "In the old days, changes would bubble up through internal review; they would go through a change board and, only then, they'd be transmitted to the contractor," Ahlberg said. "Then, they'd have to go through the whole internal process at that end, and that would take some time. We'd get into misinterpretations and problems in translating the design for their systems and processes. We would be able to work it out, but it took time. Even a couple of years ago, it could take two weeks to get a design change made."

The ability to make production changes in real time has helped to shift the focus of production from the manufacturer's needs to the customer's. When you have demanding customers, like General Motors, Cisco Systems, or the United States Marines, that ability can be an important selling point. "In every market there is a move toward what is called customer pull as opposed to manufacturer push," Schwartz said.

"It's now possible for customers to specify what they want and when they want it. Vendors with better supply chain integration can build to order more predictably."

For a company like JCI, which manufactures interiors for several automakers, that translates as flexibility. The Ford Explorer design team might want to put a cup holder in one place, while the Chevrolet designers might want it somewhere else. "There's been this incredible improvement in collaboration that allows everyone in the supply chain to see the drawings and schematics and design in real time," Suman said. "The production line responds almost immediately. You can't go to a launch meeting once a week and then say you didn't know about a change — you just didn't look. The information is all there, growing and changing. You have the ability to keep up with it, so you have to."

However, the technology is only part of the equation. The new supply chain has forced many companies to rethink the way they do business. The technology has nurtured a new kind of supply chain relationship. Customers aren't just buying products anymore, they are participating in their design and production. "There are really two important ingredients in a successful e-business supply chain," said Celestica's Blom. "There are systems and technology, but what's also important is the way you have yourself organized — that's the management part of supply chain management. We've made all the systems investments. And we've organized ourselves in 'customer focus teams.' In our supply chain, we'll have managers and teams dedicated to Cisco, Sun, and Lucent, and they won't work on any other customers' products."

With eSCM technologies evolving toward ever-tighter integration, the great science fiction promise of automated, robotic manufacturing may be getting a little closer. With CAD, digital prototyping, and modular tooling, a company like JCI or Celestica is in a position where the assembly line itself is just another facet of electronic commerce. However, it will be a long time before that becomes commonplace, said Darren Meister, an operations management specialist at the Queen's University School of Business in Canada. "The place where you see the on-line CAM exchange is where the product is just so complex, like in the high-tech industries and aerospace," he said. "A company like Celestica doesn't want to be told, 'This is where this goes and this is where that goes.' They want a file that will drive their pick-and-place machine."

Evolving EDI

Superficially, electronic data interchange is an obvious solution to the integration problem. After all, the venerable message standard is already widely deployed, and far from disappearing like the smart money predicted, its use has been growing in recent years. EDI defied the predictions of its impending demise by moving to the Internet, where small companies that couldn't afford the expense of a leased VAN connection could participate on a more casual basis through Internet-VAN gateways set up by the main EDI service providers and through corporate hubs like General Motors and Procter & Gamble. "The Internet is a huge opportunity for our customers," said John Lee, IBM's program director of Electronic Commerce Services, at the launch of IBM Global Solutions' Web-based EDI offering in 1997. "While mission-critical business may not be quite ready to go to the Internet, when you get to very small business partners sending one or two messages a week, the Internet may be very appropriate. It gives the EDI hub the capability to extend out to small and medium-sized companies. [They don't] have to change platform. In effect, we're trying to tie the network types together."

EDI has proven itself to be admirably adaptable to the new Internet business environment. Because it is simply a question of sending messages back and forth, the venerable technology doesn't care what kind of network infrastructure carries its traffic. EDI transactions can travel just as easily over the Internet as over a VAN or a direct dial-up connection. However, the carrier medium isn't the problem, so much as the messages themselves, and despite its phenomenal staying power — almost a quarter of a century and counting — it is becoming clear that EDI just isn't the ideal tool to tie the supply chain together.

EDI relies on rigidly structured messages to get information from one point to another. Because they're simple text files, each message must conform to predefined transaction sets in order to be understood by the receiver. In effect, it's like sliding a square peg into a square hole; if the peg is round, or if it's just not square enough, it won't fit. In EDI terms, an improperly formatted message would simply be rejected by the receiving system, or it would result in an error. The problem is that EDI messages are devoid of context, except the transaction set definition in the header. A (completely fictional) UN/EDIFACT message might look something like this[3]:

```
UNA:+.?
UNB+UNOA:1+JANE SMITH+BOB MACDONALD+921201:2100+00005'
UNH+NR123+ORDERS:1:10'
BGM+105+PS/996767+895656
NAD+BU+++EPHEMERATECH,INC.'
NAD+SE+++COSTLYPARTS,INC.'
LIN+1++9002:VP+3456:BP+21:100'
UNT+6+NR123'
UNZ+1+00005
```

In order for the receiving computer to understand this message, it has to understand the form of the message. To the human eye, and to any EDI system that doesn't recognize the appropriate transaction set, it's just a line of gibberish. However, if the receiving system understands the UN/EDIFACT standard, it can match the cryptic text to the right transaction set and feed the information into its system. Thus understood, the message reveals itself as a purchase order:

```
Buying Company:    EphemeraTech, Inc.
Buyer Contact:     Jane Smith
Buyer account:     996767
Vendor:            CostlyParts, Inc.
```

```
Sales Rep:          Bob MacDonald
Vendor Part #:      9002
Buyer Part #:       3456
Quantity:           100
```

However, if one "+" or any other character is out of place, or if the sender inadvertently specifies the wrong transaction set, the result would be at best an error, and at worst, utter supply chain chaos. Indeed, most EDI messages are considerably more complex than a simple purchase order, and the demands of electronic commerce supply chain integration require even more complex, richer communication. Forecasting and scheduling messages, for example, can contain huge amounts of information, and if the format of the message sent fails to match the format understood by the receiving system by even the slightest degree, the supply chain breaks down.

To make matters worse, EDI standards are specific to industry verticals, so a company that straddles industries has to implement two systems for two different EDI standards. For example, a company that manufactures rubber seals for automobile windows might require separate EDI implementations for the automotive and chemical industries. And the potential for chaos doesn't end there. The standards themselves can be subject to subtle variations. "That's a headache," said Wescast's Tim Armstrong. "Even using X12, the Big Three [automakers] each have their own variations on EDI, and it's hard enough to keep all of that straight. But there's variation within the companies, between their plants. That's where they've blown EDI."

It's not a trivial problem, suggests Sally Fuger of the AIAG. "The automakers, and divisions within companies, like to think of themselves as independent and do things their own way," she said. "Some of the big players, like General Motors, have done a good idea of commonizing the standard among their own plants, but compliance can still be a nightmare. The larger the number of plants and partners you have, the large the number of variations, and the larger the problem with compliance. It's just another reason why the little guys in the supply chain are often so bad off."

The bottom line is that EDI simply lacks the flexibility to adapt to the new realities of business in an age of global connectivity, rapid cycles, and close partner collaboration. Though it's effective enough, and likely to continue to be used for the steady exchange of roughly uniform data between arm's-length trading partners in the same vertical industry, it is simply and utterly inadequate for drawing the links of the supply chain together for real-time collaboration and response.

The Next EDI? Not OBI

Developing a supply chain technology optimized for the Internet business environment hasn't been easy, however. To some extent, it has been a problem of applying metaphors and models from pre-Internet procurement to the new realities. For example, the World Wide Web appears, at least on the surface, to be a publishing medium analogous to print media, and a logical consequence of that metaphor was the on-line catalog. Somewhat similar to a consumer-oriented electronic commerce site like Amazon.com, the business-to-business on-line catalog got a big push from software vendors and erstwhile EDI providers eager to stake out a piece of the Internet in the mid-1990s.

General Electric Information Systems, a long-time VAN operator and, along with IBM, one of the undisputed leading providers of traditional EDI services, made a big splash in 1997 with the announcement of its **advanced retail catalog** service. The idea was to provide distributors and industry trade organizations with a centralized, searchable, and flexible catalog database for their retailer customers. "This is the next EDI in electronic commerce," Joe Mirecki, GEIS's manager of their Retail Industry Segment, said at the time. "It provides a functionality that has been missing in traditional supply chain systems. It gets the right information to everyone at the right time. And it doesn't just have to be UPC numbers, prices, product descriptions, and suppliers. The real advantage is that the advanced retail catalog can add other functionality and value-added information."

Catalogs also held out immense promise for indirect procurement. In 1996, some of the biggest companies in the United States, including General Electric, American Express, and the Ford Motor Co., got together in a consortium named Open Buying on the Internet (OBI) to establish a cross-industry standard for low-cost, high-volume procurement over the Internet. OBI focused mainly on **maintenance repair and operating (MRO)** supplies, and though it wasn't a strategic procurement issue, and hardly essential to the supply chain, it was an area that the participants could streamline quickly and easily. Moreover, once they had the MRO part of the process nailed, the consortium believed OBI had a great future throughout the supply chain. Indeed, in the trade journal *Purchasing,* writer Mark Vigoroso cautioned critics in 1999 that "by virtue of its youth, OBI should not be hailed as the e-commerce silver bullet, but it exposes some of the shortcomings of today's offerings and, if nothing else, may be a step toward leaner, more universal Internet purchasing."[4]

Well … perhaps. OBI's main focus was, and remains, the occasional catalog. Like EDI, it provides a common language for buyers and sellers to communicate purchasing and transaction information over the Internet. Its great play was as a technology for centralizing a company's departmental and individual MRO procurements on a seller's on-line catalog, permitting the deployment of sell-side catalogs with traditional buy-side functionality. Departmental paper-clip purchases, for example, could be managed without requiring the buyer to host the catalog. All of that added up to greater simplicity for the vendor, who only had to deal with one catalog, and greater flexibility for the buyer, who was no longer tied into a buy-side system. Paperwork is reduced, both buyers and vendors have control, and everyone's happy. Unfortunately, OBI went nowhere fast.

Aside from some pilot projects, OBI has withered from lack of interest. MRO procurement just didn't turn out to be important enough for buyer or sellers to get excited about. By and large, existing systems — either paper-based or buy-side electronic catalogs — seemed to do the job, and major institutional MRO suppliers set up Internet storefronts that provide searchable databases and accept corporate accounts and purchase orders in plain HTML. Indeed, by the time the consortium published OBI 2.0, the first "implementable" version of the would-be standard, in 1999, three years after the first OBI announcement, other more promising supply chain integration technologies had reached maturity. By 2000, almost no one, not even the consortium's biggest sponsors, was talking much about OBI anymore.

As an electronic commerce supply chain technology, OBI had another serious shortcoming. For all of its paper-reduction promise, its main focus was on enabling human-to-computer interactions. A company employee would log onto the vendor's catalog and purchase supplies that would then be charged against the company's account. While this was, and still is, an ideal way to buy photocopier toner, paper clips, and stationery, it does little to break down the barriers between partners and integrate the supply chain as a single, frictionless, productive organism. Interactions in that model are, like EDI, computer to computer. What the integrated supply chain needed to become a reality was a technology that both linked systems and provided enough flexibility to communicate the myriad processes of business-to-business electronic commerce. That technology, it turns out, is something called extensible mark-up language.

Is the Answer Spelled X-M-L?

Context is everything. Without it, words are gibberish, data is meaningless, and communication is impossible. The contents of a document make sense only when you know what *kind* of document it is; the meaning of a message is clear only when you know who sent it; and system-to-system integration in the electronic commerce supply chain is possible only when those systems share a common method for presenting and understanding information. EDI creates context by arranging data in a specific, predefined structure; any system that understands that structure can, in theory, understand the data. However, any deviation from the structure makes the data unreadable, and that rigidity makes EDI fundamentally unsuited to complex supply chain integration.

But what if you could find a way to bury the structure in the message itself? Instead of matching it to a template of predefined transaction sets, the receiving system would simply look at how the incoming message defined itself. Both systems would be liberated from the straitjacket of reliance on predefined message structures, allowing for more flexible and more complex interactions. As long as everyone knows how the document expresses itself, it should be a fairly simply matter to share data of all kinds without too much difficulty. That's the whole idea behind **extensible mark-up language (XML)**.

Most Internet surfers are familiar with hypertext mark-up language, the technology used to build Web pages. HTML uses tags — text meant to be read and interpreted by a Web browser, but invisible to the user —to define a Web page's format. For example, the text that appears in figure 3-1 *in* your Web browser actually looks like the text in figure 3-2 *to* your browser.

Figure 3-1

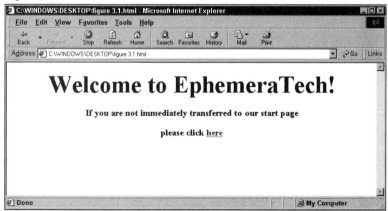

Figure 3-2

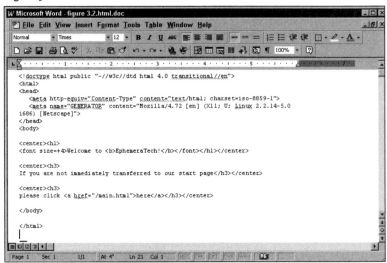

All the formatting information, like font size and style, the required character set, and the hyperlink to the "main.html" page, are embedded in the text document as tags between <> brackets. A Web browser simply interprets the tags as formatting information. The tags themselves are hidden to the user, but all text following the "<b>" tag is bold, and the text following "<a href="/main.html">" is a hyperlink to the "main.html" Web page.

XML meta-tags work in basically the same way except that, instead of defining the format of a Web page, they define the *context* and *meaning* of text. For example, a purchase order might have the purchaser's name indicated by a <purch> tag and the quantity defined by <quant>. A schema, a kind of XML vocabulary, defines just what the tags mean and which ones are used. A specialized software program called an XML parser simply interprets the tags according to the schema indicated in the message header. Unlike EDI, which demands strict compliance to a predefined message length and field order, the information in an XML document can appear and be in whatever order or length the sender desires. The

XML parser will still make sense of a purchase order if the name of the seller precedes the name of the buyer and even if the order quantity appears in the first line and the catalog number in the last.

"XML is an enormously flexible description language," said Scott Woodgate, technical product manager of Microsoft Corp.'s BizTalk XML server. "The fragmentation of EDI was caused by the fact that its messages are not self-describing. The key thing with XML is that it is self-describing, so I don't have to know the structure of a message before I receive it; I only have to parse the message when I receive it. And there's a standard mapping technology that lets me take messages from one schema to another." Functionality like that can provide the foundation for far deeper and easier integration than EDI, and because XML is designed to support exchanges between machines rather than people, it can support a level of automation impossible with OBI and catalog-type systems.

Commerce Web sites built with HTML will still be the interface of choice where human intervention is required — such as in the first phases of procurement, or when individuals have to access data stores — but XML is a more powerful technology that is also Internet-based and easily integrated with the Web. "The obvious conclusion from EDI is that it's not appropriate for business-to-business electronic commerce on the Internet because it never caused a B2B explosion," Woodgate said. "XML is designed for Internet transport; it provides the tools to abstract from a descriptive language and focus on business processes. It's the right technology at the right time, and it *will* cause the explosion."

If it all sounds just a little overheated, that's because, for all its promise, XML is only just being deployed in the supply chain. It's new and it's hot. Vendors like IBM, Hewlett-Packard, and Microsoft Corp., whose XML application servers have just been or soon will be released, have been talking up the technology since 1998. In 2000, Microsoft Corp. made XML — and the BizTalk server — a central part of its next-generation .NET strategy. Database integration and enterprise resource planning vendors like Oracle Corp., SAP AG Inc. (SAP), and PeopleSoft have been promising, and sometimes delivering, XML functionality in their products, but the technology itself is still very new. The hype has it that XML will be the perfect foundation for commerce interactions between and within enterprises in the supply chain, and it's easy to fall for the hype.

"Far too many executives, even the really seasoned ones, tend to fall for it," said Chris Pickering, a senior consultant with the Boston-based Cutter Consortium. "It invariably happens that, when a new technology comes along, vendors promise that, with their products, it will do everything including making the best cup of coffee. They promise that, with their products, it will be easy to deploy. But the reality is that there are always a lot of implementation issues with every technology and the results will always be disappointing."

Indeed, you won't be using XML to make a tuna sandwich and send flowers to a sick co-worker. It can't and it won't do everything, but what it does — such as permit users to send complex and richly structured data across the supply chain — it does very well. And that reality has begun to clear away the hype and misconceptions surrounding what Pickering said may be the "killer app" of the electronic commerce supply chain. "What I think is beginning to happen with XML is that we're getting past all the hype of the early adoption phase," he said. "People with more realistic expectations will use it as a tool rather than expecting a panacea. We're either on the cusp of the stage where XML becomes a tool, or we've already entered that stage. XML is at the point where people are really assessing its potential use within their supply chains. So it may be at the make-or-break point."

One of the things that promises to make XML work, and help realize its vast potential in business-to-business commerce, is the enormous interest that industry groups have shown in adapting the technology to their own uses. There are initiatives in the automotive, consumer products, and financial services industries, to name just a few. RosettaNet, a consortium established in 1998 to create a schema for supply chain interactions in the information technology industry, numbers almost every major vendor among its participants. With that kind of support,

RosettaNet has been able to map most of the industry's most important inter-enterprise supply chain interactions as partner interface processes, or PIPs. "In the IT business right now, there are about 100 touch points between companies, and we want to have those covered," said Mary Schoonmaker, the consortium's vice president of marketing. "We will be expanding the scope of RosettaNet further in 2001 to include processes like quality information and forecasting."

The fear, however, is that XML will go down the same path as EDI, with every industry pursuing and developing its own schemas. As flexible as the language may be, there is a limit to *how* different each implementation can be before its dissolves into chaos. "The good news–bad news part of XML is that you can create your own tags," said the AIAG's Fuger. "That's great for flexibility, but it proposes a whole new set of problems. I definitely see a need to develop common tags and schemas, otherwise we'll see the same Tower of Babel that kept EDI from being more widely implemented."

That seems to be happening. Many of the XML initiatives have begun to grow together, intersecting like ever-growing circles in a Venn diagram. In the summer of 2000 for example, RosettaNet expanded its focus in an obvious direction by setting up a semiconductor industry working group, and in a not-so-obvious direction by starting a similar collaborative initiative for the automotive industry. That kind of inter-industry synergy is becoming common, said Kimberly Knickle, a senior analyst with AMR Research in Boston, and not a moment too soon. "Some people have counted more than 30 standards initiatives, and that kind of proliferation can add up to a lot of confusion," she said. "The question is whether everyone's XML will be different. Yes, there will be a lot of different flavors, but that doesn't matter. Even with all of that it will be an awful lot easier to achieve integration than by mapping every company's internal processes."

Moreover, XML is now an official W3C (World Wide Web Consortium) standard, so everyone has a common benchmark to work from, eliminating some of the early confusion about *how* the technology would be implemented. The key issue now, according to main XML schema developers, is ensuring that the technology doesn't become tied to vertical industry silos like EDI. "There are layers and layers of things that still have to happen," said Mary Schoonmaker. "One thing that we need is a dictionary among the players. As you get up to the server level, you get the PIPs. That's what we're focused on. We're concerned about interoperability with other standards. As long as the standards can talk to each other, that's the key." Until recently, however, the upsurge in interest in XML resulted in a proliferation of inter-industry coordination efforts, which effectively defeated their stated purpose.

In addition to the XML.org portal and schema library established by the Organization for the Advancement of Structured Information Standards (OASIS), the electronic commerce consortium CommerceNet had its own repository of document type definitions, and Microsoft Corp. had begun promoting its own XML electronic commerce framework called BizTalk.org. In the wake of the 2000 anti-trust decision in the United States, critics were wary of the Microsoft-led initiative, despite its support from industry heavyweights such as SAP, Commerce One Inc., and the Open Applications Group. And it didn't help that Microsoft's pre-announced XML application server was, itself, dubbed Biztalk.

Nevertheless, the splintering of the various efforts never actually occurred, with each pledging allegiance to a non-proprietary and interoperative standard. Despite its suspicious product name, Microsoft Corp. continues to maintain that it isn't trying to dominate the world of XML. Indeed, said Microsoft's Woodgate, the whole idea is to get together to maintain a common standard, rather than the fragmentation of XML. "The name tends to cause confusion because they're related, but they're not the same," he said. "The initiative is to get companies to adopt XML, whichever technology they use to deploy it, and the BizTalk product isn't limited to XML, by any means."

Is XML ready for prime time in the electronic commerce supply chain? Efforts like the XML/EDI Group and CommerceNet's own

EDI-over-XML project have shown that the technology can integrate the hoary old standard in a more flexible supply chain environment. Initiatives like RosettaNet and the financial services industry's fXML are well on their way toward mapping the essential commerce processes, and most of the pilot implementations sponsored by industry consortia have been encouraging. The ebXML consortium, organized by OASIS and including IBM, Sun Microsystems, and Sterling Commerce, successfully demonstrated a working version of its e-business-specific schema at the end of 2000. Products incorporating ebXML were expected to start shipping in the spring of 2001. The technology is there, it seems. The management part of the eSCM equation just has to catch up.

Focus on the Supply Chain

Sandy Jap: An integration state of mind

The more things change, the French say, the more they remain the same, and that is just as true of the traditional supply chain as anything else. Supply chain management is hardly a new idea; it's still a question of making sure you have the supplies and material to do your job, just as it always has been. But electronic commerce, with its constant flow of information, global reach, and ultra-compressed cycles, has given the same-old a new twist, in the opinion of Sandy Jap, a professor at the Massachusetts Institute of Technology's Sloan School of Management.

"Supply chain management is not a new idea — it's been around for decades," Jap said. "I think the idea of collaborative relationships among various members of a supply chain working together to serve an end customer is a great idea, and it has been around for a while. What is new is *electronic* supply chain."

The "e" in eSCM changes everything. It might simply be a new way of doing the same old thing, but that new way brings a whole new set of challenges in its wake. "It presents supply chain management with new constraints," Jap explained. "One new feature is you now have complete information sharing, which you couldn't have before — or instant feedback.

All these things present new parameters we need to practice in supply chain management. The challenge now is *how* to manage the supply chain with all these constraints that we didn't have before."

The electronic commerce possibilities for supply chain management are endless. Procurement can be integrated with scheduling; design can lead directly to the production line and then to the customer's loading dock in a single, perfectly choreographed motion. Science fiction's promise of products never touched by human hands is coming true ... almost. Getting there can be a gargantuan task. "Integration is the ability of various independent organizations in the supply chain to collaboratively work together and have efficient processes across all of them," Jap said.

A large part of eSCM integration is the automation and integration of these processes in production, and manufacturers — particularly in industries like high-technology and aerospace — are already seeing the benefits. But those benefits can't be realized by deploying technology alone. "It's much more than just a technology issue," Jap pointed out. "The technology is just a tool. The real issue is a management issue. Their role is to understand how to leverage these technologies so they can create organizational advantage. They have to think when it can be most valuable and use it that way, and how best to marry this technology to factory and supply chain processes."

Nevertheless, many companies are feeling the pressure to keep up with their partners and competitors. eSCM is on every manager's lips, and the technology, more than the management ideas required to take advantage of it, is on everyone's mind. "You hear people saying 'If they're deploying this technology, then we have to deploy it'," Jap said. "While companies have moved quickly to integrate processes and automate production, the progress has been more in deploying and using technology and less in management. Companies are using a lot of technology, but they're not thinking about how it matches with the processes and management strategies. They need to think creatively about how to use technology in relationships with suppliers."

That only begins when corporate culture moves toward a culture of collaboration — and it's a tough first step. "Supply chain integration requires reorientation of your thinking," Jap said. "You've got to get rid of win-or-lose mentality, the zero sum orientation. Managers have to get over that and think *we* instead of *me*. There has to be a change in your processes in terms of how you structure with and meet with and communicate with other supply chain partners."

One of the biggest challenges of integration is not technological but psychological. For it to become as prevalent as some analysts believe it will, managers will have to overcome the traditional insularity of business. Supply chain integration implicitly requires companies to not only share data, but to open up their systems to their partners. Even in the name of greater cost savings and efficiency, that can be difficult for many companies to accept. "Managers who execute transactions on a daily basis have to understand what the norms are — that it's okay to share information, and collaborate," Jap said. "There has to be a sense that we're going to seek out new ideas, scout opinions, and try to understand the capabilities of the other party."

That begins with communication. Like any two parties entering into a relationship, partners have to know what they expect from each other at the outset. "Be clear about what you want to get out of the relationship and what you are expecting for yourself and from your partner," Jap said. "Both sides need to be frank and set goals, see what they have in common and what motivates the capabilities they have. If you do this early, it can pay huge dividends."

The eSCM Challenge

For all its promise, the electronic commerce supply chain is still more of a goal than a reality. It's one thing to decide to integrate your processes with your partners for greater efficiency and visibility, but it's something else to actually do it. The problem is that, even though supply chain management has been on just about every manager's lips for the last two years, they're not always even sure what their supply chain is, never mind how to manage it.

Despite the hype from the technology press and consultants, and the pressure from CIOs to get on the bandwagon, the technology still isn't quite there. "Supply chain management is a very broad term," said Joanne Friedman, vice president of electronic strategies for the Meta Group, a research firm based in Stamford, Connecticut. "It can mean a whole range of things in the business and manufacturing process. In some places the technology is in place, but it's not being used. Of the world's top 2,000 companies, maybe half of those who've adopted business-to-business technologies are about 35 percent of the way to fully using it. It's still emerging."

That hasn't stopped supply chain management and integration from becoming one of the hottest markets for e-commerce solutions vendors. Young companies like i2, Manugistics, and Descartes Systems, and established players like Oracle Corp. and IBM have been falling over each other to bring the latest and greatest tools to market. Yet, for many businesses, an integrated supply chain remains an elusive goal, hampered by a number of factors, including the slow adoption of e-commerce, a corporate culture that resists change, and a lack of clear vision or definition of the supply chain and its processes. Recent studies reveal that many industries are lagging in their adoption of electronic commerce and are not making extensive use of it, even though they may acknowledge its importance to their business.

In early 2000, the National Association of Manufacturers (NAM), based in Washington, D.C., polled 2,500 manufacturers of varying sizes and found that many were not making extensive use of business-to-business electronic commerce. Sixty-five percent were not using e-commerce as a forum for business transactions, only incorporating the Web into business activities at the most basic level. While 80 percent said they had a Web site, most sites were used solely for corporate information. Only 10 percent said their business systems were fully automated. When asked how they were making use of e-commerce, only 7 percent said they used it for procuring raw material, only 5 percent for integrating their supply chain.

"I didn't think we were that far behind in moving to an e-commerce environment. It was a bit of a surprise," said Thomas Orlowski, vice president of information systems at NAM. Orlowski pointed to the lack of automated business systems as one factor holding up total supply chain integration in the manufacturing sector. "True integration means that each person has to have truly integrated systems, but many smaller companies may not have that, which means they aren't able to participate. Not automating means being left out of the supply chain. If you are automated, you assume the other guy is too. If they aren't, you have to take a step back and find a different supplier."

According to Orlowski, smaller and medium-sized manufacturers continue to lag behind in integration and automation, effectively excluding themselves from the electronic commerce supply chain. One problem is the misconceptions that many smaller manufacturers continue to hold about electronic commerce, particularly eSCM — that it's only for larger companies, that it requires huge investments, or that it's all just another techie fad. "They're desensitized to all the hype about the Net and e-commerce," Orlowski said. "They think it's created by vendors to sell their product, and they figure they'll just wait until they absolutely have to do it."

Nevertheless, the emergence of Internet-based eSCM has created a significant opportunity for smaller and medium-sized enterprises, Orlowski said. The expense of EDI may have excluded them from the big industrial supply chains in the past but the Internet promises to get them online. They only have to get over their mistrust of and misconceptions about supply chain technologies. "Larger manufacturers can't get smaller suppliers to participate because it's expensive," Orlowski said. "The Net is less expensive for those who can't afford EDI. It is feasible and solves problems quicker. The tools are easier to work with. It's important [for them] to get over their reluctance about technology and make an effort to participate at even a minimal level, even if it's just taking orders on computer."

That may be easier said than done. Released in the summer of 2000, the Cutter Consortium's study *E-business: Trends, Strategies and Technologies* showed just how far electronic commerce, not to mention the integrated supply chain, has yet to go before it becomes an everyday way of doing business in the United States. Business still has to be convinced of its value. Fully 19 percent of companies surveyed were not using e-business technologies because they felt the benefits were still unproven to them. Only 2 percent of the sample group was using eSCM, and only 12 percent of the rest were *planning* to use it.

One of the greatest obstacles — the complexity of even implementing the technology — will become apparent to most users only once they've actually decided to go ahead with deployment. The vendors for solutions to supply chain management problems may promise an easy transition to the next stage of electronic commerce but that, Friedman said, is just a sales pitch. Integration is not just a technology issue. "This is incredibly complex stuff, and not just from the technology-enabling point of view," she said. "The business side of it is enormously complicated. You can have as many as 25 people, even more, in a company's cross-function team deciding what their processes *are* to begin with. And this is even before you get into deploying the technology to enable those processes."

Indeed, enterprises that see supply chain integration as a simple matter of software deployment are in for a nasty shock. The problem, Friedman said, is that most managers aren't even sure what their supply chain is, let alone how to integrate and automate it. They may know that it's important, but most are still at a loss to explain just how it functions and who is responsible for what, or they don't see it as an integral part of the overall business strategy. The Cutter Consortium found 51 percent of the respondents were not even aware of the status of eSCM in their organization. Moreover, there was little satisfaction with eSCM, as noted in the Cutter study. "Most users are totally dissatisfied or totally disappointed with eSCM ... Given [its] youth and immaturity, this is not surprising. As industry experience grows and product maturity improves, satisfaction should improve as well."[5]

There is little doubt that supply chain management is more difficult and complex than originally envisioned. It means re-examining the supply chain in order to determine what needs to be done, and it is more than simply automating processes. One of the common problems is the complexity of the supply chain initiative, which can lead to failure. "We're not always seeing a huge amount of success with the big supply chain management efforts," said the Cutter Consortium's Pickering. "After all, you're talking about integrating the processes of a lot of different companies whose processes have evolved over a long time, most of whom deal with other companies. It's a lot tougher than integrating a single company's processes internally, and *that* can be extremely difficult."

Moreover, it's tempting for companies to buy into a solution vendor's best-practices approach. But all supply chains are as different as their varied mixes of players and disparate products. There is no single model for success, so eSCM success depends, to a large degree, on the ability of an enterprise to understand itself. It's like advice from a new-age, spiritual self-help book for companies — they have to look within themselves for the truth. "There is no one right answer for supply chain management," said PWC's Schwartz. "The biggest challenge is optimizing in a kind of way [that you think is best]."

That often means re-thinking your whole approach to business, and the relationship with your partners. More than a technology issue, a successful eSCM deployment requires thinking of your partners as equals and considering their needs along with your own. "We're very careful to avoid deploying capital where our customers are," said JCI's Suman. "Sometimes we have to jettison a product or process that we've become attached to. It's part of an on-going process of aligning ourselves with our partners."

Some analysts suggest mapping out the supply chain initiatives to determine what the goals, performance measures, and resources are, and to determine what your customer's needs will be. It can also help to determine where costs can be lowered. "It's a good exercise for any company to do," said Joanne Friedman. "Whether for inter-enterprise integration, or in growth or acquisition. It's something they should be aware of, anyway. Most aren't."

Improvements continue to be incremental. In its 1999 supply chain survey, KPMG found that 17 percent of the companies surveyed reported no improvement at all from the previous year. On the other end of the scale, 3 to 5 percent showed gains of 30 to 40 percent. They also found a wide gap between supply chain haves and have-nots; while some reap the benefits of supply chain improvements, some have not even initiated a supply chain improvement program. It's the smaller companies that continue to feel the most left out. "The larger companies need to educate and assist the medium and smaller guys, and pull in the same direction," Orlowski said, adding that the Internet is a factor in moving the process along. "The Net has changed it — there is more complete integration of the whole thing."

That, at least, is the goal. The problem, Orlowski said, is that manufacturers may not have the luxury of time to work out all the issues. In the constant rush of new technologies and the increasing pressure of ever-broadening markets, eSCM integration and automation is a prerequisite for survival. In effect, the time may have come when companies have to choose between joining a supply chain team, or sitting on the global economic bench. "You can do it well, or do it without automation," Orlowski said. "Supply chain integration is the Holy Grail everyone is looking for. Instead of company competing against company, it's going to be supply chain competing against supply chain. Those who aren't automated are going to lose out on market share."

And that may require a new way of thinking about partners, buyers, and suppliers — more as teammates and fellow travelers than sometimes partners and potential competitors. The question is: Are businesses ready to play that game? Supply chains often fail because companies don't sufficiently collaborate outside their own organization and focus instead on their internal supply chain. Another error is the belief that the supply chain ends at procurement, while procurement really only accounts for 20 percent of supply chain processes. "Everyone jumped on the procurement orientation to get compression," said Friedman. "But a supply chain is more complex than that. The focal

points need to change. You need to look at the activity stream throughout the process."

Attaining the supply chain Holy Grail may still be a long slow effort,
since introducing change into the business processes of a company can
take time, education, training, and investment. Orlowski concedes as
much, but he sees more manufacturers participating in electronic commerce. "The big thing is the culture change," he said. "There is a resistance to changing. It's not fast and it's not easy. It'll reach critical mass but
it will take several years — it's not going to happen tomorrow."

Key Terms
original equipment manufacturer (OEM)
file transfer protocol (FTP)
electronic supply chain management (eSCM)
advanced retail catalog
maintenance repair and operating (MRO)
extensible mark-up language (XML)

4

Business in the Material World: e-Logistics

At some point, the supply chain runs headlong into the real world. It's the point where electronic commerce becomes logistics, where the supply chain is no longer about moving bits of data around a network, but becomes a matter of moving real products and material to real customers in the real world. Unfortunately, it's also the point where the chain is most likely to break down. Nevertheless, the same electronic commerce technologies that have created a crisis for customer fulfillment are part of the solution. Meet e-logistics ...

Making the Trains Run on Time

At the height of the information revolution, the survivors of the industrial revolution are facing a challenge — how to move into the 21st century.

You don't tend to think of locomotives and Web servers in the same sentence and, compared to other industries, the railway freight industry is a relative latecomer to electronic commerce. Since the late 1990s, however, the rail freight industry has discovered that the Internet is the ideal environment to communicate with customers, order equipment, and process customs clearance documents — all the tasks that previously were paper heavy and time intensive and that have slowed rail traffic for decades. The rail freight industry is waking up to the reality that the Internet can link with steel rails in quite a comfortable partnership.

This paradox is embodied in the Burlington Northern Santa Fe Railway Company (BNSF). With 33,500 miles of track covering 28 states and two Canadian provinces, shipping coal, grain, metals, chemicals, minerals, forest products, automobiles, and a variety of consumer goods, it's one of North America's largest rail carriers. It's also one of the oldest — its roots date back to 1849 with the creation of Burlington Lines. Paradoxically perhaps, this aging giant is at the forefront of the rail freight industry's move to electronic commerce, which has helped them trim the fat from operations by increasing efficiency throughout. "One thing we're focused on — driving toward becoming easier to do business with," said Kathleen Regan, vice president of electronic commerce development for BNSF.

And that's what the railroad has done by tailoring on-line services to the needs of specific markets like the lumber industry. In 1999, BNSF was the first railroad to go on-line with the Loading Origin Guarantees program. As its acronym suggests, LOGs is a service targeted at the forest products industry. It allows customers to reserve rail car capacity from 4 to 24 weeks in advance through a weekly on-line capacity auction. Prior to its deployment, customers had to fax or phone in orders, and with the higher likelihood of errors, there was no guarantee of successful delivery. "Now they get assurance," said Regan. "The customer gets a commitment that we will deliver that car when they ask for it." If it doesn't, BNSF pays a penalty. Automating the lumber-loading process was a crucial logistical innovation for BNSF, whose track serves more of North America's lumber-producing regions than any other railroad.

LOGs made it easier for BNSF to allocate cars more efficiently. "We can see where the highest demand is because we're posting our supply and allowing demand to react to supply," said Regan. "We want to know as far in advance as possible where cars are going to be positioned, and we see a higher utilization of equipment. Satisfaction has gone up, and we've improved cycle time."

In the spring of 2000, BNSF took another big step into electronic commerce-enabled logistics when it began to post weekly specials on the Internet. The railroad's ValueTrax service is targeted at intermodal customers — companies that move containers from trucks to rail and from rail to trucks. Every Thursday BNSF posts discount prices on excess rail car capacity. ValueTrax lists the discounted rates along with a list of which days customers can bring loads to BNSF intermodal terminals, as well as the origin, destination, and availability time for each lane special. "If we didn't respond to that need, equipment would get out of sync," Regan said. "It helps to keep equipment in a nice flow and spread the demand, keeping an even balance from west to east. In yesteryear, we wouldn't have been able to dynamically react, to communicate to customers where we have excess capacity and find out their shipping needs. The key there is we're communicating this to the marketplace."

BNSF's customers can use their Web site for tracking and tracing orders, paying bills, pricing equipment, and determining freight rates — and while they may be at the leading edge of the rail industry, they aren't alone. BNSF's partner, the Canadian National Railway Company (CN), which, since its merger with Illinois Central, runs 16,000 miles of track from New Orleans to the Alaska Panhandle, moved to electronic commerce to solve a cross-border customs crisis. Faced with increasing rail traffic, the fifth largest railway in North America was confronted with massive delays as trains slowed to a crawl at the world's longest undefended border, with their wheels jammed in the paperwork of Canadian customs clearance.

Upon crossing the border, incoming railway cars would proceed to rail yards where they were held before Canadian customs officials released them. Since the NAFTA agreement 10 years earlier, cross-border traffic had increased by 10 percent annually — with the result that yards were jammed with 600 to 800 holds across the country on any given day. Cars languished in the yards for days at a time, forcing CN to put more cars on the tracks. With the higher inventory of cars, rail costs increased — in other words, increased trade was biting CN in the bottom line. For CN the challenge was to update their customs clearance system by a couple of centuries. Using electronic commerce technologies, CN reasoned, it could speed up the documentation process that connected it to Canadian and American customs and to brokers in the main rail destinations. Cars could be cleared and released faster, and CN wouldn't have to keep as much rolling stock on the rails, thus lowering costs and raising profits.

In 1998, CN launched the Automatic Manifest System or AMS, an end-to-end EDI-based system that would allow Canada Customs and CN to preprocess incoming rail traffic. Canada Customs would now receive an electronic waybill before a train even left the United States and would be able to determine when the cargo could be released. With AMS, when the train arrives from the United States at the Canadian border, Canada Customs receives an electronic arrival message and notifies the customs broker, who can file declarations with AMS as much as 10 days before the cargo arrives. The system is completely transparent, allowing anyone in the chain to follow the clearance process from the beginning to end.

AMS was revolutionary according to Mike Tamilia, CN's systems manager of customer and trans-border operations. Before AMS, he said, "there was no sense of urgency in getting the cars processed." With AMS there was a dramatic reduction in delays at the border — with clearance completed even before the cargo left the United States, cars were processed in 10 minutes instead of hours or days. The number of cars detained at the border was reduced to 40 from as many as 800, and car cycles and connections were improved. The accelerated process and the consequent reduction in paperwork brought costs down, and the cars can now handle an additional 7,000 loads per year, adding a potential CDN$38 million to CN's bottom line. "The customers benefit because the goods are delivered faster," Tamilia said. "There is a flow of accurate electronic data, right there on the screen."

CN simply wanted to speed things up, but streamlined logistics has additional benefits. With an automated manifest system, the railway, customs brokers, and customs officials can efficiently monitor shipments and track documents. Assuming the trains run on time, shipments can be pinpointed anywhere along their route from the United States. The system is speedy, efficient, and transparent. Other carriers are doing the same. For example, Federal Express Canada converted to Target, a custom EDI-based notification system. With Target, FedEx's hubs worldwide can keep track of incoming freight anywhere in Canada, while related software sends arrival data to the customs brokers and tracks the trade and customs movement. Target liberated FedEx employees from a predominantly paper-based system, reduced the customs clearance process to three minutes in duration, and made it easier for the company to track and archive its customs and trade data.

Updating the customs and logistics processes is not merely a question of convenience; it's a condition of survival. The customs clearance process only takes minutes, eliminating 90 percent of Fedex's paperwork, and the EDI-enabled system has sped up Canada Customs' own cargo-reporting process. Expenses and paperwork are down, freeing customs inspectors for inspections. It may not be the best of all possible worlds, but it has oiled the wheels of international trade, and that, after all, is what electronic commerce is all about. The global, high-speed, real-time Internet economy is forcing enterprises to streamline their logistics and fulfillment operations for electronic commerce. The immediacy of electronic commerce has habituated everyone in the supply chain to a kind of commercial instant gratification. It's not just a good idea to fill your orders quickly. In the new business-to-business supply chain, it's the price of survival. "E-commerce has so much opportunity," said BNSF's Regan. "If done properly we can communicate with customers, communicate products and goods more than we've done before. Look at e-business and rail — there's a huge opportunity to go after new customers, become more efficient, and become hooked to the customer's supply chain."

The Logic of Logistics

Listen to the rhythm of electronic commerce. It goes, *hurry up, hurry up, hurry up ...* wait. You've probably heard it before; it's the sound of the well-oiled machine of business hitting a brick wall. At some point, the bits and bytes of the electronic commerce supply chain will collide with the hard reality of the material world. Data that whizzes from one end of the Internet to the other has to be converted into real products, and those products have to get from one location to another. Think of the place where the electronic commerce supply chain collides with the real world. **Logistics,** the process of crossing that divide, from bits to atoms, from orders to shipping products, is one of the biggest challenges for electronic commerce. It's not as exciting as XML, or as obvious as procurement, but there are few operations as strategically important as the flow of goods and materials within the supply chain. After all, your customers live in a material, and not an electronic, world.

Electronic commerce logistics is a complex process, involving both inbound and outbound movement of material, and crossing over a wide range of operations from the order desk to customer service, warehousing, production, planning, and procurement. The process is all about getting goods to their destination within a specific time frame and keeping customers happy. Even in the disembodied world of e-business, where companies may not even physically touch the goods they sell, they still have to keep the goods moving through the supply chain and get them from one place to another geographically. In fact, e-business has changed the demands on logistics and supply chain. Not only do you still have to get the goods moving but you have to move them faster. Your customers demand it.

The accelerated pace of electronic commerce has created a whole new set of expectations. The focus of electronic business has gravitated away from the product toward the customer, and your customers are demanding specialized, personalized service, with more direct business. That means shorter cycle times and changes in distribution patterns for manufacturers and distributors. With tighter order fulfillment, you need a carrier who can bring your product to market — faster.

According to Boston-based AMR Research, the volume of global business-to-business electronic commerce will reach $5.7 trillion by 2004, and though not everyone agrees on the exact numbers, everyone agrees on the coming electronic commerce surge. The Boston Consulting Group estimates that by 2003, business-to-business commerce will grow by 33 percent yearly to reach $2.8 trillion; the Gartner Group, in a report issued in March 2000, described the business-to-business explosion as imminent and predicted the worldwide market to grow from $145 billion in 1999 to $953 billion in 2001 and $2.18 trillion in 2002. Any way you cut it, that means the volume of material goods passing through electronic commerce supply chains is going to go through the roof.

With that kind of growth, companies have to ponder whether their **fulfillment** systems and logistics will be capable of handling the predicted growth. In the retail world, merchants have learned the hard way that, unless they have a logistical strategy to keep up with the growth, they may as well not be in business at all — and it's a lesson that shouldn't be lost on companies in business-to-business commerce. Electronic commerce is almost defined by the struggle to keep up with the demands created by doing business on the Web. Retailers felt that pressure particularly painfully during the 1999 Christmas season, and their experience is equally instructive in the business-to-business space. That holiday season is a kind of logistical low-water mark that analysts still use as an example of what can happen when you show up unprepared for the electronic commerce revolution.

THE E-GRINCH THAT STOLE CHRISTMAS

In the months leading up to Christmas 1999, analysts were predicting an on-line retail shopping boom for the holiday season. Ernst & Young predicted that the number of on-line shoppers would triple during the holiday season, and Jupiter Communications projected that consumers would spend $6 billion on-line in the months of November and December 1999. The Christmas shopping tide came as no surprise, but despite the warnings, many retailers — including some giants in the business — struggled to meet consumer demand and consequently risked alienating their longtime customers. Analysts' opinions were almost unanimous. Retailers were advised to optimize their distribution systems for the imminent surge in on-line traffic, streamline their Web sites, be prepared to pay attention to the additional needs of customers, and ease up on returns policies for items purchased on-line. Few merchants heeded the advice, and the hottest shopping season of the year teetered toward disaster.

Indeed, widespread logistical and order fulfillment problems were evident to anyone who took the time to look. Not many did. Just before Christmas, researchers at Andersen Consulting (now Accenture) conducted a study in which they attempted to purchase 480 gifts from 100 popular retail Web sites. They were able to complete only 350 orders. Andersen found that many retailers had not readied their on-line businesses for the peak shopping season — they just weren't prepared. Poor Web site performance was a serious problem; not only were many of the sites unable to complete orders, some crashed or were incomplete, blocked, or just inaccessible. The result was that only one-quarter of the on-line transactions actually ended with a purchase. However, the Web site problems were only the tip of the iceberg. Andersen Consulting also found that traditional retailers were accurate with projected delivery dates only 22 percent of the time, and that few Web sites could accurately provide a delivery date — crucial information at Christmas time. Robert Mann of Andersen's Supply Chain Practice division warned, "Success depends on fulfillment operations that can meet high levels of customer service. Companies run a high risk of losing customer loyalty through poor performance."

Analysts red-flagged brick-and-mortar retailers that had opened Internet sales channels in time for the holidays. It was a memorable season for retail giants who had thought they had all their e-tailing ducks lined up in a row. Toys R Us's troubles during Christmas 1999 are legendary. The retailer's distribution system encountered a "glitch" that overestimated the company's ability to ship gifts in time for Christmas. Unable to meet the December 24 deadline, Toys R Us had to contend with legions of angry customers who had not received their gifts in time for Christmas and who had to invent stories about bad snowstorms in order to explain why Santa had not arrived. Even Macy's, the New York department store famous for kicking off the holiday season with its annual Thanksgiving Day parade, encountered similar embarrassment. Many customers who had ordered gifts from the Macy's Web site found themselves empty-handed at Christmas. Wal-Mart was unable to guarantee delivery after December 14, the peak shopping week, even though it had outsourced its fulfillment processes. Surprisingly, Internet-only e-tailers without a bricks-and-mortar operation fared better. According to the Andersen study, they were better at inventory tracking, and shoppers completed their orders 20 percent faster than on bricks-and-mortar sites.

Toys R Us later admitted that it had accepted too many orders on its Internet site, and that turned out to be a costly admission. The company offered $100 gift certificates to customers who wanted to cancel unfulfilled orders and allowed customers to keep gifts that arrived after it canceled their orders. However, this did not prevent Toys R Us from being hit with a class-action lawsuit in Washington. A woman named Kimberly Alguard accused the company of accepting Christmas orders while knowing it would not be able to ship the toys in time. There were serious discussions about the possibility of sanctions against American companies under the Federal Trade Commission's Mail Order Rule.

E-tailers took stock after the holidays, and analysts said, "I told you so." Electronic commerce had changed everything, and the merchants who were burned in the Christmas logistics meltdown were the ones who thought they could just do business as usual. "The Internet changes expectations," wrote Heather Green in *Business Week*. "Customers want products to arrive faster than with catalog purchases. They want every order to be right and won't accept a note in a box telling them that all their items weren't in stock after all ... Forecasting and inventory management are key things that companies are going to have to work out [in 2000]."[1] Planning and forecasting were indeed a problem. Retailers that didn't have years of experience with Internet commerce — and few did — were unable to assess customer demand. Others who had problems with poor performance had not sufficiently integrated e-commerce servers and fulfillment systems and had not factored in the heightened need for customer service. "What happened with Christmas 1999 was that a lot of companies moved from a traditional model to an Internet model," said Bruce Strahan of the Roswell, Georgia–based consultants The Progress Group. "In order to be fast and effective from a logistical standpoint you can't do that out of a garage." To avoid chaos, said Strahan, companies have to begin at the beginning. "That means preplanning instead of reacting to things. Many companies tend to react when the order hits the floor. The successful companies are those who poll continuously and make changes before the order hits. It has to start with company-to-company planning, knowing what the future will bring so there is less chaos."

B2B Lessons Learned?

The 1999 Christmas meltdown should also be a wake-up call for enterprises doing business-to-business commerce. What happened then involved retail commerce where customers order one or two items at a time. If you can imagine the disappointed faces of children who didn't get their Christmas presents, imagine the far grumpier faces of business managers who didn't get a shipment of parts in time to assemble their order. Visualize the scenario if a shipment of several tonnes of raw materials fails to arrive at its destination, or has to sit in a warehouse awaiting customs clearance. As bad as Christmas 1999 was for the retail industry, the stakes are potentially much higher when the business-to-business supply chain collapses. If raw materials, goods, capital, and information don't keep flowing, there may as well not be a supply chain at all.

Having said that, cracking the logistics nut can be a substantial obstacle to businesses just making the move to on-line sales. Many, after all, are e-commerce novices. Referring to the Christmas 1999 debacle, Green wrote, "Fulfillment is hard because on-line merchants are shooting at moving targets — a lot of them. E-tailers are adding new customers, systems, products, suppliers, and distribution centers all at the same time."[2] Manufacturers and other participants in the supply chain are being warned of an imminent boom in their own in business-to-business transactions, and businesses attempting to keep up are adding a number of different pieces to their fulfillment systems. Early in 2000, as part of an ongoing study, Hackett Benchmarking and Research surveyed 25 companies, two-thirds of whom earn $1 billion yearly or more. While many realize they must adapt their distribution strategies to the demands of electronic commerce, at least 73 percent of those surveyed said they had not changed their traditional shipping methods and 40 percent said they had not integrated their supply chain systems with their e-business systems. It's not good news. Despite the obvious warnings, all too many businesses continue to neglect exactly what analysts are telling them to focus on — logistics. All the red flags are still there; ignore logistics, and your Internet sales channel will be a disaster.

The Internet economy has made it possible for companies to go virtually global, virtually overnight, simply by adding "dot-com" to their names. But selling on the Net is hardly a guarantee of success when a company can't accept or fulfill international orders. The global market is an enormous opportunity, but it also brings new technological and logistical demands. The reality is that many electronic commerce companies simply aren't prepared to go global. Thirty-eight percent of companies surveyed by Forrester Research cited global distribution as their biggest fulfillment challenge in 2001, and 85 percent said they can't fill international orders because of the difficulties inherent in international shipping. The Internet may be borderless, but countries are not; goods have to be shipped to and from countries with different trade regulations, tariffs, and product classifications. There are the issues of screening orders for boycotts and embargoed countries, international regulatory compliance, and the ability to calculate the total cost of a shipment. Some manufacturers are reluctant to ship globally because their systems don't process international addresses and postal codes or else they can't accurately price the total landed cost of delivery. And there are concerns about customs clearance: If you are shipping perishable or quickly dated goods, you don't want to run the risk of having them sit in a warehouse for days awaiting the all-clear. Because tariffs and rates can — and frequently do — change rapidly, there is a need for a constant flow of available information between all points, from the point of origin to customs, governing bodies, the shippers, and the receivers. Enterprises that have done relatively small volumes of international shipping in the past may be hamstrung by outdated systems that they never considered upgrading, or have smaller staffs that simply can't keep track of trade data. Shipping internationally may not be part of their core operations, and they may never have contemplated what's involved until their first order from Buenos Aires arrived. Companies that fail to retool for international trade will find themselves unable to do business overseas or risk violating international trade rules, and being on the wrong side of international trade law can result in more than just delays or lost business. It can mean fines or jail time.

This also applies to large companies that actually have shipping departments and some experience with long-distance orders. Just imagine the damage done to a smaller, newer enterprise that has only started trading on the Internet and has never had to navigate the labyrinth of international order fulfillment. Any enterprise that wants to survive the e-commerce boom is going to have to look at the failures of their existing fulfillment systems and determine a strategy to resolve their logistics issues.

Focus on Logistics

Gary Allen: Third-party logistics

So you've set up your B2B Web site and you're listed on one of the biggest international trading exchanges. You've seen the ad with the Italian olive oil shop that sells in the United States, and the other one with the little guy in Texas who outbids everyone else for a big Japanese contract. You're all set to transform a regional business into a global electronic commerce powerhouse. Except for one thing — one of your new customers is in Korea, and you haven't the faintest idea how you're going to get your products to the other side of the Pacific Ocean.

"Selling to customers on the other side of the world is realistic; how you get it there and how you fulfill that order is a whole different matter," said Gary Allen, senior manager of Cap Gemini, Ernst & Young's supply chain practice. "That's the real logistical challenge for electronic commerce, because it's enabling anybody to sell anything anywhere. But the fulfillment is complex. How you do that — whether you actually invest in an entire network, or you outsource — there are a number of different operating methods by which you can execute. But people aren't necessarily considering all of the factors behind how you fulfill orders. That's the big challenge, especially on a global scale, because these smaller mom-and-pops in Texas don't necessarily have the capabilities, or they may not have thought through all of the international tax implications and all the other stuff that goes along with it."

No matter what happens to your business, the bottom line of electronic commerce is that you still have to move stuff. As marketplaces are formed, as the Internet expands for additional capability, that means moving stuff all over the world. "But the business of logistics is changing as well," Allen said. "Logistics providers are changing their partnership and outsourcing strategies, and they're continuing to increase in capability. You have third-party logistics providers and you have the fulfillment providers who are trying to change and adapt to those needs at the same time. That means global e-commerce is do-able, but it's complex. The olive grower in Italy trying to fill orders all over the world is [doing something] complex, but if [he has] the right approach and the right strategy behind it, and [he selects] the right partners, he can do it. Of course, you get into an issue of are you going to do it yourself, or are you going to partner, and what are the costs and benefits associated with doing that?"

The main advantage of outsourcing to a third-party logistics provider (3PL) is that you don't have to invest in the infrastructure and the resources and the competencies yourself. You can focus on growing olives in Italy, if that's what you want to do, rather than having to build up your own infrastructure and technology behind it. "The benefit is that the 3PL can leverage its network and its capabilities across multiple companies and customers, because they're already established," Allen said. The value of that can continue to expand, in the sense that "they can expand the network, they can fill assets, use their own planes, trucks and whatever, while a single olive grower in Italy can't do any of that himself. And how long would it take you to build up to that capability and size?"

It's an economy of scale, of course, but there are advantages for large companies as well. Why divert resources to keep rail cars on track, trucks on the road, and planes in the air when planes, trains, and trucks aren't even what you're really good at? "A large automotive company like Ford or GM's focus is designing and manufacturing automobiles," Allen said. "They may not want to invest in the resources and the capital behind doing [the logistics] themselves, and this creates much more flexibility."

Part of the problem — a big part, in fact — is that the immediacy of electronic commerce has raised customer expectations. Instant buying has created an anticipation of instant fulfillment, and that has a whole lot of managers running scared. It's worth considering whether your own shipping department is up to the challenge. "In general, from a customer's perspective, expectations are increasing; that's the reality," Allen said. "Think of the amount of time people spend on the Internet, even in their own homes, and the ability businesses and consumers have to find out where their order is, look at their product, look at their inventory. They expect to be notified about when it's going to be delivered and, oh boy, if it doesn't hit that delivery date, they want to know. That started on the retailing side, but those expectations are really carrying over to the B2B side now."

In the business-to-business market, moreover, customers are demanding complete visibility at every step along the way from your loading dock to theirs. "Visibility is becoming much more of an opportunity for the 3PLs on one side, and an expectation from a customer standpoint," Allen said. "Five years ago, especially on the B2B side, if you talked to people about the need for visibility and for putting value propositions together around inventory turns and reduced cycle times, you'd just get this blank stare. But now, it's becoming an important part of the whole logistical process."

How do you actually go about hiring a logistics provider who can take the load off your mind? The selection process is never easy, simply because a 3PL can be anything from a small provider who ships one box at a time to large warehouse-based and transportation-based providers who will take over your whole loading dock. "We have companies claiming to be 3PLs, when they actually have different incentives and goals for establishing that service offering," Allen said. "The approach that companies *should* take is certainly to look at the history, the track record, the customers in place; do a pretty thorough analysis behind expectations and goals from a customer's standpoint and why you'd want to outsource — and what's the baseline behind it. Even before companies start that process, they should understand what their current costs are today, and what they really want to achieve by [outsourcing] it."

Nevertheless, as electronic commerce continues to create a near-insatiable demand for logistics specialists, and as existing companies become better established, the decision is getting easier. "The challenge is that 3PLs market themselves differently, so trying to peel back true competencies and capabilities is a different story," Allen said. "And then there's the issue of all the mergers and acquisitions going on around the globe — every time a 3PL acquires another, there's a certain amount of integration that occurs, and that definitely impacts a 3PL's ability to serve its customers. You just have to keep your goal — finding someone who can help you serve your customers — in mind."

UNTYING THE GORDIAN KNOT

In traditional commerce, if your customers don't like your service, or their orders are not being fulfilled, they can just walk away. If you're lucky, you're the only business of your kind in town, and they'll have nowhere to walk away to. It's called a captive market, a phenomenon that allows supermarkets to let their shelves go bare, lets office supply companies run out of fax paper without notice, or permits your unscrupulous supplier to let his inventory run out. There is an economy in keeping stocks down to the point where they are likely to run out and in shipping at the very last possible minute. That way, suppliers don't have to keep surplus inventory gathering dust rather than profit. And if you don't like it … well, more often than not, there's nowhere else to go.

But that's not true anymore. Procurement decisions don't have to be made on geographic proximity when the next supplier — one that can fill your orders efficiently and on time — is a mouse click away. For suppliers, the message is simple. In the interconnected, real-time world of the electronic commerce supply chain, they ignore the logistical management part of the supply chain at their peril. The new sine qua non of logistics in electronic commerce is the fully transparent fulfillment system that provides visibility and a continuity of service from purchase to delivery.

However, streamlining logistics is putting pressure on carriers, who are having trouble keeping up. Compression of cycle times is also creating pressure on carriers. "We're creating a lot of peak management situations we didn't have in the past," said Bruce Strahan. "We see a whole lot more business being compressed in a smaller amount of time. You'll see 60 to 80 percent of volume going out of a warehouse between 4 and 7 p.m. That is changing logistics from what happens inside four walls to what happens to transport mechanism."

The same electronic commerce technologies that have created such a crisis for logistical management can provide the solution. "Federal Express ships 3.1 million packages a day," said Tim Kibbey, a manager of electronic commerce and customer convenience at Federal Express. "The only way we can fulfill our value proposition is by using information."

That, of course, was the lesson FedEx learned with Target. However, it goes further than that. Few companies have as many logistical issues as an international courier — it is, after all, logistics in the raw — and FedEx's solution is a kind of paragon of transparency and streamlined logistical management.

Every time a FedEx package changes hands, couriers or handlers enter a tracking number in their portable Supertrackers. That data is routed to the company's central information system, allowing anyone at FedEx — and anyone expecting the delivery of a package — to pinpoint its location on the delivery route. The process isn't completely automated yet; it can't be. Kibbey notes that there are some places in the world, like Mongolia or the jungles of Burma, that aren't yet networked enough to permit the complete elimination of paper documents. And a lot of processing by FedEx clients in the wired world is still done by hand. However, the company is encouraging its e-commercial customers to network directly with the shipping database. "We absolutely recognize the need for integration with customers' back offices," Kibbey said. "We're moving to be part of the process so that the moment a customer makes an order it's ready to go. There are exciting things we're doing with electronic commerce."

Indeed, a whole industry has emerged to move paper and telephone-based logistics systems to electronic commerce-enabled e-logistics. What's new on the block is something called **e-fulfillment,** complete solutions that integrate seamlessly with enterprise and procurement applications to automate supply chain and logistics management and provide high speed and transparency, much like CN's AMS. The whole idea behind e-fulfillment is to synchronize the business process across the enterprise, thus providing better logistical management with excellent customer relations and package visibility (whereby you can track the progress of an order or transaction from beginning to end). It represents a revolution in logistics that promises to transform the enterprise from the outside in. "Any move to e-commerce or e-business forces the company to focus and evaluate their existing processes," said Heather Ashton of the

Hurwitz Group, a Boston-based research and analysis company. "The first step is to optimize their existing processes before they translate those into technology."

The typical goal of logistical automation within the supply chain is increased productivity, a reduced paper trail, more accurate inventory tracking, and reduced costs. When Ericsson Communications' radio division upgraded its delivery system in 1996, for example, the communications equipment manufacturer wanted to be able to determine locations and arrival times for orders already in transit, and to be able to provide their customers with that information. What Ericsson wanted was end-to-end package visibility, nothing less than the Holy Grail of logistics. The company deployed DeliveryNet FSM, an integrated logistics package from Waterloo, Ontario–based Descartes Systems Inc., in 1997. The new system provided backbone systems integration and global visibility management software out of the box, and permitted the exchange of logistical information over EDI. That kept Ericsson's shipping and order fulfillment departments in the loop, taking advantage of a messaging technology the company had been using for decades. Account reps could supply customers with order information, and above all, the company was able to reduce transportation costs and speed up worldwide delivery, cutting lead times by 72 percent.

Shipping domestically is one thing, but managing logistics across national borders is a Gordian knot of its own. "Not automating your global logistics puts you at risk," said Greg Stock, vice president of marketing for Vastera Solutions, in Dulles, Virginia, a company specializing in Web-based e-commerce solutions for streamlining international trade. Stock has seen the need for automated trade systems grow rapidly in recent years. "NAFTA made it harder, not easier," he said. "The documentation it created is horrendous. Trade logistics is a big problem, especially since firms go global overnight and don't have the systems in place to deal with it. A lot of them are using homegrown or manual systems — and that can be a problem." They can be a problem because even a whole office complex full of workers devoted to logistics simply can't keep up with the pace of electronic commerce. Vendors like Vastera have begun to offer Web-based solutions to optimize a whole range of global trade processes, from managing shipping documents to screening, tracking, and tracing orders. Vastera's TradeSphere system, for example, provides a landed-cost optimizer, letting a shipper sum up the entire cost and calculate profits before the order leaves the loading dock. With Global eContent, Vastera users can check a global trade information bank, which provides expert assessment in real time of the constantly changing international trade data — tariffs, taxes, duties, and regulations.

Stock pointed to one of Vastera's success stories, the New Zealand Dairy Board, which ships more than 4,000 products yearly to over 1,000 destinations in over 120 countries across six continents. They had to process international orders on a 10-year-old system and contend with a huge amount of paper documents — each shipment required a dozen. They considered hiring additional staff to handle the documents, but instead automated in 1998 with Vastera's TradeSphere and Global eContent solutions. The dairy board was able to reduce the total number of shipping documents from over 5,000 to less than 300 and virtually eliminated documentation errors by 1999 — all of which allowed them to increase their total exports to 1.13 million tons from 300,000 without adding to their documentation staff.

The benefits of automation are numerous — reduced costs; faster, more accurate shipping; increased productivity; and a smoothly running, integrated system. However, the move to automation can be tricky for smaller businesses or novices who don't have the infrastructure and don't want to automate bad processes. Most providers of e-commerce solutions offer consulting as part of their service package, to help each company determine what is the ideal product suite for them. The most successful e-commerce deployment will involve enterprise-wide integration and a carefully planned, coherent implementation strategy. It's not just about technology — it's about the strategy that benefits your enterprise. That means starting at square one to create a technological foundation your company can build on today and leverage in the future.

Key Terms

logistics

fulfillment

e-fulfillment

5

THE GLOBAL VILLAGE: VIRTUAL TRADING COMMUNITIES

*Electronic commerce changes everything. The traditional adversarial rela-
tionships between competitors are giving way to collaborative market building;
the rigid, linear interactions between companies, their suppliers, and clients
are becoming multifaceted and diffuse. This new business paradigm is embodied in virtual trading communities and e-marketplaces, the digital kas-
bahs of electronic commerce.*

SLEEPING WITH THE ENEMY

The news hit computer-industry watchers like a ton of bricks in the
summer of 1997: Microsoft Corp. had agreed to invest $150 million in
non-voting stock in Apple Computer Corp. and collaborate on technology development. Apple's co-founder and acting CEO Steve Jobs,
called back from the wilderness to revive the ailing company only months
before, may as well have announced that he and Bill Gates had renounced
technology and were joining a Luddite commune; the U.S. government
could have appointed Iraqi strongman Saddam Hussein to the Supreme

Court, and it would have made more sense. After all, Apple and Microsoft were mortal enemies, whose whole philosophies and raisons d'être had been diametrically opposed for more than a decade. Apple, once described as a cross between a cult and a public utility, was the great computer revolutionary, on a crusade to build "the computer for the rest of us." Microsoft was the Evil Empire, whose stated goal was to put "a computer on every desk" — a computer running Microsoft software.

At Apple's annual sales conference in October 1983, Jobs pulled a stunt that haunted the company for more than a decade. Before the assembled multitudes of Apple's corporate faithful, Jobs hosted a spoof of "The Dating Game." Gates, Mitch Kapor of Lotus Development, and Fred Gibbons of Software Publishing Corp. — then the software industry's leading players — came up on stage and vowed to "go steady with Macintosh." The Macintosh had yet to go on sale, and Apple needed all the support it could get to convince potential customers that there would be a considerable supply of application software available for the new personal computer. Unfortunately, things didn't quite turn out that way, and the dating game stunt has been a bit of an embarrassment for more than a decade. Apple has never succeeded in attracting many suitors, and today, software companies are increasingly reluctant to develop products for the Mac.

Fourteen years after the dating game, the Mac simply couldn't get a date, and that was showing on the bottom line. In many ways, the company was back where it had been in 1983, trying to convince potential customers that the software industry was lining up to develop products for the Macintosh. The Mac's principal shortcoming had long been the paucity of third-party applications for the platform. Without a wide range of application software, it was difficult to attract new customers. Macintosh sales were going down the toilet, while cheaper personal computers running Microsoft's Windows operating system were selling at unprecedented rates. There were more applications for Windows, with the prospect of more to come, and that hurt Apple.

In fact, $150 million is pocket change in the computer industry, but Apple benefited far more than the numbers would suggest. The investment was a desperately needed vote of confidence in the long-embattled company. The message — more than the investment itself — was that Gates believed in Apple, and that the world's biggest software company was committed to producing applications that would run on its rival's machines. The immediate performance of Apple's stock, which reached an 18-month high the day after the announcement, reflected that. The turnaround in Apple's fortunes, driven by new models like the iMac and Macintosh G4, dates from the investment. The company was, in effect, saved by its traditional enemy.

The benefits of the deal were subtler for Microsoft, but the company hoped they would be just as substantial. Microsoft is like the successful, popular, good-looking classmate that everyone hated in high school. For all of its success, it has few friends in the computer industry. Companies work with Microsoft because they have to, not always because they want to or because they believe that it has the best technology, and that attitude had begun to exact a price. Aside from opening a potentially lucrative market for Macintosh software — to this day, Microsoft makes almost all of the serious business applications available for the Mac — Microsoft needed Apple to provide a viable, though relatively small alternative to the Windows operating system. Gates's legal troubles had only begun, and he doubtless reasoned that, as long as Apple continued to exist, American regulators couldn't pursue Microsoft for anti-trust violations. He was, as it turned out, wrong.

Nevertheless, for $150 million and the promise of cooperation, Microsoft had bought a friend — Apple was conspicuously quiet during the anti-trust trial — and Apple got a date for Saturday night. Seeing them dance was a subversion of natural laws … but the laws were changing.

CO-OPETITION?

It shouldn't have been so much of a surprise. Only a year before Gates and Jobs dropped their $150-million bombshell, Boston-based business consultant James Moore informed the world that competition was dead.

In his book *The Death of Competition,* Moore wrote that the traditional boundaries between industries and companies had collapsed in the wake of globalization and technological change. The traditional dog-eat-dog competition that once characterized American — and global — business was no longer practical nor even desirable, he argued. Indeed, what companies had to do now was find a way to co-evolve, to work together to create markets, collaborating at times and competing at others.

Much of what Moore wrote was hardly news. His conception of a new form of enterprise organization, the self-contained **business ecosystem** that cut horizontally across a number of traditional industries and that existed to create, nurture, and exploit a wide range of markets, though audacious in its presentation, was familiar to any student of the Japanese business alliances known as the *kereitsu.* Admittedly, Moore's ecosystems are less a formal alliance than a federation of companies anchored by the sometimes-ruthless influence of one powerful corporation, but he seemed to be saying that, to compete on an equal footing with the *kereitsu* of the then-powerful Asian economies, North American corporations had to become more like them. From that angle, it was a familiar cant — something big American corporations had, in fact, been saying since the late 1970s.

In the few years since *The Death of Competition* came out, much of Moore's thesis has begun to seem hopelessly dated. The Asian economic crisis of the late 1990s seemed to debunk his contention that horizontally integrated business ecosystems — or *kereitsu* — were the key to economic growth. Indeed, at least a year before the Asian economies collapsed, Hiroyuki Tezuka argued in a prescient essay that traditional cooperative Japanese business structures were a brake on innovation and entrepreneurship in the Japanese economy.[1] Moreover, some of Moore's paragons of business ecosystems in the U.S. context, such as Microsoft and Intel, have either failed to maintain their ecosystems or failed because of them.

Microsoft's legal woes are the result, in large part, of the corporate behavior that Moore so admired. In June 2000, Judge Thomas Penfield Jackson ordered the software vendor to be broken up for uncompetitive business practices. These practices — using its dominant market position to influence PC vendors and dictate to software developers — were precisely the strategies Moore recommended for the creation of business ecosystems. It seems that some business ecosystems have yet another name — monopolies.

Less dramatically, but perhaps more importantly, Intel's subservient confederates in the personal computer industry went out of their way to court rival Advanced Micro Devices Corp. in 1998 and 1999 when the chip maker failed to meet production and price expectations for the Celeron and Pentium III microprocessors. Compaq Computer Corp., long Intel's staunchest ally, announced in the spring of 2000 that it had also allied itself with Transmeta Corp., a maker of microprocessors that can mimic the functions of anyone's, including Intel's, chips. Far from anchoring a vast business ecosystem, Intel has become one equal — though perhaps still the *most* equal — among many in a complex, highly diffuse trading environment.

However, there is something to the idea of business ecosystems that's right on target, exemplified by the Apple-Microsoft deal and, perhaps paradoxically, by the complex web of alliances and partnerships that characterize the personal computer industry. Competition, though not dead, has become just one ingredient in the mix of 21st-century business strategies. The convergence of several trends, namely the liberalization of global trade, the establishment of vast international trade zones, and the emergence of technologies that not only enable but require companies to respond to those markets immediately, has created a new commercial imperative of corporate cooperation. As Donna Fenn observed in *Inc.* magazine in 1997, "While advances in technology, communications, and transportation have created an unprecedented number of opportunities for growing companies, it's now nearly impossible for entrepreneurs to take advantage of those opportunities on their own."[2]

Corporate cooperation is not a new idea, of course. Cartels rose and fell throughout most of the last century; industrial associations and standards bodies set the rules of corporate engagement and quality standards;

competitors collaborated on the great 20th-century public mega-projects, such as the St. Lawrence Seaway, the hydroelectric development of northern Quebec, and the space program. What is new is how cooperative efforts — or **co-opetition**, the annoying but accurate consultant-speak neologism popularized by Adam Brandenburger and Barry Nalebuff in their 1997 book of that title — have become a common, if not dominant, mode of corporate interaction, even without the compulsion of a public works contract.

Far from being a fluke or an isolated incident, the Apple-Microsoft deal was symptomatic of a more general trend toward building business ecosystems. Apple also collaborated with IBM and Motorola in the 1990s to develop the PowerPC microprocessor; telecommunications carriers regularly share network capacity with other carriers in vast "fiber swaps"; consumer electronics manufacturers work with each other and with network operators to develop broadcast standards. Whether "co-opetition" represents the future of North American business strategy remains to be seen, of course, but the trend has already had profound implications for the electronic commerce supply chain. The smart money — including the leaders of the automotive and steel industries — has seen the future of business-to-business electronic commerce, and it is the virtual trading community. The horizontally integrated *kereitsu* is passé. Another Japanese idea — the **wa**, or mutual commercial support network — is in. "Co-opetition" has triumphed, and North American business will never be the same.

On the other hand, the realities of the new economy have created a new kind of competition, no less cutthroat than the rivalries between industrial empires of the age of steam and steel. As Don Tapscott has noted, "In the digital economy, competition doesn't just come from competitors only — it comes from everywhere. When information becomes digital and networked, walls fall and no business is safe."[3] Your competitors may be traditional rivals, national economies, or virtual consortia that come together for one project. But competition has come to mean something different. That enterprise which is most flexible, and most able to leverage its position both vertically and horizontally without over-committing its resources, is the one most likely to succeed. Paradoxically, the very flexibility that enables and empowers your competitiveness can only be achieved in the context of a new paradigm ... at least that's what the smart money is saying.

COMMUNITIES OF INTEREST

It's one thing to proclaim the emergence of a new business paradigm, but it's something else again to make it happen. Nevertheless, it was perhaps inevitable that co-opetition would meet the Internet, fall in love, and have a baby they'd call the **virtual trading community** (or **e-marketplace**, or **hub**, or whatever). Indeed, the whole philosophy is predicated on how the immediacy of computer and telecommunications technologies has created new opportunities that companies can take advantage of only by using the same technologies. The Internet and electronic commerce create both the need for and the ability to build commercial support networks in the tradition of *wa*.

A peer-to-peer network with no central authority or single focus, the Internet is perhaps the ideal place to build virtual *wa*. From its earliest days, the Net has been touted as a kind of global village, a congenial neighborhood with no national borders. In *The Virtual Community*, cyber-guru Howard Rheingold praised the Internet — or more generally "computer-mediated communication" or CMC — as the perfect vehicle for a new kind of social organization. "The experience has to do with the way groups of people are using CMC to rediscover the power of cooperation," he wrote of the Well, one of the first consumer-oriented network services, "turning cooperation into a game, a way of life — a merger of knowledge capital, social capital, and communion."[4] Over-heated utopian rhetoric, perhaps, but there is something to what Rheingold observed at the Well. The Internet can create a *simulacrum* of community, even if it's not a community in fact. And that's all you need for co-opetition.

Admittedly a virtual trading community is indistinguishable from the partner **extranets** that have been an electronic commerce fixture for several years — except for one thing. Rather than being focused on the procurement needs of a single enterprise, the community provides a secure extranet environment and software infrastructure to support many companies' procurement processes, at the buy side and the sell side. And that's a big deal. In effect, these e-marketplaces provide a single point of contact, a portal for many companies to interact and transact. The idea is to open up the supply chain, so that sellers can work together, compare products and prices, and make deals as required with a number of buyers, rather than locking them into a proprietary relationship with just one. The flip side is that buyers, no longer tied to their regular suppliers, can shop their procurement needs around. The market, rather than one powerful buyer or vendor, sets the price. "That's the big attraction," said analyst Kirsten Cloninger for Cahners In-Stat Group. "It's the ability to turn around procurement from the tactical perspective and make it strategic. It can make procurement both more responsive and more flexible."

And it's a powerful attraction. Since 1999, virtual trading communities have proliferated at an astounding pace, and the number of terms that have emerged to describe them is a sure indication of the importance they have assumed in electronic commerce. Just as the Inuit have specific words for snow in all its forms, almost everyone in electronic commerce has his or her own term for the same basic idea: e-business networks, e-marketplaces, network exchanges, hubs, business-to-business portals. Despite all their names, however, virtual trading communities fall into just two basic categories — third-party marketplaces and public exchanges sponsored by industry verticals.

The typical trading community of the former variety is an on-line service set up by an entrepreneur to serve a niche market. The market builder acts as a kind of shopping mall developer, providing the software, information, transaction services, and servers in exchange for a membership fee, or some kind of profit share on transactions, or both.

These services can be a great boon for smaller companies that want to extend their supply chain but may not have the money or resources to build their own partner extranet. "In an extranet situation, a company usually has to do its own setup," Cloninger said. "Third-party industry marketplaces are different. Someone is building that part of the supply chain *for* you."

And it's a different *kind* of supply chain. By providing a virtual environment where potential collaborators and partners can connect and interact, market builders are nurturing *wa*. Though that may superficially seem like a fringe benefit, it's really the big attraction of the phenomenon of the virtual trading community. It puts the supply chain out in the open, where all participants can share the same market information and act on the same intelligence. The big challenge for market builders is to provide enough information and value-added content, while making the exchange and transaction process transparent enough to foster a sense of trust and community. "My sense is that there are four key components for success — the four Cs," said Dan Latendre, vice president of marketing and business development for OpenText Corp.'s B2Bscene.com trading community. "You need a sense of community, compelling content, and a sense of collaboration, and you have to be able to do commerce. You see a whole lot of companies getting together in marketplaces not just to sell, but to build the industry."

That sense of community is easier to build from *within* an industry, however, and the biggest trading communities are the ones set up by the industries themselves. To some extent, it's a question of making a virtue of necessity, as when the private hubs proposed by each of Detroit's Big Three automakers were folded together under the sponsorship of the AIAG into the Automotive Network Exchange (ANX). Illustrating the reality of co-opetition, perhaps, the three traditional rivals realized that they couldn't go it alone and so opted to work together to build a secure, real-time, one-stop-shopping trading environment for the whole North American auto industry. ANX itself — whose management the AIAG spun off to Science International

Applications Corp. in 2000 — is a secure network infrastructure that automakers can use to build their own procurement portals and hubs.

The idea is that, by opening their traditionally closed, linear supply chains to a wider range of potential suppliers, the automakers will be able to benefit from a far more fluid and responsive procurement process while consolidating network applications, like messaging, EDI, CAD/CAM data transfers, and digital prototyping, in a single, secure network infrastructure. It is quickly becoming the network foundation for any number of virtual marketplaces, like Covisint, the procurement portal launched by Detroit's Big Three in February 2000 and joined by Nissan Corp. and Renault the following April.

The ANX's value for the automakers' suppliers is both more fundamental than a secure network and, in its own way, revolutionary. In theory, at least, the exchange provides a single point of contact to the procurement process for the whole North American automotive industry. "It's just a transport mechanism," said the AIAG's Sally Fuger. "It's just the road, and it exists independently of the cars that go over it, whether that's EDI, CAD/CAM, or whatever. It creates an infrastructure for all the tiers." Instead of having to set up, maintain, and pay for EDI links to each manufacturer individually, suppliers can reach all of the big three — and then some — at once, as well as reaching to the industry's outer tiers. That means smaller suppliers that had been locked out of the supply chain by the cost of highly compliant VAN-based EDI systems can now play with the automotive big boys.

That doesn't mean that the old way of doing things — like dedicated EDI connections or direct feeds of prototype information to the CAD/CAM-enabled production lines — will be immediately supplanted. "That's not going away," Fuger said. "It still works, and there's something to be said for inexpensive, dial-up EDI. But it brings it all together." More importantly, perhaps, the existence of a single, common transport medium for automotive electronic commerce promises to greatly simplify the IT management equation at all levels of the exchange by reducing the number of parallel connections.

The automotive industry is only one of several verticals that have opted to create industry-wide virtual trading communities. Similar hubs have been or are being developed by the chemical, plastics, mining, and steel industries. Whether they will fundamentally change the way these industries conduct their business is anyone's guess. At a very basic level they're all about making and closing deals between multiple buyers and vendors in a fluid, flexible environment, but even their biggest boosters concede that, for now, at least, the big hubs like the ANX still have to rely on traditional processes. "Applications that were previously working over a proprietary connection will usually be implemented to operate similarly over ANX," observed automotive industry watcher Jeff Sabatini. "The only thing that's really changing in this case is the path over which the data travels."[5] What these exchanges need to really enable co-opetition, however, is a new transaction model that breaks down the old linear supply chain relationships and lets the whole community participate in an open market. And to build the future of electronic commerce, market builders have pulled their model from the past.

Focus on Virtual Trading Communities

Piyush Bhatnagar: A new way of doing business

You can feel the sense of urgency out on the frontiers of electronic commerce. You can even smell fear. There's a palpable sense that things are changing, that the time-honored conventions of commerce and competition are changing. Virtual trading communities like Detroit's ANX seem to be rewriting the rules of business, and no one wants to be left behind. "You have all of these competitors that are trying to play nice and trying to get all together because they know that if they don't play nice, somehow, they're going to die," said Piyush Bhatnagar, manager of Accenture's (formerly Andersen Consulting's) Toronto Business Launch Centre. "They have this sense that, if they're late adopters, then they're not going to survive."

Yet, for all the speed with which the new generation of electronic market-places has begun to emerge and the enthusiasm with which the dot-com set have embraced the idea, there remains some resistance. Collaborative market-building and industry-wide cooperation may be fine in theory, but for companies used to doing business the old way, it can all be very confusing. "They know that they have to do something; they just don't know what that something is," Bhatnagar said. "So they're wading in slowly, and they're seeing how it's going, so they can say, 'Yes, I'm a part of this.' But I don't think a lot of them have completely bought into the process."

The problem, Bhatnagar said, is that the new e-marketplace order promises to upset the whole business food chain. Frankly, the big fish are scared. "The bigger players have monopolies," he said. "The networks are allowing all the other players who are number four or five in the market to have equal representation and start playing in the big boys' game, as opposed to not even being able to get in the door. And it's the number fours and fives that are pushing things because all the number ones don't want to have to play nice. They're profitable already, and they don't want to weaken their position."

They may not have the choice, however. The rise of virtual trading communities represents more than a simple change in electronic commerce applications. It's part of a transformation that runs to the heart of the new economy, Bhatnagar said. The information revolution that brought a computer to every desktop and a global network of information to every business person's fingertips has subverted the traditional virtues of market domination and control. Every business is interconnected; data and capital move around the world at the speed of light. There's a new business virtue — it's called efficiency. "In the last 50 to 70 years, I don't think business has ever been efficient," Bhatnagar said. "Companies got monopolies; they had the first mover advantage; they got great brand recognition ... and they didn't need to do anything else. Now they're realizing that people are a little smarter and better informed than they were. They're realizing, 'People actually know how I do business, I'm no longer protected.'"

In the new networked business environment, Bhatnagar sees the old measures of business success fading to irrelevance. It's an environment where a company with fewer than a hundred employees and minimal business infrastructure can become an industry leader. "The distinctions between small and large businesses aren't meaningful anymore," Bhatnagar said. "Those definitions definitely have to change. There's got to be some other scale by which you define a company's influence or success. Small, medium, and large don't mean anything. Size won't matter, it'll be all about profitability."

But it won't happen all at once. Virtual marketplaces and, more generally, electronic commerce are only the first steps. The linear supply chain that connects suppliers and buyers one link at a time will inevitably change, Bhatnagar said, "but it's not going to change overnight, maybe not in my lifetime. Linearly is the only way we've known, traditionally, to think in terms of supply chains. Even the phrase supply chain implies a linear process, and we always think of a chain. But the future is the supply network, and it's not about a linear process." Suppliers and vendors alike will have to be able to respond quickly, changing direction, retooling, and above all, scaling to meet the needs of an infinitely more fluid market. "It's the kind of environment where you need to be able to call in all sorts of different processes at different times to increase your scale. You have to be able to build strategic alliances and partnerships and outsource. That's not a linear process. If it's a linear supply chain, you're done."

The supply network may not become the dominant way of doing business overnight, but according to Bhatnagar, it will happen. The seeds have already been sown in virtual trading communities like ANX and PlasticsNet; companies that are small in infrastructure but big in their ambitions are forcing the old tier-one giants to follow their lead. The technological infrastructure for networked business and market-building collaboration are in place. Most importantly, a generation of managers weaned on electronic commerce will be tomorrow's industry leaders — and that will make all the difference.

"In the next five to ten years, a younger generation will be leading business," Bhatnagar said. "Networking, trading communities, and all that is bread and butter to them, it's all they know. They don't know all the stodgy, old-boys' club stuff, and they don't want to know. When they're in the more senior roles — and it's going to happen sooner rather than later — they're going to say this is the only way to do business."

VIRTUAL AUCTIONS

Revolutions in EDI and the automated shop floor in the 1960s, and new supply chain technologies, have made a virtue of tightly controlled, predictable, and linear procurement processes. However, virtual trading communities demand a more open model that lets large numbers of vendors and buyers bid, make deals, buy, and sell in real time. "We're seeing the traditional supply chain becoming more open," said Liron Petruska, vice president of auction services at Commerce One, the Pleasanton, California–based company that hosts Covisint. "Companies are realizing that they have to open up. Auctions are natural for that kind of business."

The fact is that the auction, in all of its forms, is the only model of exchange flexible enough to adapt to all the virtual marketplace's transaction needs. With its huge volume of buyers and sellers, the ANX needed a transaction process that could, in effect, be all things to all people. In fact, the ANX uses the basic auction model as the template for one-to-many, one-to-one, and many-to-one transactions. A **reverse auction**, with one buyer and multiple sellers, is essentially the traditional tender and procurement process. There are **forward auctions** in which single sellers invite multiple buyers, and there's the **exchange**, where multiple buyers and sellers match up against each other. The key is that the basic auction model — and its software infrastructure — is flexible enough to support any one of those types of transactions as needed.

Keep in mind that this is the automotive industry, and not the livestock pen at the farmers' market. The volumes can be enormous, and the speed of the deals relatively instantaneous. Commerce One hosted a reverse auction for General Motors for automobile window seals. The automaker closed a $150-million deal in nine minutes. That kind of transaction efficiency is what will make on-line trading communities like the ANX indispensable, Petruska said. "The advantage to doing procurement this way is the speed of the transaction and the scalability," he said. "In the past, companies could only receive and review a handful of RFPs, and it took time. Now they can work with thousands in an afternoon."

However, as much as auctions — in whatever direction — may be the ideal approach for virtual marketplace transactions, no one believes that it's enough to sustain a viable on-line trading community. If the otherwise heterogeneous virtual trading communities have anything in common, it's that the auction, the actual transaction piece of the puzzle, is a small part of their value proposition. Their main attraction is as business-to-business matchmaking services, said Cloninger of Cahners In-Stat Group. "What we're seeing is that the auction is principally a negotiation process within the context of an e-marketplace," she said. "And most of these marketplaces are for sourcing and infomediaries. They're for services and not for transactions. Often, once you've done the negotiation, you have to take that off-line."

Despite the phenomenal success of consumer-based auction Web sites like eBay, the on-line business-to-business auction is still in its infancy. Big players like GM may relish the ability to close multimillion-dollar deals in minutes, but that may not be enough to attract the smaller companies that need to participate for the trading communities to realize their promise. Indeed, market builders are still trying to find the right mix of interactivity, services, and speed that will make their trading communities thrive, said Forrester Research analyst Laurie Orlov. Every business-to-business auction is still something of a work in progress. "The jury's still out on how people are going to do this," Orlov said. "The short-term approach is the interactive browser portal. For the next step, you'll see partnerships in the supply chain. There's a strong interest by software vendors in some kind of integration, with results of the bidding process being fed back into supply chain systems."

In fact, that is happening. Commerce One has begun to use XML to simplify the process of integrating auction transactions with the corporate supply chain. However, XML integration won't likely be a major competitive advantage for long, Cloninger said, since it is quickly becoming the de facto e-business interface standard. It won't be long until everyone offers it. Rather, she said, the key to success may ultimately be to offer a unique service that both justifies the transaction and streamlines the procurement or sales process.

That will vary from one industry to another. It may be live industry information, or real-time quotes and listings. For the construction industry, the killer app seems to be kicking the tires of backhoes and front-end loaders. In the wake of the Asian economic crisis, Dominic Johnson set up Philadelphia-based Assetline.com in order to sell idle equipment in places like Singapore and Hong Kong to American builders. The problem is that his potential buyers weren't about to spend $100,000 or so on a bulldozer that they'd never seen. "What we really offer are the services around the transaction that you need to buy something sight unseen," Johnson said. "We have to go out and assess equipment and then guarantee it. We're moving into warranty and financing."

If you're in the market for that kind of equipment, those value-added services can be quite appealing. Randy Conklin, president of the O'Leary Company in Southampton, Massachusetts, needed more than a slick Web site and a chance to shop from his computer to put his trust in electronic commerce. Perhaps more conservative about electronic commerce than other verticals, the construction industry has been slow to catch the Internet wave. The value to Conklin wasn't so much the convenience of shopping on-line, but the fact that he could use the Assetline.com community to suss out a deal on a concrete forms truck. "The dealers around here had nothing," he said. "I wouldn't have trusted Assetline.com if not for the inspection, assessment, and certification, but I was very impressed. That's where the value was in this deal."

On-line auctioneers may also take a tip from consumer-based auctions, like eBay, that provide escrow services to protect their customers and to keep them coming back. Financial services may be — along with information and assessment — the business-to-business auction's killer app. It may also be the most efficient and lucrative way for on-line auction houses to make money. The catch is that no one who actually hosts an auction likes the term. Indeed, "auction" carries an unfortunate stigma in business-to-business commerce. It's associated with cutthroat bidding and cut-rate prices. Auctions, in their various forms, may be just the thing for virtual trading community transactions in a digital economy.

PULLING IT TOGETHER

A market builder need not be an industry giant like the AIAG or Detroit's Big Three — and the virtual marketplace doesn't have to be a massive institution like the ANX. By virtue of the Internet's global span and relatively low connection cost, a marker builder can conceivably aggregate almost any commercial activity into a virtual market *from* almost anywhere in the world. Traditional geographic centres of business activity have begun to shift to the Internet en masse, and sometimes with startling results. But how do you aggregate a whole industry especially when you come to it as an outsider?

You can call it what you like — market building, portal management, e-business networking — but if electronic commerce is about anything, it's this. The dominant theme of Internet business is pulling things together. Internet fortunes have been made simply by gathering all the resources your customers want at one location. Aggregators like Yahoo!, Content.com., and Deja.com offer little in the way of tangible products, but what they do so well is provide a single point of access to products sold and information produced by other people. With so many information sources and options out in the wilds of the Internet, providing access to an organized, searchable directory of everything is simply a brilliant sell. If Internet users are using on-line services for the sake of convenience — as the vast majority are — then the entrepreneur who provides that convenience will be sitting pretty…

Take the example of Yahoo!, and apply it to business-to-business commerce. The relationship between buyers and suppliers in the traditional supply chain is a kind of Western line dance, with partners spinning, pairing off, and do-si-do-ing two at a time. What if someone set up a portal for business-to-business commerce, where a whole gang of suppliers could meet up with multitudes of buyers, or where a whole industry could link together to offer mutual commercial support and a single point of contact to their market.

That's what Veredex Logistics Inc. is trying to do for the same-day shipping business through its United Couriers network and the HotShip.com portal. "Same-day shipping is a $15-billion business in North America," said vice president of business development Court Carruthers. "There are about 50,000 companies and about 90 percent of them make less than $150,000 each year. You can have a cell phone and a bike and be a same-day courier — and that's the problem. The top two companies have 5 percent of the market; it's very fragmented, and most of the players are too small to do electronic commerce."

By bringing buyers together with suppliers — in this case, same-day couriers — and then give them the tools to find the cheapest, most direct route for their package, Carruthers believes he has an unbeatable value proposition for both sides. "About 95 percent of the ordering and dispatching is done manually in this market — only five percent is automated," he said. "Our value proposition is automating that process for the couriers." For the shippers, the value proposition is even clearer. The HotShip.com portal gives shippers access to United Couriers, a network of 1,300 same-day couriers in every state and every Canadian province; Veredex simply streamlines the process, providing one-stop shopping, least-cost routing, and, for the first time in the industry, on-line tracking from pick-up to delivery.

It all works because independent same-day couriers are just as eager to get in touch with shippers as shippers are to get in touch with them. "What we're doing is leveraging the Internet to bring together the distributed capacity of the whole industry," Carruthers said. "It sounds simple, doesn't it?" If it was, of course, then everyone would be doing it and there wouldn't be any margin in aggregating the industry. But it isn't simple. The idea is to insulate both shippers and couriers from routing and scheduling, and making all the parts play together like a string quartet. "The aggregation engine is a pretty significant piece of technology," Carruthers said. "The part we bring to the table is our ability to bring everything together. Each courier has his own way of dispatching and pricing. But we can standardize all of them despite the fact that one courier prices per mile, and another does it from zip code to zip code."

If you're sending a package to the outskirts of Chicago, you only want to know when it's going to be picked up, when it's going to arrive at its destination, how much it's going to cost, and whether it will arrive in one piece. You most assuredly don't want to be party to the nuts and bolts of the shipping process.

And neither do the independent couriers. They just want to know where and when to make their pick-ups and deliveries. The big sell for the independent couriers is that, by creating a single point of contact for the industry as a whole — or a least for those couriers who wish to participate — HotShip.com can amplify their individual market reach far beyond their local markets. That means that the hottest, fastest, cheapest courier in Cleveland can promote and use its strengths across a national market, without having to set up branch offices in Wichita and Kansas City.

There is a price, of course, but Carruthers said that his courier partners are willing to pay it to get into the nation-wide loop. Moreover, Veredex has ample opportunity to expand the community beyond the original single-shipper, single-courier relationship. "We're wholesaling the offering to other transportation procurement streams," Carruthers said. "We're a single-source plug-in for procurement portals. If they have procurement, we have same-day shipping. It's like we're a portal for portals."

THE SUPPLY CHAIN OF THE FUTURE?

What if you opened a market and nobody came? That's the challenge facing market builders as virtual trading communities spring up on the Internet with the inevitable frequency of suburban shopping centers. By some estimates, there were already a thousand e-marketplaces, trading networks, and exchanges at the beginning of 2000, and analysts were confident that that number would continue to rise in the early years of the new century. The problem is that, like suburban shopping malls that open before the surrounding communities are developed, too many virtual trading communities are marketplaces in search of markets.

In the rush to create new trading communities and cash in on the e-marketplace hype, many market builders are trying to attract buyers and sellers before they actually have any services to offer. It's a risky strategy for the builders, and it doesn't offer much to their prospective clients. "The philosophy is that many of these e-marketplaces first wanted a critical mass of customers, and then that would be followed by functions," observed Forrester Research's Orlov. "Part of the hype is a willing suspension of disbelief. Participants who have something to gain from the process of building critical mass will gain something. I'm not so sure about everyone else."

Part of the problem is that many of the trading communities that emerged in 1999 and 2000 may be long on vision, but they're short on commerce applications; in effect, they're like shiny new malls, but without much more than a lone cash register — and some don't even have that. According to Forrester Research's April 2000 report *eMarketplace Hype, Apps Realities,* while most of these communities offer some basic information-related functions, their transaction features are, on the whole, surprisingly thin — and it's not likely to improve substantially in the near future. Only 40 percent of surveyed marketplaces had catalog or negotiation features, and that was expected to rise to only 50 percent and 48 percent, respectively, in 2002. Even more surprising was that procurement, arguably the virtual trading community's raison d'être, seemed to be an afterthought. Only 6 percent offered e-procurement features, and only 16 percent expected to offer them in 2002!

Admittedly, as Clinton Wilder observed in *Information Week,* "frontiers are not easy places in which to thrive."[6] Virtual trading communities are attempting no less than a thorough redefinition of the electronic commerce supply chain. It would be naïve to believe this could be accomplished overnight. Unfortunately, many of them are making it up as they go along, hoping to attract customers to create the all-important critical mass, and then asking the participants to pay fees so they can develop practical and useable features. Industry-sponsored trading communities, established by organizations like the AIAG have built-in relevance, and the implicit support of a whole industry from day one, but most e-marketplaces are independent ventures — and that, believes Cloninger of Cahners In-Stat Group, makes them dodgy propositions, particularly if they are asking participants to contribute to their development. "Where the marketplace model might break down is that the dot-coms don't have the pull or strength to support an industry," she said. "And make no mistake, the place where they make the most sense is in vertical industries."

Even those communities established by industry leaders to be the commercial loci of their verticals have had more than their share of problems. Exchanges set up for the plastics, mining, and chemical industries have been slow to build critical mass. Even the mighty ANX has met considerable resistance. Many of the automakers' traditional first-tier suppliers are hesitant to abdicate their traditionally favored place in the EDI supply chain to an open exchange that might favor their smaller competitors. Conversely, with so many overlapping marketplaces, smaller companies face the very real possibility that they will have to participate in a number of trading communities. Adapting your internal processes to participate in one is difficult enough, said Cloninger. "But they're coming out daily ... and most of them are targeting niche markets," she said. "But they fail to see that buyers and suppliers will have to integrate their existing systems. It costs to participate in one marketplace, and it costs a whole lot more to participate in many. That's the real weakness of the proliferation."

Nevertheless, most analysts believe that the proliferation of trading communities is just a transitional part of the start-up phase of the marketplace supply chain model. According to Orlov, we're looking at the Burgess Shale[7] of e-marketplaces where, in the first flush of evolution, the market is experimenting with hundreds of possible strategies and approaches. It is somewhat analogous to the proliferation of computerized travel reservation systems in the 1960s. Dozens of companies, most backed by individual airlines, set up competing systems and, like most of the virtual trading communities, invited companies to join, but with the requirement to fund the start-ups. Mergers, acquisitions, and competitive pressures soon winnowed the field down to one industry-wide service. "We're still in the start-up groundswell," Orlov said. "We'll see a lot of competition and consolidation, and the marketplaces with the best services will win. Only some will achieve critical mass."

When they do, will they completely revolutionize the business-to-business supply chain? Probably not. Virtual trading communities, when they get their suite of applications in order, will certainly revolutionize some supply chains and enable smaller suppliers to participate in once-closed, once-proprietary marketplaces. Large buyers, like Detroit's Big Three automakers, will benefit from a wider range of expertise and the economies that come from a broader supplier base. With an infrastructure to support it and communities to nurture it, corporate cooperation will likely become easier. However, if the remarkable persistence of EDI is an indication, the traditional electronic commerce supply chain is unlikely to change radically any time soon. Existing supply chains will continue simply because of the investment companies made in them, and because they work. No one wants to throw out something that works.

That, Cloninger said, will have a profound impact on how virtual trading communities will evolve. "Every buyer is going to have a core group of suppliers who are already in the supply chain," she said. "What some of the others — the companies jockeying for the buyers' attentions in the marketplace — are doing is spot selling, and those folks will eventually be folded in the supply chain as well." Indeed, where virtual trading communities will ultimately show their real value isn't as a replacement for the traditional supply chain, but as a complement to the main procurement stream, or a portal to the existing supply chains. The virtual trading community, e-marketplace, corporate portal — or whatever you want to call it — will be an important part of the future for most enterprises, but the traditional supply chain will be there too.

Key Terms

business ecosystem

kereitsu

co-opetition

wa

virtual trading community

e-marketplace

hub

extranet

reverse auction

forward auction

exchange

6

THE INTEGRATED ENTERPRISE: ERP AND CORE INTEGRATION

Electronic commerce has placed new demands on the enterprise. To play in the supply chain, you have to be quick, agile, and responsive. Orders have to move efficiently from the front end to the back without interruption. Electronic commerce seems to demand enterprise integration, but many enterprise managers are wondering if it's all really necessary. Is enterprise resource planning the IT panacea, or is the cure worse than the disease?

E-BUSINESS INSIDE OUT

There was a time — it seems so long ago now — when they actually used books in bookkeeping. Records of accounts receivable and payable, payroll, and human resources were indelibly inked into paper ledgers, page after page and book after book. But businesses grew, and keeping track of their processes grew increasingly complex. What was once a simple question of a couple of account books became manufacturing resource management, payroll and human resources, and enterprise financial planning.

It was the demands of managing these increasingly complex internal business processes that gave the nascent computer industry its first big push in the 1960s, starting in the data processing departments of the world's biggest corporations. A decade later, the smaller enterprises with the same big number-crunching requirements provided a built-in market for minicomputers and, in the 1980s, personal computers. Indeed, it was the spreadsheet — specifically Lotus 1-2-3 — that took the PC out of hobbyist computer clubs and onto office desks everywhere. The spreadsheets soon gave way, as all technologies do, to smarter and faster tools: standardized, prepackaged, infinitely customizable financial and business management software ranging from off-the-shelf small business products to professionally integrated application suites.

The Internet and electronic commerce are propelling a fifth wave of technological change at the company core, one that promises to make the spreadsheets and financial management practices of the 1980s and 1990s look as quaint as the dusty ledger books of the 19th century. The conventional wisdom these days holds that, unless your enterprise's internal processes can take advantage of the speed and fluidity of electronic commerce, the value chain will come to a screeching halt at your front door. It's more than a question of putting your own house in order. The electronic commerce supply chain effectively turns the enterprise inside out ...

The Lean, Mean ERP Machine

Even before electronic commerce was a gleam in anyone's eye, there was **enterprise resource planning (ERP)**. All the good names must have been taken when the ERP pioneers came up with the name, because the main thrust of the concept isn't planning — though you still have to do plenty of that — so much as integration. ERP originally evolved to meet the information-processing needs of the world's largest companies. In one of those cases of corporate synchronicity, SAP, a German software developer, was contracted to integrate the IT infrastructure of the giant chemical conglomerate ICI Group, at almost the same time that Amsterdam-based software developer Baan Systems Inc. and Mercedes-Benz began doing the same thing. From those starting points, Baan and SAP, together with PeopleSoft, another software company, created the technological foundation of ERP.

Mercedes-Benz and ICI provide just two examples of the technological chaos that can follow in the wake of rapid computerization. The problem is that companies often deploy IT assets to meet specific contingencies or to perform specific operations, but without a consistent plan. Consequently, while each department within the enterprise might have moved toward computerized efficiency — and that's far from certain — the enterprise as a whole becomes a patchwork of often-incompatible technologies. Business processes originating in research and development, marketing, human resources, or purchasing screech into a dead end as they move from one department to the next. Data keyed in on one department's systems has to be printed to hard copy and re-keyed as it moves through the enterprise. Though this creates boom times for the data-entry profession, it utterly subverts the efficiencies that computers and networks are supposed to provide. In fact, without some kind of common ground, some sort of corporate IT integration, you might even be just as well off doing it all by hand, the old-fashioned way.

It goes almost without saying that a consistent, enterprise-wide IT infrastructure, one that cuts across all departments and employs centralized **data warehouses**, is inherently more efficient than a department-by-department hodge-podge ... at least in theory. The idea is that, by integrating each department's processes, sharing data resources, and putting all its enterprise data in a central repository where it can be matched and cross-matched across departments, a company can eliminate wasteful duplications and streamline operations to create, in effect, one efficient, enterprise-wide application. And that is supposed to create a more intelligent, more responsive, more organic enterprise. That, in a nutshell, is the whole point of ERP.

When your sales department takes an order, it automatically matches the information to the customer database, checks the inventory database, sends requisition information to the factory floor, and informs the loading dock that you have an outgoing shipment; human resources automatically allocates the personnel, and when you receive payment, the financial system automatically updates the budget. In the best of all ERP worlds, there is complete transparency throughout the enterprise, so every department knows exactly what every other department is doing, and everyone knows what resources are available when. In fact, in a finely tuned ERP system, by the time your sales representative finishes taking the order, he is not only able to say when the product will ship, he can be confident that it's already being built on the factory floor.

Perhaps not surprisingly, ERP won enthusiastic converts, mainly among the Fortune 1000, in its heyday from the late 1980s to the late 1990s. Most early ERP systems were planned, developed, and deployed in-house or by system integrators hired to develop custom solutions in the 1980s. Off-the-shelf packaged software began to dominate the market throughout the 1990s. Vendors who developed custom systems for huge multinationals were able to adapt those products for a wider audience. Conversely, the vendors could — and can — benefit from their experience working out the IT kinks of the world's most successful corporations. In effect, by buying into the ERP solution that makes Mercedes-Benz or Timex tick, users can buy into a whole system of best practices … again, that's the theory.

Ironically, the ERP market's rapid growth in the 1990s was probably driven as much, or more, by the fear of the impending millennium as by any interest in best practices. In 1997, for example, when enterprise resource planning became a bona fide high-tech catchphrase, Air Canada embarked on a massive IT restructuring project that would take most of its core operations off its Honeywell Bull mainframe computers and onto a spanking-new client-server system running PeopleSoft's ERP software. The principal objective of the project was to ensure that the airline's systems were Y2K compliant; if the new software permitted greater efficiencies, so much the better. "Nineteen ninety-nine is a brick wall," Air Canada CIO Lise Fournel observed at the time. "If we haven't completed the project by then, we will still not have converted our existing systems to Year 2000. That would be a problem."

The problem for the ERP vendors was that the sense of urgency that accompanied the end of the 20th century could not last forever. After about the middle of 1998 — the drop-dead date to begin Y2K compliance projects — the ERP market began to nose dive. A more serious problem, perhaps, was market saturation. By 1999, ERP had become a fact of day-to-day business in its core market of billion-dollar-plus companies. Mercedes-Benz, ICI, and Air Canada wouldn't be buying much more in the way of ERP technology for many years to come, and smaller companies weren't quite convinced of the technology's return on investment.

Though SAP, PeopleSoft, and a handful of other vendors had established themselves as the masters of the enterprise's core functions, electronic commerce and the Internet came along to change everything. While ERP is fundamentally inward looking, everyone else started looking outside the enterprise at the supply chain. The big ERP vendors seemed somehow out of the loop. "These guys were doing their own closed, proprietary thing," said Martin Marshall, director of San Francisco–based Zona Research. "Then the Web smacked them in the face and they said, 'What?!' Now their customers are demanding that these closed ERP systems have interfaces that can draw data from core processes to the Web. They know they'd better listen." It isn't clear if the major ERP vendors actually learned that lesson. But starting in 1999, the new catchphrases were e-business- and e-commerce-enabled. The big push with third-generation ERP solutions isn't just about the traditional virtues of efficiency and organization; vendors are now making a case for the benefits of an e-business-enabled enterprise core. It seems they have decided that ERP's whole purpose was now to integrate enterprise processes with each other and with partners on the supply chain. In effect, the core has moved to the network edge, and ERP is turning inside out.

Chastened by the growth of electronic commerce, ERP vendors have been falling all over each other to re-invent themselves as electronic commerce solution providers. The casual exchange of information between companies has evolved into tight supply chain integration. XML, which has already become a ubiquitous feature of supply chain systems, and latter-day, evolved EDI have emerged as the key technologies in this transformation. All of the major ERP packages, and most of the minor ones, support XML to one degree or another — and those that don't almost certainly will soon. XML provides the interface to the Internet and heterogeneous commerce processes at the transaction front end, while the database interfaces provide integration with legacy data at the back end.

This double-ended interface isn't just a convenience, but it reflects necessities imposed by the transformation of the enterprise itself. Corporations are decentralizing, reorganizing themselves in autonomous business units that have to be able to access and share data among departments, managers, and employees, but they are still dependent on data that they have accumulated over a period of years or decades. The relationships between internal departments have taken on much of the character of partner communities, the technological foundations of the enterprise intranet are exactly the same as the Internet itself, and the operations of the internal supply chain have begun to mirror the external supply chain. Except for one thing — unless you're a dot-com, you still have a vast investment in data to be shared within and without the enterprise.

The Internet is the ideal transport medium on both sides of the network. While the Web was the medium of choice for a relatively small number of enterprise intranet applications during the great ERP surge in the 1990s, in the 21st century it has become the vehicle for almost every business process. Supply chain partners want to know where their orders are, and how long it will take to get from the order stage to their loading docks. For existing ERP users, the ability to leverage their substantial internal IT infrastructure investments to the supply chain can be a big selling point. E-business-integrated ERP offers the opportunity to perform Internet-based transactions without having to re-engineer core processes that were already re-engineered to deploy ERP in the first place. After all, no company of any size wants to go through a re-engineering process more than once a decade — and preferably less frequently than that.

The experience of Cybex International, a fitness equipment manufacturer based in Medway, Massachusetts, is instructive. Cybex wanted to get into electronic commerce, to maintain a consistent around-the-clock relationship with its distributors and with its big institutional customers. According to Thor Wallace, Cybex's president and CIO, it was imperative to make a quick, seamless turnover to electronic commerce. After evaluating "dozens" of electronic commerce solutions, Wallace said, the deciding factor was the fact that his ERP system's vendor was now offering electronic commerce functionality. "The thing we wanted to do was expose the ERP functionality residing in our backbone to the Web, and it made sense to leverage our existing systems rather than invest in something new that we'd just have to integrate with what we already had. It certainly didn't make sense to start all over again."

However, the relatively nimble, medium-sized companies like Cybex that have been straining at the leash to push their businesses into cyberspace are more the exception than the rule in ERP. The technology's traditional champions tend to be large corporations, and up until recently, they were cautious about embracing the possibilities of electronic commerce. That has put vendors in an interesting position, in which they have to maintain their traditional sales pitch while, on the one hand, expanding into electronic commerce solutions and facing stiff competition from established vendors and dot-coms alike, and on the other hand, making a pitch for traditional ERP products to a new market. And that new market — one composed of small and medium-sized companies — typically sees electronic commerce as the justification for ERP, and not as its logical extension.

The big ERP vendors are hoping that the electronic commerce boom among small and medium-sized enterprises will translate into a revitalized ERP market. The big problem for SAP, PeopleSoft, and the rest is that ERP is not typically a high-growth market, and with the widespread adoption of ERP by large enterprises in the 1990s, it has become dangerously saturated. There may be a market for upgrades, but SAP and the others won't have much of an opportunity to sell to new customers — unless they can eke out a new market niche. So they're trying to find a way to move downstream to a hot new market. They've been down that stream before. As early as 1997, both PeopleSoft and SAP tried to make their case to small businesses, but without much success. For one thing the whole idea of enterprise resource planning had only just begun to penetrate the mainstream business mindset. Moreover, with electronic commerce still just an intriguing concept for most small businesses, it was hard to come up with a compelling justification for the expense of an ERP deployment, no matter how focused the products were. However, in the intervening years, the Internet and electronic commerce have become small business obsessions. It probably isn't much of an over-statement to say that the small business that isn't looking for ways to use electronic commerce to enhance its business doesn't exist.

For vendors like PeopleSoft, that's an opportunity too good to pass up; they can use the Internet as both the justification and the medium for a new kind of ERP offering — a pay-as-you-go **application service provider (ASP)**. That means software and systems vendors whose whole focus was, until two years ago, on billion-dollar corporations that bought solutions that they typically deployed and managed with their own IT staffs are suddenly in open-ended, on-going relationships with a large number of small clients, each of whom requires a great deal more hand-holding. "These are companies that are used to dealing with the Fortune 1000," said Darren Meister at Queen's University. "It's going to be hard for a small-money client to get their attention."

In fact, some analysts believe that the ERP-ASP strategy is more of a response to shareholder pressure than to any compelling evidence that smaller businesses want or need ERP. With so much happening in the high-tech industry, and particularly in electronic commerce, vendors have to show that they're keeping up with the digital Joneses. The problem is that this new market might not be interested. Existing ERP customers, who are only just opening their closed core processes to the outside, will be a hard sell no matter what their size.

According to Kneko Burney, manager of markets and opportunities for Cahners In-Stat Group, mid-sized companies that have already invested millions in ERP see those investments as strategic assets that they're reluctant to leave in someone else's hands. In fact, she expects outsourced ERP to be even less attractive to small companies that probably don't need ERP services to start with. The whole idea of enterprise integration for small businesses is an oxymoron, Burney said. "Small businesses aren't enterprises," she added. "There's a bit of a play in the high end of the mid-range, and the dot-com companies may be interested. But ERP evolved in the first place because large companies needed to manage huge amounts of data about their core processes." Indeed, a small enterprise would probably be better off buying a copy of QuickBooks at the local computer store.

Misfits at the Enterprise Core

Enterprise resource planning promises to integrate a company's IT assets in a single infrastructure, effecting tremendous efficiencies and economies of scale. The ERP-enabled enterprise is technologically leaner, meaner, and more competitive, better prepared to bring its partners into an automated supply chain and take advantage of the new world of electronic commerce ... or so they say. In many cases, most in fact, ERP succeeds in delivering exactly what it promises. Unfortunately, that isn't always the case. For all of its technological logic and built-in best practices, ERP can often be both a black hole for your IT budget and a dangerous misfit with your company's core processes.

Enterprise resource planning systems are an enormously complex, expensive technology. It is the single most costly IT investment many companies will ever make. In a 1999 survey of 63 companies, the Meta Group found that the total cost of ownership of ERP ranged from $300 million to $400,000, with the average costing a staggering $15 million. Admittedly, the survey subjects ranged from very large to very small companies, but $300 million is a lot of cash, even for the very largest companies. The main reason that ERP is so expensive is that it isn't just technology; it involves the complete re-engineering of your business processes, a philosophical shift in corporate culture, not to mention testing, employee retraining, and the migration of departmental data stores to centralized data warehouses. In effect, "going live" with SAP, PeopleSoft, or Oracle's technology is only part of a lengthy and often difficult process.

How difficult depends on the enterprise and how deeply entrenched the old business processes are. In a study conducted in the summer of 1998 for Deloitte Consulting by Benchmarking Partners Inc., almost half the respondents said that they don't expect their ERP implementation and integration programs ever to be completed! That makes it very difficult to assess the return on investment, and it isn't uncommon for enterprises to experience a kind of corporate depression when their ERP system is finally operational. Moreover, the actual benefits of the system are often, initially at least, intangible, while the costs — consulting, re-training, changes in management style and personnel — are all too concrete. The Deloitte study found that a quarter of respondents actually experienced an IT performance decrease immediately following the operational deployment of the ERP systems. While this is usually a temporary phenomenon related to the teething process or to an insufficiently planned deployment, it can stop a company dead in its tracks.

Because ERP involves, in essence, a complete business process overhaul, its implementation has to be carefully planned and modeled. Though that used to be part of the process of developing a system in-house, the packaged solutions that now dominate the market come with a whole set of new issues. As August-Wilhelm Scheer and Frank Habermann observed in the pages of *Communications of the ACM,* "ERP systems are more or less easy to install, yet users must also determine which goals (strategies) they wish to reach with the system, how the functionality of the system can achieve this, and how to customize, configure and technically implement the package."[1] In fact, Scheer and Habermann estimate that the cost of implementation is typically five times the cost of the ERP product itself. That is money well spent, because an improperly or incompletely implemented ERP system can spell disaster.

How bad can it be? Once again, that depends on the company, but in the case of Hershey's, it was very bad indeed. The chocolate company blamed its disastrous third quarter 1999, in which its profits took a 19 percent nosedive, largely on problems attending the deployment of its spanking-new ERP system. In a textbook example of Murphy's Law, almost everything that could go wrong did go wrong — just in time for Hershey's boom-time Halloween-to-Valentine's season. In effect, the company's internal supply chain just broke down; orders weren't being filled, products weren't being shipped, while almost a third of the confectioner's sweet stock waited in warehouses.

While a carefully planned and modeled deployment will normally go more smoothly than that, part of the planning process should include an assessment of whether your company can actually be re-engineered along the lines demanded by packaged ERP solutions, and whether you can even benefit from the level of integration they provide. The best practices promised by the major ERP packages are a kind of one-size-fits-all-with-alterations approach. And while they may be attractive —who wouldn't want their enterprise to run like a well-oiled, German-engineered machine like Mercedes-Benz? — they may not be appropriate.

In fact, all the ERP packages impose a process model derived from the experience of other companies. That may not be a bad thing, of course — rare is the enterprise that operates so smoothly that it can't stand some improvement. However, the basis of each package's process models should be a major consideration in the ERP purchase decision. The problem is that these models often reflect practices that evolved in different industries and management and national cultures than your own. The problem with best practices, after all, is that they lead to the question "Best for whom?"

However, the big vendors, with their large enterprise expertise, are not the only game in town. Perhaps responding to the needs of small and medium-sized enterprises that can't or won't benefit from Mercedes-Benz–sized solutions, the ERP market has seen the emergence of many smaller vendors that straddle the space between the big packages and custom solutions. Though they can't offer the kind of cross-platform, cross-enterprise ubiquity of an Oracle or a SAP, they often provide a much closer and more comfortable fit with smaller businesses and lower-volume processes. And with standard interface and transport technologies like XML promising the potential of seamless integration with Web-based commerce, they are often those enterprises' best choice.

Focus on Integration

Anindya Datta: Data warehousing

At the heart of the integrated enterprise is data: integrated, aggregated, consolidated data that can be accessed, manipulated, and queried across company divisions or from outside the enterprise itself. Indeed, though data warehousing — the practice of consolidating data in an integrated data store — can exist without enterprise resource planning, you can't do ERP without data warehousing. "ERP systems necessarily have to rely on large volumes of enterprise data, which would, of course, be stored in warehouses," said Anindya Datta of the iXL Center for E-Commerce at the Georgia Institute of Technology's Dupree College of Management. "ERP is basically about tying together your organizational processes, it's a glue; data warehousing is a system. ERP systems must rely on underlying data and therefore, they must rely on some kind of data repository system — and that happens to be a data warehousing system."

From the perspective of managing an enterprise's information assets, data warehousing and ERP have similar — and complementary — goals. Just as ERP traditionally promised great efficiencies and economies of scale by tying enterprise processes into a single application, data warehousing's principal value is the way an enterprise can leverage all its information assets quickly and effectively.

"The whole raison d'être of data warehousing is to make the retrieval of large amounts of data quicker, and to support interactive data processing, if you will, between a user and a large data repository," Datta said. "When data warehouses came into being, the question that would often be asked was 'We have relational databases, why do we need these specialized systems called data warehousing systems?' The reason was that if you stored ten terabytes of data in a traditional database system and you asked a question, it could take two days to get back an answer."

That may not have been a huge problem in the days when deals were made over the phone and procurement orders came on paper. Electronic commerce changed all that, by compressing cycles and accelerating business processes. Though data warehousing was slow to catch on outside the realm of ERP in the mid-1990s, the growth of electronic commerce has made it an IT imperative in its own right. "One of the reasons why data warehousing systems didn't take off right away was that a basic relational database could get you an answer in five minutes, and no one could understand the benefit of getting it in less than a minute," Datta said. "In the context of electronic commerce, getting an answer in a minute just isn't acceptable. You've got to get an answer in a few seconds, or even a few milliseconds. Electronic commerce takes this interactive data processing to its limit. Every e-commerce user session is basically an interaction with a data repository — and response times are critical."

Nowhere is this more critical than in the integrated business-to-business supply chain. Access to integrated data has become a crucial part of supply chain interactions as new ideas like build-to-order and just-in-time crank up the complexity of manufacturing and distribution. There just isn't any other way to ensure that your partners' CAD systems have access to your shop floor's CAM, or to synchronize every phase of production with suppliers' and buyers' shipping schedules. "There's no doubt that there is a very distinct shift in the data distribution paradigm," Datta said. "There is a push overall to centralized data services. In electronic commerce, you have transactions whose data get updated in real time, and if you have large, distributed databases, it can be a huge pain — maybe even impossible — to keep them all consistent."

Because of its close association with ERP, data warehousing was tarred by some of the bad press generated by failed or difficult enterprise integration deployments in the 1990s. In fact, Datta is quick to point out that, for all of its benefits, data warehousing has traditionally been a difficult project to pull off. "But it's much easier now than it was a few years ago," he said. "When the term 'data warehousing' came into vogue, it was primarily a consultant-driven thing. Organizations would have accumulated gigabytes of data and all of a sudden, someone from Price Waterhouse or Ernst & Young would come and tell you. 'Hey, you've got all this information and you can use it to do cool stuff.' Investment in your data warehousing project would essentially be the investment of hiring this consulting team."

Today, data warehousing has become a packaged technology, making it easier to plan and deploy. With the emergence of specialized, off-the-shelf software and tool sets to manage for and overcome the classic problems attending data integration, it has lost a great deal of its peril. "Data integration is the kind of thing that never happened well," Datta said. "But tools have emerged now that do this kind of specialized data integration and that run on top of different systems and bring them all together. So now I think data warehousing deployment has become easier."

That doesn't mean that it's safe to start a data warehousing project lightly, without considering its impact on enterprise processes. In fact, Datta firmly believes that there is little value in data warehousing for its own sake. "A data warehousing project should always, always, always be application-driven," he said. "An organization, in a strategic-planning meeting, may decide that it needs to do better customer tracking; or they may say, 'Hey, we need to do cross-promotion between our products.' And 99 percent of all applications boil down to looking at the data underneath and making some decisions based on the data."

The bottom line is that the implementation of a data warehouse in even a medium-sized enterprise is a complex, long-term project. Failure to plan carefully is courting disaster. Moreover, once begun, it's the kind of project that you can leave half-done. "IT people will say that the problem is that these projects are often so long and so intricate that management people change and priorities change before the project is completed," Datta said. "People get promoted or leave, and these projects often simply suffer under the stewardship of multiple layers of management. That's where they often get screwed up. But that's the fault of management, not of the technology, and these projects don't have to get screwed up, as long as they're managed carefully."

HEAVY METAL

An implicit part of most ERP systems' architecture is the assumption that your systems will migrate — if they haven't already — to a **client-server** model. The idea that centralized enterprise data should be processed by a network of powerful workstations with their own application logic, rather than by a centralized data-processing system, seems obvious. Dave Urban, an IT specialist with management consulting giant Towers Perrin, would beg to differ. It's not that he has anything against the flashy servers and networked workstations that were supposed to have replaced the big mainframe systems long ago. It's just that heavy metal comes with the job. "Part of that is the fact that we have a lot of legacy applications that are simply resistant to migration," Urban said. "Part of it is just that mainframes continue to be the best platform for some applications."

For the better part of the last 15 years, the smart money has been betting on the big iron's impending demise. Writing in *Computerworld* in 1987, William Zachmann, then vice president of research at IDC, described mainframes as an "endangered and probably doomed species."

In fact, he confidently predicted, "Mainframes are headed the way of the horse and buggy and steam locomotive." Things didn't look any better in 1992, when *InfoWorld* editor Ed Foster opined that IBM, by far and away the dominant mainframe vendor, was a "walnut-brained dinosaur" doomed to extinction because "personal computers and PC networks are doing the work that IBM's vaunted mainframes once did with far greater cost efficiency."

It was all very clear. The day of the hulking giants had come and gone. The "glass rooms," where mainframe computing power was kept forever beyond the reach of ordinary computer users, would come crashing down. Soon, enterprises that were heavily invested in big mainframes would simply migrate to the more highly evolved client-server architecture. That was the theory. In practice, the migration was extremely difficult and often fraught with peril. "It didn't play out well at all," Urban recalled. "We placed mainframe expectations on client-server systems, and they didn't stack up. But we were being driven by business decisions and not technological concerns, so we kept building out this client-server infrastructure. It would have made sense to just stick with the mainframes all along."

Far from marching into a dead end of technological evolution, mainframes — often called large servers, **legacy systems**, or heritage systems — have maintained their essential position in the corporate core. It doesn't make sense to throw away something that works, and mainframes are a proven technology. Moreover, as e-business applications become mission-critical, many enterprises are being attracted to the big iron's traditional virtues. There's an old joke in mainframe circles that Windows NT and UNIX workstations don't keep track of system crashes in an exception log — a record of unusual occurrences — because they're not unusual. In contrast, mainframes are designed to run continuously for years without interruption. "I think our customers are finding that this new e-business arena is just as mission-critical as running payroll," said Rich Lechner, vice president for e-business strategy at IBM's Enterprise Servers Group. "Mainframes have always offered the highest scalability, availability, and security, so there's a lot of renewed interest in the platform."

They're also designed to serve far more simultaneous users than Windows NT, and that can be a major benefit for e-business. "At any one time we could have 30,000 to 40,000 sessions in some state of process on our IBM S/390 G-5 mainframe," Urban said. "Our developers could be using it, while it acts as the core of our interactive voice response system, a Web server, a database engine for most of our Web applications, and a few other applications. I think the top end of an NT server is 1,200 users at one time."

That's good news for e-business people who manage huge amounts of data and serve huge numbers of customers. "What happened is that e-business and the requirements of e-business have driven the market back to mainframes," Lechner said. "A lot of people in e-business are finding that they have to re-engineer their processes and change their business models and integrate their systems. At the same time, they're experiencing phenomenal growth in the number of customers and in the volume of transactions. It's all putting a lot more stress on the infrastructure. So what has happened is that the market's requirements have moved back to a place where the mainframe has always shined."

Nevertheless, the people buying mainframes today are more likely to be existing users seeking to update or expand the systems they already own, rather than first-time buyers seduced by the inherent virtues of heavy metal. Though Lechner likes to talk about dot-com users who adopted mainframes when they "hit a brick wall" with their workstations and PCs, the vast majority of mainframes in use today remain in use because they perform operations that simply can't be moved to another system, or manage legacy data stores that have accumulated on the platform for several decades.

In spite of that, few current users of big iron would migrate to another platform, even if they could. Today's mainframes, particularly IBM's S/390 family and, to a lesser extent, the AS/400, represent the culmination of 30 years of centralized computing power. Designed to handle heavy-load applications and provide robust availability security and data integrity, mainframes are still the platform of choice for large-scale applications in the financial services and airline industries. Analysts estimate that some 70 percent of mission-critical corporate data continues to reside on legacy systems — almost every financial transaction on the Internet passes through a mainframe at some point. Despite the reports of their imminent demise, mainframes continue to sell — and sell well. "We're seeing, year after year, incredible growth in terms of the capacity we ship into the marketplace," Lechner said. "Some of the predictions were made by people who *wanted* the mainframe to disappear, and some of the alternative technologies didn't mature as people expected. It's also worth noting that this isn't your father's mainframe. We've made significant investments in the software layer. We have the best-performing Java virtual machine and the best TCP/IP in the industry. This is an e-business machine."

It wasn't always that way. In the early days of electronic commerce, the mainframe's unique virtues made it an awkward fit with the Internet. While the Internet is an open, distributed, and comparatively chaotic environment, the big iron was closed, centralized, and secure. As late as the mid-1990s, getting a mainframe to even talk to IP-based networks like the Internet was a lesson in frustration. That changed when IBM began to integrate internetworking features into the OS/390 (formerly MVS) and OS/400 operating systems, the software that runs the S/390 and AS/400 mainframes, respectively. That's an attractive option for some users, and IBM has gone to great lengths to port its most important e-business applications, like Lotus Notes and Domino, to OS/390 and OS/400. "The open version of MVS was a *very* important step," Urban said. "It opened the mainframe up as a large server option for people wanting to do open system stuff at a scale that just wasn't available before."

On the other hand, a good number of mainframe users would be just as happy to keep the Web at arm's length from their mission-critical systems. In an inversion of the whole ERP philosophy, these users like the way their business works on the inside, thank you very much. They just want to find a way to get those existing business processes, tied as they are to the big iron, to work with the Internet without upsetting the apple-cart. "The big issue for our clients is translating the way they work to e-business on the Web," said Justin LaFayette, president and CEO of DWL Inc., a developer specializing in legacy system integration for the insurance industry. "Insurance companies organize their data by account, and not by customers. The challenge is to get that data off the mainframe and onto a Web page in a form that customers will understand."

For insurance companies seeking to enable their independent agents to use the Web or offer services directly to the consumer via the Web, integration doesn't mean re-engineering business processes. Rather, the goal is to consolidate data from multiple accounts on the fly in a Web browser, then direct transaction data to the appropriate accounts on the appropriate systems in the back end. And they want to do this without having to change the way they've been working for decades. But it's not that easy. For companies invested in legacy systems, the big question is whether to treat their legacy systems as data servers, or to integrate the big iron's application logic itself into their e-business systems. Moreover, both approaches can be done in a number of ways — from replicating legacy data on an NT application server, to building e-business components on the mainframe itself.

"The reason why there are so many ways to integrate legacy systems with e-business is that no two companies are alike," said Carl Greiner, vice president of the Meta Group's enterprise data strategy practice. "But full integration doesn't come until you're pretty sure of what you want to integrate, and not a lot of companies are quite there yet. That's why the real push is to externalize the data from legacy systems."

In a loosely coupled integration architecture, the mainframe's data is simply exported to an application server. The back-end database on the mainframe is updated periodically, but not in real time. A tightly coupled architecture uses a Web application server to mediate e-business trans-actions that interact directly with the legacy back end. Which approach is most appropriate depends on the situation. A system that manages annually updated information doesn't have to act on live data. If you're managing a manufacturing supply chain, your data has to be updated in real time, and most of your business rules are probably on the back end. In a tightly coupled architecture, you can have the commerce-specific rules on an external application server and all the business rules on the mainframe in back end. That way, commerce transactions can interact with core processes in real time, request inventory, and, if you've gone that route, interact with ERP.

The most direct way to externalize legacy data is by simply integrating the mainframe's terminal interface with an e-business system — **screen scraping**. In fact, this kind of software, which allows users to interact with the mainframe through a Web browser, has become fairly common. Typically, screen scrapers just dump the mainframe "green screen" terminal interface into a browser window, and that can be a problem. Mainframes were designed to be operated by the IT elite from the comfort of the glass room. Consequently, green screens are usually incomprehensible to ordinary users, whether they're co-workers, employees, or prospective customers.

More advanced tools take screen scraping to the next level. They can take a data stream from the mainframe and convert it into a small Java routine that a Web developer can present in a greatly simplified, user-friendly context. **Java** is an interpreted programming language whose applications and routines can run in any Web browser on any computer running any operating system — including smart mobile phones and handheld computers — making it an ideal tool to bridge the gap between technologies. Having something like that mediates between the mainframe and Web developer worlds, so each doesn't have to know what the other is doing. That means you can deploy your e-business solutions using data from the glass room, without making the traditional IT guys jump through hoops to adapt.

But what if you don't know exactly what that front end is? It shouldn't be much of a surprise that the smart money is betting on XML. Just as it has begun to do with EDI, XML is emerging as the killer app for tying the back end to the Web and any number of other commerce interfaces. Because each XML document's structure and format are implicit in the document itself, it can, in effect, connect anything to anything, providing an ideal data transport vehicle for loosely coupled legacy integration. It can tie legacy systems to the Web, to cellphones equipped with **wireless application protocol (WAP)** micro-browsers, or to virtually any other incoming or outgoing datastream available now or in the future. The application server becomes more of a portal that mediates the big iron at the core, across the enterprise network, or out to the Net.

As we've seen in EDI and across the supply chain, XML can integrate data across the enterprise from a variety of content sources. And whether the enterprise core is ERP-enabled or running on the big iron, the goal is integration. At the end of the day, the supply chain shouldn't have to know what hardware or software you're using. And it won't if you can strip away all the application interfaces until you get down to working with the real lifeblood of electronic commerce — not systems, not applications or philosophies, but data.

Key Terms

enterprise resource planning (ERP)

data warehouses

application service provider (ASP)

client-server

legacy systems

screen scraping

Java

wireless application protocol (WAP)

7

THE INFORMATION SUPPLY CHAIN

The hard truth is that a supply chain is only as good as the information that supports it — and information is everywhere in electronic commerce. It can make you more competitive and more intelligent, and it can help you serve your customers better than your competitors can. Information can make you a better business person; you only have to know where to find it, how to analyze it, and where to apply the intelligence. That process is the information supply chain, and it's the real backbone of business-to-business electronic commerce.

THE INTELLIGENT ENTERPRISE

There's one idea central to electronic commerce that has become so much of a cliché that it's almost not worth repeating. It's the idea that the most valuable commodity of electronic commerce is not the products you sell, the services you offer, or even the cold hard cash that accumulates in your corporate bank account. It's something far less tangible. Call it data, information, the knowledge capital of your combined workforce and of every customer or partner with whom you have ever done business. We all know that information is power in the new economy. What is sometimes less obvious, however, is the idea that the strategic application of that information as intelligence is often far more important.

Information informs every step of the electronic commerce supply chain, from the initial procurement transaction to its final logistical consummation. The manager in the electronic-commerce-enabled company has to be a lot like a professional athlete, bouncing on his toes, alert to every sound, every bounce, every change in the momentum of the game and the ball, ready to dive into the melee, and conscious of when to stay out. Every RFP, customer query, contract, shipping manifest, memo, and closed deal can be leveraged to make your enterprise more efficient and its products more compelling. Indeed, the supply chain, whether linear or diffuse, depends entirely on the information flow across the enterprise and between partners.

It's the **information supply chain,** and it is, in its own way, the lifeblood of electronic commerce. The challenge is to integrate all the sources along its length, to combine intelligence about your business processes, intelligence about your customers, and intelligence about your marketplace and competitors in one strategic whole. There is, typically, a whole encyclopedia of neologisms to describe each phase of the chain — business intelligence, customer intelligence, and competitive intelligence are just three — but they all basically refer to the same thing. The **intelligent enterprise** must have the strategies and tools to collect and analyze information right across the business process, and then be able to act on it. It is business intelligence (BI) in the broadest sense, and it all begins and ends with your customers.

THE CUSTOMER RELATIONSHIP

Add the phrase **customer relationship management (CRM)** to the neologism encyclopedia. Unlike so many other jargon terms, however, this one actually means something, and it's worth remembering. The concept — managing the relationships with your customers — is one of the fundamental tasks of commerce, electronic or otherwise. "The formula for success in e-business stands upon the twin pillars of e-commerce and customer intelligence," observed Wayne Eckerson, an analyst with the Patricia Seybold Group, a Boston-based, high-tech market research firm. "An e-business strategy that unites these two disciplines is sure to succeed."[1] Conversely, of course, the strategy that ignores the customer is likely doomed to failure.

It's not really a new idea, of course. Companies have been managing their customer relationships as long as there have been customers and companies. What's new now is that, in electronic commerce, you have to throw technology at the customer to get it done. "Hey, this thing has been going on forever," said Curt Hall, editor of the Cutter Consortium's *Business Intelligence Advisor* newsletter. "You have to tailor your interactions with your customers or lose them. The difference is that you don't actually see your customers anymore."

To some extent, that potential boils down to being able to replicate the interactive touch and intuition of a human sales representative with computers. Though no eCRM vendor would promise to make your Web servers warm-blooded, they can leverage all of the information collected from an on-line transaction. It may not be a human touch, said Bob Runge, chief marketing officer for Vancouver-based Pivotal Systems Inc., but it's a touch. "The very essence of the technology is understanding the context of how business is conducted," he continued. "It's not about trying to turn a multibillion-dollar corporate conglomerate into the corner drugstore. The goal is to match functions to customer convenience, and trying to pull back into the company all the knowledge that allows you to be more competitive."

Conventional business wisdom holds that it is five to ten times more difficult to attract a new customer than to hold onto an existing one, and attracting new customers into business-to-business relationships can be doubly difficult. Unlike the music fan with $20 burning a hole in his or her pocket who surfs over to the HMV Web site to look at the specials, the people behind business-to-business procurement are not quite as prone to impulse buying. They're procurement professionals, looking for more than the best price on a low-margin product. Moreover, business-to-business vendors typically have considerably fewer customers than consumer-oriented merchants, but they're customers with a lot more money to spend. Consequently, the relationship you have with each one assumes greater importance. Amazon.com can afford to lose the customer who buys $20 worth of books; you can't afford to lose the company that buys $500,000 of your product. That means you have to ensure that your customers' experiences on your site are always productive; you can't waste their time, and you have to anticipate their needs.

Managing the customer relationship involves much more than intelligence, of course. Francis Buttle of the Manchester Business School in England has observed that the CRM value chain involves a series of links, from identifying your strategically significant customer — the long-term buyers, the trend-setting "benchmarks," the customers that make you work better, and the bulk buyers — through the development of an intimate, mutually beneficial relationship. He argues, "CRM at its most sophisticated has the potential to integrate all business processes around the requirements of strategically significant customers ..."[2] However, the nature of those requirements, and the strategic significance of your customers, whether they are a few or your whole marketplace, begins with their identity. You can't develop a relationship with them until you know who they are. "E-businesses need CRM more than ever," said Aaron Zornes, executive vice president of application delivery strategies at the Meta Group. "There's an increasing demand to know the customer. On the Internet, companies don't just compete on price; service is the big differentiator. Customers are much more fickle on-line, and you need CRM to keep them from clicking over to someone else's site."

Customers' identities are somewhat easier to pin down in business-to-consumer transactions, of course. When you're selling books or audio CDs on the Internet in ones and twos, your customers are all discrete, identifiable individuals with unique interests and needs. On the other hand, when you're selling shiploads of titanium ingots, your customer is a corporation, an organizational abstraction of individual identity. Yet it is vital to remember that behind the corporate identity, behind every click on your extranet site or in the virtual trading community, there's an individual. For all of the automation in business-to-business electronic commerce, decisions are still made by people, not by machines. In order to nurture that all-important customer relationship, you still have to know the person behind the transaction, and track his e-commerce behavior. In that sense, at least, there's not really a whole lot of difference between selling CDs and titanium. "The B2B system must map relationships within the customers' organizations between individual people and their roles in the procurement," observed Tom Hennings in an article in *e-Business Advisor.* "It must have the ability to connect them with each other, as well as tie them back to the corporate entity."[3]

Customer-tracking technology has evolved from the crude process of counting "hits" — the number of file requests that individual users make to a Web site — to become one of the essential analytical tools of electronic commerce intelligence. In fact, "hits" have precious little value in the information supply chain. One single Web page might contain a half-dozen graphic images that could account for as many as seven hits. In the old days, before finer analytical tools became available, that information only had moderate value if you were willing to dig through your server logs, estimating how many files made up each page. "The initial forays into Internet commerce were just a question of getting a Web site up, so hits at least meant people were visiting your site," said Mike McClure, vice president of marketing for Marketwave Inc., a customer-tracking technology vendor. "But as business people got involved, and as the Web became a business issue, they had real questions. How much money should I pour into this thing? How will it affect my bottom line?"

Those are tough questions in what is, after all, a new way of doing business, and many of the old methods of gauging customer habits and measuring business success just don't apply to the Web. "People are moving away from **brochure-ware** [non-interactive, advertising-oriented Web sites] to doing real business on the Web," said Mark Brewer, vice president of sales at Andromedia Inc., a vendor of on-line customer-tracking software. "People in electronic commerce are really interested in behavior. Your customers might be sitting in front of their computers anywhere in the world, and unless you can measure what they do at your site, you have no way of knowing if you're serving them well."

Every time an Internet user visits a site, the browser informs the server software of what kind of Internet software is being used at the time and which site the visitor just came from. **Cookies** — small pieces of identifying information — can be placed on users' computers so they can be recognized individually, tracked as they visit different parts of the site, and logged every time they return. Web servers have been able to log cookies and refer information for a couple of years now. What's new is the ability to analyze that data for customer behavior and preferences. Combine that with dynamic Web servers that create special content on the fly, tailor-made for individual users and, the vendors say, you have a powerful tool. "There aren't 100 million people on the Net, but 100 million individuals," said Jim Ingratta, general manager of electronic commerce solutions for IBM Global Solutions. "All electronic commerce sites are getting into personalized service, and the only way you get that is by **data-mining** your customer-tracking information."

A key proposition of CRM is that, if you know your customers well, you can keep them coming back again and again. And the first place you encounter them — the interface to both your commerce processes and your on-going relationship — is on your Web site. "A customer-specific Web site is essential to successfully managing your B2B, e-commerce customer relationships," Hennings wrote. "To effectively manage and fulfill orders, a B2B site must reflect buyer preferences, pricing, and historical purchases."[4] Their habits and needs can streamline your own processes and optimize the customer interface. Does XYZ Corp. need more information than EphemeraTech for you to close a deal? Do some customers want a graphical catalog, while others just want detailed specifications? If

XYZ Corp. only buys plastic widgets, why clutter the page he sees with information about steel widgets?

By keeping track of their preferences, you can make buying recommendations that match customers' tastes and streamline the procurement process to fit their habits. And that can be a powerful part of building a lasting relationship. "It's all about the behavior of the individuals, but also whether individuals are coming to my site creating meaningful relationships," Brewer said. "A year ago, the big issue with e-commerce was getting people into your site. Loyalty is becoming even more important. You have to find a way to make people want to come and stay."

Perhaps more important, however, is the Web's ability to provide companies with the kind of detailed business intelligence they need for long-term strategic planning. Your customers are no more anonymous on the Internet than they would be at your front desk. Even the traditional business-to-business customer relationship was built on a solid foundation of information. You've always known, to a greater or lesser degree, who you're doing business with, how to bill them, and where to ship your products. Your sales staff may have additional information, like the name of their contacts' kids, and what kind of music they listen to. Every piece of identifying information has always gone into the process of making a deal. Customer-tracking and data-mining technologies just automate that process in an environment where you never actually see your customer contact's face or hear his or her voice. However, what you see in electronic commerce, or rather what your system sees, is just as important when it comes to clinching that sale.

The ideal is to refine the intelligence down to the point where you know your customers almost better than they know themselves, where you can anticipate their needs before they ask. The benefits are increased efficiency and the ability to respond immediately to every procurement query without having to maintain unnecessary inventory. At this time, that kind of sophisticated, completely synergistic relationship is still the ultimate goal of CRM.

That may be all well and good, but it does raise the question of whether CRM is a technology issue at all. Can a company that doesn't subscribe to a customer-relationship philosophy and have a customer-relationship strategy expect customer-relationship technology to do anything more than add some complexity to the IT department? "The strategy issue is gigantic," Hall said. "If you really want to do CRM right, then you have to know what you want from it before you start. One figure everyone's throwing around right now is that 70 percent of eCRM deployments have failed. Most companies are pretty unsatisfied."

Unsatisfied? You have to wonder if they even know what they want. The problem is that eCRM is such a buzzword right now that everyone wants a piece of the action. Hall continued, "Companies feel that they could be left behind, and they're jumping on eCRM in much the same way that they jumped on ERP in its heyday. They've heard the marketing campaigns, but they don't know exactly what they want. There are hundreds of CRM product categories. Most companies' Web strategies aren't even thought out, not to mention their whole enterprise strategies."

CRM embraces so many functions, processes, and technologies — from customer tracking and data mining to computer-telephony integration and call centres — that the big issue is integration, more than anything else. "CRM is a series of piece parts that are assembled to provide service for your customers," Zorne said. "It's like an ecosystem. You're no longer just automating marketing, service, and sales, but you're blending them together. Service is just part of the product these days." The bottom line is that, not only do companies have to integrate their front ends with their back ends and manage all their sales channels equally, they're under pressure to integrate the channels by which their customers interact with them, and that's a tall order. "If you're in business on the Internet, there's a good chance that your Web site isn't your only point of contact with your customers," Zorne commented. "What that means is that they're going to want to have the same level of service, maybe even a similar experience whether they're reaching you on the phone, at your brick-and-mortar store front, or on the Web."

Focus on the Information Supply Chain

Peter Fader: E-business as usual

At the University of Pennsylvania's Wharton School of Business, Peter Fader is a rebel. The high-tech, on-line marketing orthodoxy says that the Internet and electronic commerce have raised the curtain on a new age of one-to-one marketing, that dynamic Web sites and customer personalization are allowing businesses to tailor their sales pitches more effectively than ever before. Fader just isn't buying it. "I've been saying that this stuff is nonsense since the summer of 1999, and people were saying, 'Oh no, you're wrong ... you don't understand ... it's a new economy ... markets operate differently now ... there are increasing returns to scale ...'," Fader said. "And I've been saying balderdash! The problem is that now I'm starting to look right. Yet there are still a lot of people out there who say that 'markets operate differently now'."

Fader doesn't mince words. "One-to-one marketing is a myth," he said. "It's one thing when you have a trusted advisor, who not only knows exactly what you've purchased and when, but knows what mood you're in, and knows what the weather's like that day, and can anticipate your needs. The idea of reading someone's log file and just running some dopey program on it and saying 'Aha! This is what you need!' is not only not one-to-one marketing, it's bad marketing." All things being equal, and technological change being what it is, Fader expects that on-line marketers will get smarter and their software will get "a little less dopey," but he's not holding his breath. "People keep talking about that — maybe the technology will catch up — yeah, maybe it will," he said. "But it'll be a long time to get there and a lot of companies will waste a lot of money before that golden day arrives."

Make no mistake, it's not that Fader has anything against the Internet or electronic commerce — he thinks they're just dandy. What he has a problem with is the unreal and unreasonable expectations created by software vendors and the prevailing orthodoxy that business on the Internet is somehow a new *kind* of business. E-business is business-as-usual. "I might be skeptical about people's use of the Web, but the nice thing about it is that it gives us viewpoints into business-as-usual that we never had before," Fader said. "That's why I love electronic commerce. The ability to observe traffic patterns, the ability to know how many unique visitors a site has, regardless of whether they buy or not, is great, it's really insightful. So if we were willing to view e-commerce as business-as-usual and just put on our old glasses, we could do fantastic things with the new data. Instead, everyone says, 'No, no, no, it's different; we have to throw out the old models,' and that more than counterbalances the good things about electronic commerce."

The problem is that data mining has its shortcomings despite vendors' hype, and every electronic commerce manager should be aware of them. "Data mining is very good for certain, specific tasks," Fader said. "Like when it's used to determine whether you should get a credit card — for that, it's terrific. When you just have a bunch of variables — you know, the 300 demographic and psychographic variables — and you just want a yes or no answer, it's fine."

That kind of information can be extraordinarily valuable for an e-business, but it has its limits. Data mining has no regard for the *process* of buying or selling, Fader said, and *that's* the kind of information you *really* need. "What's the histogram of the number of your customers' visits to your site?" Fader asked. "It alarms me that I can pose that question to people in this business, and they don't know what it looks like. What's the histogram of clicks-to-bail, how many people leave after one click versus ten clicks, or whatever? There are fundamental things that, before we try to explain them away by saying 'It's a Tuesday, so people leave more quickly,' we should understand. We should understand these basic patterns and tell simple stories about them. If our simple stories are inadequate, *then* we should bring in all those explanatory factors."

Having said all that, Fader is nevertheless quick to point out that customer tracking, business intelligence, and CRM are no longer optional. "You do it for the same reason you bother with having a good return policy," he said. "It's just a prerequisite of doing business on the Web. However, it really should be kept in mind that it's more about competitive parity than about trying to boost sales. Part of it isn't only that it will perhaps create a few incremental sales, but it's more that it sends a message to your customers and other constituents that you're committed. Otherwise, you might as well just burn a $10,000 bill. It's just that most companies are just throwing big money at it and they don't know what they really want out of it. They don't know how to compare a good vendor with a bad one."

But what do you do with all the data generated by customer-tracking and CRM systems? If the information supply chain is about anything, it's about the massive volumes of information and metrics generated by every transaction. Multiply that a few thousand- or million-fold, and an e-business can stumble into a frustrating embarrassment of riches. "Be selective about what you look at," Fader said. "The good news is that we have lots of cool data that we didn't have before; the bad news is that it's like drinking from a fire hose. So you have to know which pieces to look at and how to read them. There are some really dopey metrics out there that a lot of companies have just grabbed and have become de facto standards, even though they're entirely meaningless and potentially harmful."

Data don't mean anything on their own, and the really important information-management task is to give it all some kind of meaningful, real-work context. "There are so many dopey metrics, but there's one I love best," Fader said. "Every e-commerce firm, if you look at its annual report or even some of its PR, will give you a statistic like this one from Amazon.com: '78 percent of the people who bought stuff from us this quarter are repeat buyers.' And they imply that this is a good thing. And then I ask a couple of questions, like what is that number for Crest toothpaste? It's a backwards-looking statistic. It might be that your brand, your product, or your store really sucks and you lose all but one customer, and he's the only one who hangs around. So you sell a lot of stuff to repeat buyers, big deal. When your potential market is growing as fast as the Internet is, that's not a great achievement."

However, if Fader is convinced of anything, it's that, for all its speed, the promise of supply chain integration, and the potential market reach of an aggressive e-business, electronic commerce remains business-as-usual. So, instead of looking at all the data in the information supply chain as evidence of something new, said Fader, it might just be worth looking at it through the eyes of his great-grandfather in Brooklyn. "The funny thing is that in the old world, companies looked at a seemingly similar statistic, which was 'among all of the people who bought stuff this month, how many will come back and buy again?' People keep confusing these two statistics, but not only are they different, they have no relationship to each other at all. It might be the case that you have a wonderful brand that's so good that, not only do 100 percent of your tryers come back and buy again, but you keep bringing on so many new tryers that, at any given point in time, your fraction of buyers who are repeat buyers is tiny. That's worth thinking about."

SEARCH AND DEPLOY

The problem with information is that it proliferates almost beyond the wildest imaginings of the world's most fecund rabbit. Customer-tracking information from your Web site, data in your CRM database, figures from EDI, logistical numbers from the loading dock — it all gushes into your data warehouse or, more likely, a half-dozen or more discrete databases scattered throughout the enterprise. Each datum is absolutely critical, of course, but together they build to a digital surge of cinematic proportions. Here's the paradox: You need as much information as you can possibly collect to be the quickest, most effective, and most efficient e-business in the world, yet by collecting all of that information you set yourself up for one serious case of information overload. Something's got to give. "It's a huge issue," said Reva Basch, a California-based research expert and author of *Secrets of the Super Net Searchers* and *Researching On-line For Dummies.* "What comes after information overload, but the solution? The phrase **information management** is relatively new, but it's a valid and long-standing problem."

While information overload may cause casual Internet users the odd sleepless night, it is shaping up to be a headache of epic proportions for e-business. "That problem is only getting worse on the Internet and in the corporate intranet," said David Yockelson, vice president and director of electronic business strategies at the Meta Group. "Intranets are now being used to connect people to groupware, communications, and critical data. The expectation is that people can get at it, and that's not always a realistic expectation."

Five years ago, when the first Web-based search engines came on-line, Internet information management was simply a question of creating an engine to sift cyberspace. Those first virtual librarians were relatively half-witted, slow, and inaccurate, and they were focused mainly on the public Internet. However, the business intelligence perspective has turned inward to the corporate intranet, and so has search technology. Today, the Internet search engine is an intranet tool, part — though admittedly a small one — of a revolution in networked knowledge. The latest e-business catchphrase is something called **knowledge management.** The idea is that, with all of the information out there, e-business people have to raise information to a higher level of abstraction called knowledge. In practical terms, that means that getting *at* information, and making sense of it, has to become as natural and effortless on the Internet as it is, in theory, in your own mind.

It's a lot to ask and, even though today's internal search engines are far more sophisticated than their distant ancestors of a few years ago, they're far from perfect. In fact, if your intention is to get at all kinds of company information quickly and efficiently, search engines alone are woefully inadequate tools. Reva Basch, for example, although impressed by the state of searching technology, nevertheless believes that it still has a very long way to go until companies will be able to rely on it for effective knowledge management — if ever. "The technology is far from mature," she said. "Individual search engines are getting smarter, and they're past the new-born stage, but aren't quite yet into adolescence."

It's not surprising, then, that consumer-oriented search technology on the public Internet has begun to focus on information personalization and filtering services, provided by so-called portals such as My Yahoo! and Netscape's Netcenter. Internet portals typically provide passive filters set to match each user's special interests. In effect, portal users see only the news and links that they choose to see. Though the problem is different on the corporate side — the information is typically more complex, and the question is not about filtering for special interests, but actively locating information that you need at a specific time — the same approach has been turned inward to give knowledge workers a portal on enterprise information. Indeed, the **enterprise information portal (EIP)** has become the main link in the information supply chain within the enterprise.

EIPs are knowledge management servers that present each user in the enterprise with a customized, personalized gateway to company data and enterprise applications. They are, in fact, portals to the contents of the corporate intranet. The more sophisticated EIPs amass information from a wide range of data sources, both inside and outside the enterprise, notify users of on-going processes in real time, and give access to all kinds of search and analysis applications. Indeed, the more sophisticated enterprise portals can launch any server application directly, making them ideal e-business computing interfaces.

Of course, a portal is only as valuable as the content and applications it ties together. "Being able to put a stock ticker on everyone's desktop is cool, but we're not looking to deliver MyTimeWasters," wrote Ted Gannon in *DM Review.* "We're looking for MyCompetitiveAdvantage."[5] However, once deployed throughout the enterprise, an EIP provides a unique way to customize the desktop of every user and every department in the enterprise. In effect, the EIP can be used, at the same time, to give users access to what they need to see, and close off what they don't need, or are not authorized to see, without having to actually configure each user's individual workstation. As the supply chain redefines the limits of the enterprise, the ability to provide everyone with a customized interface could become a key competitive advantage. "The reality is that the portal stuff is fleshing out," said Mark Smith, senior analyst with the Meta Group. "Companies are concerned about outputting their intelligence information to managers, employees, and even partners … You have to keep them in the loop, but you want to be able to control content access."

EIPs create a kind of one-stop-shopping computing environment, a fully-integrated enterprise desktop that lets users tie all their information and applications together at one point. "Corporate information and technology managers say the portals they're rolling out this year are already contributing millions of dollars to the bottom line," wrote Steve Konicki in *InformationWeek*. "Others say their return on investment will be measured in minutes and hours of employee time that is better and more profitably used."[6] For the electronic-commerce-enabled enterprise, moreover, the EIP ties together the various strands that make up the information supply chain, and that can provide an essential edge when it comes to monitoring your electronic commerce processes and maintaining customer relationships.

While many EIPs offer advanced features like **natural language** and **heuristic searches,** in addition to the old standby **Boolean search** technology, their principal focus is information aggregation and directory classification. Indeed, the whole idea behind the EIP is to provide a consistent and logical context for enterprise information. While you may not be able to benefit from that context when you're searching the Internet at Altavista or Yahoo!, it is both feasible and necessary within the enterprise. "Search is what you do when things are scattered at random," said Dora Futterman, product marketing director for Infoseek Inc., a knowledge management solutions vendor. "But that's not enough. When you're at Campbell Soups and you're looking for 'stock,' is that soup or securities? You really need some kind of hierarchical directory as well."

The whole knowledge management — and consequently, business intelligence — proposition is predicated on bringing order to chaos and applying some kind of structure to random data. Basch believes that, without some kind of classification structure, the Web within the corporate intranet will defy all attempts at rational organization. "That makes it impossible to turn random data into organized information," she said. "If you want to bring some normalcy to the Web, you have to look at some kind of meta-scheme. You need to have indexing." The question, however, is exactly how to do that.

The solution is fairly simple if you're starting from scratch. Most modern knowledge management systems provide for on-the-fly indexing, using a wide variety of technologies, including XML. Data produced in the marketing department may contain descriptive text and meta-tags that provide classification information. Unfortunately, older data is considerably less convenient. One solution is to manually index all of your electronic documents, but this is almost always a painful, time-consuming process. Some vendors have tried a number of artificial intelligence approaches to creating indexes, but their success is typically mixed. A more common solution is the classification server, software that applies preset rules, usually defined by the user, to organize enterprise data. Data is filtered by variables like the department or user that produced it, keywords, and context — is the word "stock" in a financial report or a recipe? — and date. However, the process is almost never perfect, and some human intervention and re-indexing are almost always required.

Down in the Data Mine

Getting *at* enterprise information is one part of the business intelligence process. The other part is turning the information into actionable intelligence. The human mind is a remarkable analytical tool, but the demands of the information supply chain, with data collected throughout the enterprise and from one end of the transaction process to the other, have created a tough situation for knowledge workers. Undoubtedly, they could go through all of the data collected by these processes and develop strategies all in good time. But there is an awful lot of data, and no company can wait to act strategically.

Data warehousing, the practice of concentrating all the enterprise's data in one, massive, core database, got a big boost from the surge in enterprise resource planning in the mid-1990s. The whole point of ERP is to integrate all of a company's processes into one, enterprise-wide application, and it naturally follows that, to accomplish this, all company data — customer information, manufacturing, shipping data, for example — must be housed in a central repository. During ERP's heyday in the last decade, the drive to data warehousing spawned specialized system integrators and warehouse ASPs and, above all, data mining. With the increasing activity in electronic commerce, data warehousing has begun to enjoy something of a revival, and so has data mining. After all, with all the information that you can gather on your customers, partners, transactions, and business processes, it makes sense to put it all together in one big database. Once there, moreover, that data can be mined for all its worth.

Data mining is, like so much jargon, a pretty vague term. Anyone who has ever queried a database for useful information — often a frustrating and fruitless endeavor — can identify with the mining metaphor. After all, excavating data can be a sweaty, grimy chore in the enveloping darkness. However, with data warehouses growing to multiple terabytes,[7] sophisticated data analysis tools are no longer optional; they are becoming an essential part of business intelligence. Data mining, in its strictest sense, is one of the most sophisticated. By applying sophisticated, automated analytical and predictive tools, it charts relationships and inter-relationships between data, and then models the interactions. If you don't know what you're looking for, data-mining systems can provide highly advanced data models and predictive visualizations. In effect, they search for patterns in vastly complex systems in much the same way that a seasoned businessperson intuitively brings order to the chaos of commerce. For all their promise, however, data-mining systems are expensive and complex technology ... and probably overkill for most e-businesses.

Few business people would even be in business if they didn't know what questions to ask at least part of the time, and **on-line analytical processing (OLAP)** is designed to sift through data when you know what questions to ask. In some ways, OLAP is a lot like more common database query interfaces such as SQL and ODBC. What sets it apart is its complexity and sophistication, and its ability to analyze complex, multidimensional relationships from diverse data sets. While an SQL query might tell you which customer purchased the most rubber O-rings at the highest average price last quarter, an OLAP system can be used to predict who will buy the most next quarter and help determine the optimal price for rubber O-rings in different industry verticals in different parts of North America.

The Lay of the Land

E-businesses have an insatiable appetite for information. They need to know — or at east they *believe* they need to know — what their customers are thinking, where their products are going, and how the market is likely to change. Finding that kind of raw data isn't so much of a problem if they're looking within the enterprise. However, the wild, unruly, and unstructured world of the Web beyond the firewall is a different matter.

And Internet search engines don't make it any easier. According to a recent report by Forrester Research, frankly they stink. Most searches at more than two-thirds of the sites Forrester surveyed turned up results that had nothing to do with the original query. This is supposed to be the information age. Information everywhere, yet most of it is utterly unstructured, and that makes it pretty useless. The Web is chaos, and it seems pretty unrealistic to expect any intelligent order of that maelstrom of data. "In fact, it's actually pretty realistic," said the Meta Group's Mark Smith. "The technology is there, and the space is converging. The challenge now is not whether it can work, but how to integrate it into your enterprise processes."

Business intelligence technologies that evolved to mine the internal data warehouse have been turned outside the enterprise to bring order and impose some kind of structure. "Business intelligence, as we've termed it, started out in the early 1990s, and it was very internally focused," said

Brant Davison, senior program manager for IBM Data Management Solutions. "The idea was to more effectively leverage the knowledge capital of the enterprise. Now customers are saying, 'Geez, there's a lot of information out there; how do I crawl it and analyze it? How do I extend my Web-based analysis outside?'"

Unlike most internal information, easily mined and searched, safely indexed and comfortably tucked away in data warehouses, the Internet is fundamentally unstructured. The challenge is to impose some kind of structure on all that external information on its way into the enterprise and to the desktop. Considering the chaos of the Net, it sounds like a tall order. "Actually, the difference between unstructured and structured data is probably less than you think," said Don Campbell, vice president of information delivery products at Ottawa-based Cognos Inc., one of the world's leading data management and BI solutions vendors. "It's sort of a garbage-in-garbage-out thing. But as you start applying filters and metadata information, you can create your own structure." It's the process of transforming data into information. By finding some context — any context — raw data can be turned into something useable. "Once you have that one piece of context, and it doesn't have to be anything really big, you open up the whole world of intelligence."

Almost every information management technology has been pressed into the service of external business intelligence. Self-propelled programs called spiders crawl the Web to build keyword or searchable content databases. Document content is matched against rules to determine word contexts. Other tools read meta-tags, identify the location of the data, and count the number of links to it on other sites to determine its relevance. At the end of the process, a knowledge management worker tweaks the categories and streamlines the indexing before serving it up to the enterprise. "We're starting to see the convergence of a lot of technologies," Davison said. "A lot of the taxonomies you want to index against are manual. Someone has to find the information, and then decide how to categorize it. But some of the really advanced data-mining technologies that tell you how information should be categorized are being applied to external information sources."

External data may be categorized according to classification rules based on how documents are indexed *within* the enterprise. In effect, all you have to do is introduce a few hundred thousand internal documents into the system, and it can use them as a template for categorizing external information. Some systems let users build context models by asking the intelligence system a series of questions. The system plots the answers and shows patterns and trends. "It's amazing what you can do with the right modeling," Campbell said. "It's all about being able to leverage the human brain."

… Or an artificial brain. The application of advanced artificial intelligence (AI) technologies like expert systems, natural language searches, and **intelligent agents** — autonomous programs capable of completing complex knowledge management tasks — takes the automation process one step further, said Sami Hero, senior director of product management at Hummingbird Technologies, a Toronto-based vendor of knowledge management systems. "Think about it," he said. "You can do a query, say, on what your competitor is doing with their SAP implementation, and the software will go to your competitor's site. The system finds keywords, matches them to cluster maps, and puts them in context. It uses artificial intelligence, so it understands natural language. Then it can automatically summarize, so you can quickly scan the information."

According to Hero, a U.S. government agency (one that he would not name) used Hummingbird's AI-driven technology to categorize, in a week, information that had once taken three years. It's all heady stuff, at the technological cutting edge. Artificial intelligence, once the realm of top-secret government black projects and cyberpunk science fiction, is going e-business mainstream. But it's only part of the knowledge management process, cautions Brant Davison, and there's still a long way for AI to go. "On a scale of one to ten, my sense is that, a year ago, we were at about one with artificial intelligence," he said. "Now we're at about two or three. That's impressive on its own, but it's not perfect."

PORTALS AND PUSHERS

Perhaps more impressive (though still not perfect) are the technologies that have emerged to share information outside the enterprise and across the supply chain. It is, perhaps, an inevitable consequence of the increasing interdependence of supply chain partners. With new enterprise information interface technologies, portals have begun to evolve from a proprietary, rigid interface to something that can be integrated into the enterprise process. "These things are getting very big and a lot of people are spending a lot of time working on the integration part," Campbell said. "In the open model, with XML and OLAP, if you think of your business intelligence content as open, it can be exchanged in a business-to-business environment, or created by your partners."

The goal, Campbell said, is to drive a tighter integration right across the information supply chain, internalizing external data, and externalizing the intelligence. In effect, with the continuing revolution in business intelligence, the enterprise portal is becoming less a window on corporate data stores than the key link in the information supply chain. Smith expects the portal to evolve into the essential business-to-business commerce interface, a **WUI (Web user interface)** rather than a **GUI (graphical user interface)**, integrating content with a wide range of collaborative functions. "Content and applications are, to some extent, two sides of the same coin," the Meta Group's Smith said. "When you're talking about an information supply chain, there isn't a lot of difference. The issue is driving data to the desktop."

That issue has also given new life to a one-time superstar technology that seemed dead for sure. A few years have passed since **push technology** was the Next Big Thing. In the waning months of 1997 and the beginning of 1998, it seemed like push was everywhere. PointCast had appeared overnight on business and personal desktops, while Microsoft Corp. and Netscape Communications Corp. tripped over each other to build push features into their browsers. It seemed like a good idea at the time. Rather than having to venture into the wild unknown of the Internet, users would be able to select the type of information they wanted to read, and it would be delivered — pushed — to their desktops. In the frenzy, specialized push vendors like Marimba Inc. and BackWeb Technologies Ltd. became high-tech industry darlings and then … no one talked about push anymore.

Anyone who used PointCast — dubbed "PointlessCast" by some wags — remembers how it tied up your computer and clogged networks. If push was dead, then good riddance. "A combination of circumstances gave push a black eye," said Marimba CEO Kim Polese. "A major part of that was that push itself was a meaningless category — it was too broad. Companies ranging from PointCast to us were lumped together. The field was really identified with PointCast, and when they had problems, we all took a hit."

But push wasn't dead, and much of the functionality that was lost in the hypestorm of 1997–98 has become even more critical with the emergence of the information supply chain. The leading push vendors had to reinvent themselves and focus their offering. At some fundamental level, push is simply about finding a better way to move bits and bytes. "We started with a core technology of moving bits around and added a whole management system," Polese said. "Now we have access control, roll-out, security, and encryption. What we've done is stay true to the vision of creating a management environment."

Push is ideal for information that can't be ignored. While a user has to go to a portal — which is not normally a problem if the portal is the user's home page — or may fail to check his or her e-mail, push content arrives right on the desktop, within or beyond the enterprise. Push systems typically comprise a server, where the administrator can control content distribution, and small client programs that can be distributed to users across the information supply chain. One of the key ideas behind push is the ability to send information with different levels of intrusiveness, depending on its urgency, and to be able to broadcast the right information to the right person. Every client program has a distinct profile defining the user's identity, privileges, and information needs. Just like personalized Web content, push systems let managers set preferences for different classes of users — managers and workers, for example — in different departments and companies. The point is to get their attention. "Attention management is extremely important," said Bill Heye, BackWeb's vice president of advanced technologies. "When we first started putting BackWeb together, we focused on how to push all the way to the user, and not just to his hard drive. When you go from the hard drive to the user's brain, you have something of a human bandwidth problem."

At the other end of the spectrum are data updates that no one needs to know about. Using push technology, companies can keep their corporate phone directories continually updated and servers synchronized, and can broadcast software upgrades across their local- and wide-area networks and extranets transparently. "Just think about it — you have hundreds of servers in your back end, and huge quantities of data and information," Polese said. "Now you have a management problem. How are you going to keep them all up to date and synchronized?" A broader question might be how to ensure that your partners, suppliers, distributors, and customers are kept in the e-business loop. Home Depot uses Marimba's Castanet system to ensure that its in-store home-decorating kiosks reflect current product and pricing information. The New York–based brokerage Bear Stearns uses the same technology to distribute a financial application to its brokers and make sure that everyone is using the same updated, bug-free tools.

The bottom line, of course, is keeping the information supply chain running smoothly and finding a quick, efficient, and transparent way to maintain e-business relationships, for relationships are the essence of electronic commerce. Vendors may need to keep their buyers updated on the latest production information; distributors might want to keep retailers' catalogs and price lists updated; a system integrator might have to apply software patches to clients' systems. Using push technology, all that information can be sent transparently and broadcast without the recipients' intervention.

Key Terms

information supply chain

intelligent enterprise

customer relationship management (CRM)

brochure-ware

cookies

data mining

information management

knowledge management

enterprise information portal (EIP)

natural language search

heuristic search

Boolean search

data warehousing

on-line analytical processing (OLAP)

intelligent agents

Web user interface (WUI)

graphical user interface (GUI)

push technology

8

In-House or Outsource

What do you do best? That's one of the key questions of electronic commerce, and it's behind one of the most profound changes in business infrastructure in more than a century. And if you know what you do best, what part of the business can you do without? A whole new industry of application service providers has begun to answer that question, by offering an outsourcing option for almost every IT and electronic commerce operation.

DOING IT RIGHT

Every serious business person knows that if you want something done right, you had better do it yourself. More than almost anything else, that dictum propelled businesses, through the course of the last century, to greater and greater feats of horizontal expansion. Ford Motor Co. and GM needed someone to lend their potential customers money to buy their cars. No problem — automakers became bankers and set up their own, internal financing operations. IBM's customers required the assistance of consultants to get their mainframes up and running smoothly. No problem — IBM jumped feet-first into the consulting business ... and then, when they had to find a way to exchange data between the home office and the consumer, Big Blue expanded into the networking services business.

From the Japanese *zaibatsu* of the 1930s and their postwar successors, the *kereitsu*, to vast, diversified North American corporations like General Electric and Dupont, the dominant operative philosophy of the 20th century was horizontal integration. Yamaha made — and makes — motorcycles, musical instruments, and digital cameras and has dozens of major and minor divisions devoted to making products or providing services to other divisions within the company. General Electric "brings good things to life" from light bulbs to jet engines, and to make it all happen, it's also in the trucking, networking services, and EDI businesses. Indeed, the sine qua non of corporate success in the 20th century was that ability to manage the whole business process, from primary resource extraction, through manufacturing, distribution, and sales, to the consumer. The really successful companies, the really important companies, were the ones who could do it all.

That's great, except it's not the 20th century anymore, and the virtues that define a successful company have changed. That's not to say that the IBMs and Mitsubishis of the world are likely to disappear, or even that they have lost any of their relevance. But the companies that best exemplify these virtues are leaner and more focused. In effect, their guiding philosophy can be summed up as "we don't do it all, but what we do, we do very well." It's what former Intel Corp. CEO Andy Grove called the clarity imperative, "which includes describing what we are going after as well as describing what we will *not* be going after."[1] In effect, success in the new economy is often as much a question of letting someone else do it right as it is a question of doing it yourself.

The really effective companies are often the ones that know what and when to outsource, said Heather Smith, an IT management specialist in the Queen's University School of Business in Canada, and that can mean a lot more than a little subcontracting on the side. "It's definitely a business model whose time has come," she said. "I think that people are discovering that they can be much more efficient by focusing on their core competencies." One such company is British Petroleum, whose workforce went from 100,000 to 60,000 employees in the wake of its 1999 merger with Amoco. "BP has consistently downsized, and it outsources a huge chunk of its organization," Smith said. "They're outsourcing their accounting, their HR, their IT. They find it makes them incredibly profitable and helps to focus them, instead of building these huge infrastructures."

Outsourcing isn't exactly a 21st-century idea, of course, but the downsizing tsunami that hit North American business in the wake of the mid-1980s recession and never quite went away has become a way of corporate life. Even one-time corporate powers like United Fruit, which once controlled its own colonial army and could set the public policies of small Latin American countries by virtue of its size and influence, has consistently downsized by outsourcing most of its business in the last two decades. Its evolution is reflected in its name changes, to United Brands in 1970 and Chiquita Brands in 1990. This company once controlled the whole process itself, from the banana tree to supermarket produce displays. It used to grow the bananas, ship them, warehouse them, and distribute them — the whole thing. "Now they have completely outsourced everything," Smith said. "They figure that the only thing that's important to them is their name — Chiquita — so the only thing they do is the distribution of bananas in the store. That's the context in which business is changing."

And the Internet and electronic commerce are part of what's changing it. On one hand, the growth of global markets, linked by high-speed networks and electronic commerce technologies, have forced companies to focus. The old economies of proximity and, to some extent, scale have been utterly subverted by a global commercial infrastructure that can pull links together in a supply chain that stretches from coast to coast. There's no reason your supply chain partners have to do business with you rather than someone else, except that you can deliver the goods.

And, as Intel's Grove discovered, that often means focusing on the one thing you do best. The 21st-century networked economy rewards clarity and agility. On the other hand, electronic commerce and networking technologies actually make it possible for companies to outsource many of their ancillary processes, even their core operations to an unprecedented extent. Digital documents and enterprise data can move just as easily, and as instantaneously, to a subcontractor a continent away as they can to an office down the hall. With properly installed and maintained security, it may even be safer to send sensitive corporate data halfway around the world on the Internet than it is to sneakernet it to the next office cubicle.

The fundamental truth of the new economy, particularly electronic commerce, is that it takes a lot of technology to become and stay competitive. However, the rapid pace of technological change and the tempo of global electronic commerce have conspired to create a business environment where outsourcing isn't just an option — it's an imperative. "You have a whole industrial shift happening," said Kneko Burney, director of e-business infrastructure and services at Cahners In-Stat Group. "There has been a fundamental change in the economy from manufacturing goods to delivering services. But companies that are used to doing business in a different way suddenly have to learn a new way to do business just to stay viable in an e-commerce supply chain, for example. So they're saying, 'Why don't I outsource this operation to someone who knows how to do it?'" Burney is quick to point out that many companies simply don't have the experience in brand-new but essential technologies to do it themselves. They're strained by change, and with the shortage of skilled workers, the best way to stay in the technological loop is to outsource.

In one sense at least, outsourcing IT and network services isn't an entirely new idea. EDI, after all, was built on a foundation of third-party VANs in the 1970s. What is new is the range and depth of applications that can be outsourced to an **application service provider (ASP).** It can be hard to distinguish between a traditional outsourcer and an ASP, and the distinction, fine though it is, is that an ASP provides subscribers with access to a specific application or suite of applications — like data warehousing, ERP, or transaction processing — for a regular fee, rather than just services like consulting or system integration.

As network connectivity margins dropped in the late 1990s, Internet service providers, in particular, rushed to re-invent themselves and increase revenues through value-added services like Web site hosting and electronic commerce application delivery. More than a few erstwhile ISPs dropped network access services completely and evolved into pure ASPs. The first applications were simple extensions of the ISPs' traditional value-added services, but it didn't take long for entrepreneurs and established IT players to take advantage of the huge potential market for outsourced applications of all kinds. Even giants like Oracle and SAP, which are more used to selling applications through traditional channels, have got in on the ASP action. It's now possible to outsource almost every IT and electronic commerce application, from transaction processing to procurement and ERP, to an ASP.

Where there's demand, there's opportunity, and the number of ASPs has surged in the last couple of years. More than 600 were listed at WebHarbor.com, an on-line portal for the ASP industry, by the summer of 2000, though Burney believes that number was somewhat inflated. "That reflects wishful thinking," she said. "A lot of companies that call themselves ASPs are just resellers and system integrators that want to be ASPs. In terms of real providers with a defined product set instead of just a **server farm** (a service that maintains servers for other companies offsite), the number is closer to 200."

PULLING A CHIQUITA

Consider EphemeraTech, the outsourced, electronic-commerce-enabled, automated — and entirely fictional — enterprise of the 21st century: It bids on contracts on a virtual trading community owned and operated by an industry association; it closes deals on its Web site, which is hosted by an electronic commerce ASP; transactions are processed by another ASP and funds are automatically transferred to its bank; the order information is transferred to its ERP provider and product specifications are sent out to the automated CNC systems at its manufacturing subcontractor's plant; when the product rolls off the line, the third-party logistics company packs the product and ships it to the customer. IT management, customer relationship management, and business intelligence services, marketing, on-line advertising, human resources, and sales force automation can all be handed off to ASPs, and public and investor relations can be outsourced to agencies. If there's anything left to do, EphemeraTech's few managers and employees can do it all from home offices interconnected by a VPN (virtual private network — see Chapter 9 for further discussion) managed by a network provider. With the myriad outsourcing options available to the outsourced, electronic commerce-enabled, automated enterprise of the 21st century, the question is not so much whether it should pull a Chiquita and simply become a brand name, but why not?

Admittedly, few companies would ever go as far as that, but with the constant pressure to adopt new technologies and adapt to ever-changing market conditions, their success in electronic commerce — indeed, their survival — depends to a large extent on deciding which processes and operations they should do themselves and which they should outsource to ASPs. There are no hard-and-fast rules, of course. Every company is going to have its own weak points and its own strengths. If you do something better than a service provider, it doesn't make sense to outsource it. It does make sense, however, when you're moving into uncharted waters where an ASP can turn an operational weakness, or even a deficiency, into a strength. "I don't know if it's for everyone," Burney said. "But a company should certainly consider it when they're making a significant change in business. If you haven't traditionally used the Web for procurement or sales, then you should look to someone who has the expertise."

The problem is that few companies actually have the expertise within the organization to venture successfully into new areas of technology. In order to gain and maintain a competitive edge in electronic commerce, companies have to be prepared to take advantage of the newest technologies, and unless they were themselves the innovators, those technologies inevitably come with a steep learning curve. Even if you want to do it all yourself, you still have to find the staff to do the work.

That problem is particularly acute for small business. While it may be entirely realistic for a small company to bring all of its operations in-house from a technological perspective, technology is never the only consideration. The problem is that small businesses don't typically have IT departments. If you have 20 employees, how many can you spare to get your e-commerce system up and running? The main problem that small businesses have in this area is finding the people who can build and integrate the system, and they are in incredible demand and tend to be very expensive. Consequently, any small company that is trying to add electronic commerce functionality should seriously consider turning to a service provider. "These technologies tend to be very complex and difficult to implement and maintain," Burney said. "The cost of failure can be high — but so can the cost of success. How well can you scale if you start doing great business? If you can't handle the volume, it may as well be a failure."

ASPs have a strong play in the medium-sized business and enterprise markets, of course. The former tends to be focused on costly applications like ERP, and on labor-intensive but not necessarily strategic operations like help desks and management. Medium-sized companies that operate from a variety of disparate locations have also been inclined to outsource major portions of their IT, networking, and telecommunications infrastructures. For big business, it's more a question of the rapid deployment of services in discrete lines of business. Though large enterprises usually have fully functional IT departments, they tend to be focused on maintaining existing infrastructures. ASPs can offer a chance to experiment with, and create prototypes of, new technologies. Having said all that, however, the hot market for ASPs is, and will remain, small businesses. In a March 2000 study, Cahners In-Stat Group found that more than one-third of ASP customers in 1999 were small or SOHO (small office/home office) businesses. It's a market that the big ASP players have been eager to tap with off-the-shelf versions of their enterprise products. IBM, for example, re-jigged its eBusiness suite of enterprise electronic commerce applications with just that market in mind.

Focus on ASPs

Colin Davies: Beyond outsourcing

Outsourcing is hardly a new idea, said Colin Davies, a financial services partner with Accenture (formerly Andersen Consulting); it was an idea whose time had come in the downsizing trend of the 1980s and 1990s. Its time has come again in the 21st century, but this time, the Internet has changed everything. "There are some things that are being outsourced now mainly because the technology has finally arrived at the point that it's actually do-able," Davies said. "It's not that it wasn't desirable before, but it just wasn't technologically possible."

With the emergence of a data communications infrastructure that can link companies in real time, from New York to Tokyo, for the first time outsourcing to ASPs has become a realistic — even attractive — proposition for processes like procurement. "Realistically, it has only been with the Internet and all of the technologies around that, that it's gotten to the point where you can actually rely on a third party to dynamically support you in an environment where you're trying to purchase things and get the suppliers hooked in and transactions processed quickly," Davies said. "That dynamic of the Internet allowing organizations to be seamlessly linked together is fairly new."

So is the nature of the services offered by the new generation of outsourcers. What sets ASPs apart is the depth and richness of the services they provide, more than the medium in which they deliver them. In fact, Davies wonders if it's even right to call them "outsourcers" at all. "Outsourcing, as it was defined, was really a phenomenon of the 1980s and 1990s, and believe it or not, what we're experiencing is a trend away from outsourcing — from the old definition," he said. "Outsourcing traditionally meant that you were coughing up resources and giving them to a third party, and then holding his feet to the fire to deliver something at lower cost and, ideally, better service than you could provide to yourself. There was no additional [value added] over and above that. The pressure right now is on these traditional players; they're under fire because it's no longer a good enough value proposition to take something off someone's hands and then give them back something at lower cost."

The value proposition depends on the function to be outsourced, but it usually boils down to being able to do something better —not just cheaper. In the hyper-accelerated world of electronic commerce, that can mean helping you stay ahead of the technology curve. "An ASP that specializes in IT maintenance has an economy of scale that many organizations simply don't have," he said. "You hold them accountable to service level agreements to keep their skills up and meet the target service levels, versus having to do that on your own. This is particularly true of a technology example, where it's tough for any organization to keep current on technology and to be continually high-end on their own."

That doesn't mean that an enterprise should outsource everything — though, with the proliferation of ASPs, that certainly is a possibility. Indeed, the list of processes that can be entrusted to an ASP is growing rapidly. "The functions and capabilities of your organization that actually aren't core to your strategic value proposition are automatically candidates," Davies said. "The first thing you have to do is understand your competitive plan to market — what is your differentiator. And what are the processes and functions in your organization that are directly relevant to that, because those are the ones you typically want to keep close to your chest, just by definition."

That definition can vary from one industry to the next, of course, and understanding that is the key to a successful and profitable ASP relationship. "There's a whole list of functions that may be strategic for some companies, and not for others, like procurement or IT maintenance," Davies said. "Procurement is not core to a bank, but it is to a manufacturing company. So there can be many different perspectives on what constitutes a core process, depending on the organization you're talking about."

Strategic or not, managers should be prepared to work in tandem with the ASP, once they've made the decision to outsource. Using an ASP's services doesn't mean that you abdicate responsibility for that function or process. "It means you change your role in it, so even if you outsource IT maintenance you still have to have leadership within your organization and people to govern that," Davies said. "You're off-loading some of the delivery capability, but you're keeping the management side of it."

Perhaps as a consequence of that, many enterprise-ASP relationships are evolving into partnerships of equals. The talk now is not so much of outsourcing, but of joint ventures. "Instead of arm's-length, hold-their-feet-to-the-fire, deliver-or-else, it's 'Let's work together'," Davies said. "'You've got value, I've got value, let's team up here and let's jointly create a value proposition.' In traditional outsourcing, the value proposition of the customers of a bank stays with the bank, even if it outsources some functions. In partnering, the bank would team up with a company and say, 'Let's create a brand together, create a value proposition, and we'll have both our names on it.' And that's how you'll see ASPs evolving; they're not just arm's length anymore. There's cross-equity ownership."

As electronic commerce and the Internet break down inter-enterprise barriers and bring companies closer together, the still-young ASP market is itself undergoing a transformation. It's a change that promises to be as profound for e-business as a whole as it is for the ASPs. "I think we'll start to see an increased stratification of what used to be a single thing called 'outsourcing' or ASP," Davies said. "Some of those players are going to evolve into an alliances model. They will partner with organizations, put skin in the game, and jointly commit to go to market with something. You'll see a stratification where some of these guys will move into that space; others will drop down to be narrow, niche players, where they will just make themselves available to the marketplace on a very narrow, skill set basis. The buzzword for that is netsourcing. That's where an organization doesn't want to give up processes so much as they want to use the capability or resources of a third party."

Davies is pretty confident that there will always be niche-oriented ASPs and netsourcers to support specialized market slices. "But general application management support and systems maintenance is getting highly eroded and commoditized," he said. As for the niche players, "the question is do they have the deep capabilities and resources that will really allow them to claim their slice?"

WHO TO CALL?

It seems like everyone wants to be an ASP these days. Not a week goes by without another handful of erstwhile software or system vendors, system integrators, or network providers announcing an "exciting ASP offering." From their perspective, it makes perfect sense, of course. With an ASP, the software vendor can bring customers into a continuing, long-term relationship that provides a constant and recurring source of income; the system integrator can develop and market a single product and sell it off the rack any number of times to any number of customers; the ISP can migrate from the no-margin business of access to high-margin services. And the traditional giants of the computer industry, like IBM, Compaq, and Hewlett-Packard, can use ASPs to seed markets and leverage their other product lines. The bottom line is that the computer business has changed and, like the ISPs, system vendors have to find new ways to turn a profit. Vendors like Compaq and Hewlett-Packard once focused primarily on selling hardware and software, and left system integration and consulting services to partners. However, as the profit margins on equipment sales have plummeted, they have discovered that there is money to be made by providing the services themselves.

For the big IT vendors, it has been a game of follow the leader. IBM pioneered the market for integrated electronic commerce and enterprise services with its eBusiness portfolio — coining a neologism in the process. That, more than anything else, encouraged the other IT vendors to take the ASP plunge both by showing the way and by making an end-run around its traditional channels. A traditional rival, HP, announced its e-Services suite in 1999, with its gaze firmly planted on IBM's eBusiness wake. IBM had built an empire on its eBusiness strategy, and HP wanted a piece of the action. "There's no question that Hewlett-Packard is going after IBM," said Steve Robins, senior analyst with the Yankee Group, a market research firm in Boston. "And they're doing it partly by adopting part of IBM's eBusiness plan."

It was a significant departure for HP, but a necessary one. On one hand, the company made its core e-Services technology open source, inviting other companies to use and alter it to their own ends with the hope that it would seed a market for HP's products and create a critical mass for its services. On the other hand, it could leverage its strong position in personal computers and mid-range systems and, above all, the on-line transactions leadership of its VeriFone subsidiary. In one of those dialectics that keep turning up in electronic commerce, VeriFone sells e-Services, while e-Services sell VeriFone. "In order for our technology to work, it has to be pervasive," said Nigel Ball, general manager of Hewlett-Packard's e-Services division. "Hewlett-Packard will make its profit from its leadership position. We'll offer brokering, consulting, and other elements that you'll need to really make it all work. As you use aggregate services and integrate your business processes, you'll need things like billing services. That's the strategy."

It's a strategy that underpins much of the action in the ASP space. The idea is that, with an integrated sell, vendors can exchange services for products and vice versa. "[HP] traditionally had all these independent but united technologies, and the idea used to be to use these individual products to get people to buy hardware," Robins said. "Now they've got a comprehensive and complete offer that isn't necessarily dependent on equipment sales."

Though the transition from products to services, from the traditional vendor channels to the ASP model, is happening quickly, it isn't complete. Barely any ASPs even existed in 1997, but Cahners In-Stat Group found that companies with ASP offerings made roughly 30 percent of their revenues from the delivery of application services in 1999. The ASPs themselves expected that to rise to 35 percent in 2000. With an eager market, compelling offerings, and the guarantee that innovations in electronic commerce will keep the demand growing for years to come, it almost appears that the ASP business will just keep expanding. But appearances are deceiving. The ASP business is poised to follow the example of ISPs, which proliferated in the first great flush of Internet mania in the mid-1990s, only to consolidate in a relatively small number of providers a few years later.

Consequently, choosing an ASP has to involve a gamble on whether the people handling your mission-critical processes will even be in business in a few years. "There is definitely going to be a lot of consolidation," Burney said. "If you look at the identities of some of these ASPs, they tend to offer one specific application. That works well for enterprises that only outsource one application, but small business wants a one-stop solution and, in the long run, small business is the real market for ASPs." Who's best equipped to provide one-stop application shopping? The dot-coms and one-application ASPs have a severe credibility problem: Burney's own research found that most small businesses don't even know what an ASP is, and that gives providers with established brands a significant edge. The big-system vendors have an advantage, of course. They have already muscled their way into the market with end-to-end offerings designed to appeal to small business. But the real ASP winners will probably be the telcos.

The advantage telecommunications carriers like MCI Worldcom, AT&T, and Sprint have over everyone else is that they actually own the networking infrastructure used to deliver application services. The deregulation of the telecommunications industry and the introduction of competition to the local exchange market, moreover, gave existing carriers an incentive to expand their product portfolios and new players an entrée to customers through their networks. And just as the once-ubiquitous telephone answering machine has given way to voice mail services offered by local telephone companies, the small business network is evolving into little more than a plug in the wall. "Outsourced network services are probably the future of the small business network," Burney said. "The problem for small business network operators is the investment in equipment they have to make as they grow. And they have to call their local carrier for a new telco line every time they add a new Web site or remote access server."

Sprint Communications Corp. introduced the mother of all out-sourced network offerings in the fall of 1999, with the launch of the Integrated On-demand Network (ION) service. Almost completely transparent to the end user, ION integrates all of a company's network traffic — data, voice, and multimedia — on a single network pipe. What makes ION so special is that it automatically allocates bandwidth as needed, so users don't have to lease separate channels for different kinds of applications. They just jack into a switch installed on their premises by the telco and pay the monthly bill. It's a brilliant play by a carrier interested in expanding its offerings into the lucrative ASP market. With access to as much network bandwidth as they need at any one time, small companies can comfortably outsource all or part of their operations. "ION is the leveling tool of e-business," said Kirk Heinlein, Sprint's ION marketing manager, when ION was launched. "It gives you the option of hosting servers on-site, or using outsourced networked servers. One of the realities of e-business is that it will have to involve companies of various sizes."

While that may be great news for the small business person who wants to build a virtual trading community or insinuate his or her company into a high-volume supply chain, it's even better news for the telco. After all, the company that provides your integrated telecommunications, data networking, and multimedia services will probably be first in line to provide application services as well. It's a powerful sell, and one that resonates loudly with telecommunications giants bent on diversification. Within the year, AT&T launched its Integrated Network Connect Service and MCI Worldcom has been gradually rolling out On-Net, a similar, though far from identical offering, since the middle of 2000.

As attractive as the *idea* might be, however, integrated networking services have been surprisingly slow to catch on, and the providers have been taking something of a hit. Far from being a major revenue center,

Sprint has discovered that the service has become something of a black hole, observed Denise Pappalardo in *Network World.* "ION revenue for the first quarter of this year [2000] totaled only $1 million, with operating expenses of $137 million."[2] It's hard to say whether this is due to teething problems, or that the availability of integrated networking services has been inconsistent, at best. Nevertheless, Burney is quick to point out that, if anything is going to be outsourced — particularly by small enterprises — it will probably be networking services. To that extent, at least, she said, the outsourced enterprise network "is inevitable."

THE END OF IT?

You could taste the fear in IT departments across North America at the turn of the century as ASPs emerged to provide applications for almost every IT and electronic commerce operation. Superficially, at least, it seems like the apotheosis of the virtual corporation — the company with no head office, no infrastructure, no concrete assets apart from its expertise and knowledge capital. In the admittedly extreme case of EphemeraTech, the enterprise is barely an enterprise at all; having shed all operations except those required to generate product ideas and maintain its brand image, EphemeraTech doesn't even have an IT department. And that, said some IT industry watchers, is the shape of things to come. Not only are traditional IT departments inflexible and slow to change, they argued, but they are also fundamentally ill-suited to the demands and exigencies of electronic commerce and e-business. One Forrester Research study even heralded "the death of IT."

At some level, it's an attractive argument — attractive, that is, if you're not an IT professional — and, on the surface at least, it has the ring of truth. Who wouldn't want to outsource that part of their enterprise processes most prone to obsolescence? Moreover, the argument goes, no one company can be expected to ensure the scalability, availability, flexibility, or ubiquity required to keep up in the warp-speed world of e-business. As processes begin to take precedence over organizational structures, enterprises will allocate resources across departments. According to Forrester Research, IT management is under intense pressure from electronic commerce technologies and e-business to evolve from an internal to an externally managed technology infrastructure. It will be supported not by IT departments, or even ASPs, but external service providers that manage the whole infrastructure from commerce servers to data warehouses. The evolution to this new paradigm will happen relatively quickly as e-businesses outsource one process at a time to realize e-business efficiencies and participate in new market relationships built around virtual trading communities.

From that point of view, then, despite the rapid pace of networking technologies, automation, computerization, and electronic commerce, the beginning of the 21st century is a bad time to be an IT professional. It's a little like being a coal stoker at about the time shipbuilders made the transition to oil-burning turbine engines. Nevertheless, as strangely compelling as the argument may be, rumors of IT's demise have been greatly exaggerated. There is certainly great value for small and even some medium-sized businesses to outsource all or part of their IT processes to ASPs or even full-service IT infrastructure providers.

The fictional case of EphemeraTech is entirely in the realm of possibility if it does not already have an investment in IT and infrastructure to begin with. However, if the experience with large-scale IT transitions and process migrations like ERP implementations are any indication, it just isn't that easy to re-engineer corporate IT, and the enterprise itself, to fit into the externalized model. Moreover, IT is, and will likely remain, an important strategic asset and market differentiator for some time to come. Even with a new market model, companies need something they can compete with, and in electronic commerce, that edge comes from IT. And with the inevitable consolidation of the ASP industry, the situation could conceivably arise where companies share identical IT services, outsourced to the same ASPs. How do you compete when your competitors have the same edge? With that in mind, it remains to be seen just how many enterprises will feel comfortable outsourcing all, or even a significant part, of their IT operations.

When you look at it that way, corporate IT is safe and, more importantly, enterprises — particularly the larger ones — can still turn IT around strategically. Saying ASPs are the end of IT is a little like saying XML is the end of EDI; it's a nice, tidy answer but, as we've seen in the supply chain, nothing is ever that tidy. "There will always be a mix," Burney said. "There's a reason for having these private networks or inside systems, and that reason is control. Companies are outsourcing because they're strained, and because there's a shortage of talents and skills. The best thing to do for now is outsource, but that doesn't mean it's the best thing to do in the long run." Indeed, in the long run the legacy of the ASP boom will be twofold. It will allow smaller companies, who would not otherwise have had the resources to play with the big boys, to enter the business-to-business supply chain. And, it will enable something different for big corporations. ASPs provide a risk-free way to create prototypes for new technologies and to expand operations without upsetting the IT apple-cart. They are the environment in which the next killer apps of electronic commerce will be cultivated. Once mature, however, they will find their place again within the thriving heart of IT.

Key Terms

outsourcing

application service provider (ASP)

server farm

9

SECURITY

The Internet can be a wild, unruly neighborhood, and if you want to do business there, you have to be prepared to take certain precautions. The tools are all in place. Security technology is effective, proven, and mature. However, security is not just a technological issue. It's also a question of planning, policy, and procedure. And, at the end of the day, the thing that's really going to save your company's bacon won't be the latest, greatest security system, it will be the knowledge and intelligence you put into its application.

THE DAY THE NET STOOD STILL

You couldn't read a newspaper or watch television during the second week of February 2000 without getting the sinking feeling that the Internet was under attack. Headlines screamed around the world — "Hackers choke Internet" and "Internet chaos as virtual terrorists swamp Web sites." Talking heads on CNN, CBC Newsworld, and all the major U.S. networks gravely warned of the threats posed by "techno-gangsters" and "cyber-terrorists" to the lifeblood of global electronic commerce.

Some of the highest-profile sites on the Internet, including Yahoo! and eBay, were brought to their knees by denial-of-service attacks on February 7 and 8. Using software freely available on the Internet, one or more high-tech delinquents hijacked dozens of otherwise innocent networked computers and used them to flood their victims with millions of simultaneous server requests. Faced with a tide of useless, often meaningless traffic, the victims stopped, seized up, and crashed.

In the wired economy, going off-line can be the kiss of death. A disgruntled user can just as easily point his browser to Haggle Online as eBay if all he's looking for is a quick and exciting auction. Indeed, shortly after the attacks hit the headlines, analysts at the Yankee Group in Boston came out with an estimate of the week's losses. After adding up the expense of security upgrades, the cost of the lost sales and commissions, lost advertising revenues, and market capitalization losses, the Yankee Group came up with a tally of $1.2 billion in losses to the Internet industry as a whole.

After a couple of expensive days of hacking, law enforcement officials leapt into high gear. In Washington, the Federal Bureau of Investigation began the largest computer crimes investigation in history. When the trail appeared to lead to a shadowy Canadian hacker, Mafiaboy, the Mounties — who always, after all, get their man — joined in with the G-men. Internet security became, for a brief, shining moment, an international public policy priority. In Washington, President Bill Clinton asked Congress to add $37 million to the $100 million already earmarked to fight computer crime. The good guys were moving swiftly, and the only people who didn't seem to be impressed were the hackers themselves.

Though it was far from a false alarm, the media reaction to the February 2000 denial-of-service attacks was vastly out of proportion to the damage that the hackers had actually done. While it's true that some of the biggest names in electronic commerce had been hit hard by the attacks, no one had penetrated their defenses. There had been no unauthorized access to sensitive information like customer profiles or corporate records; the hackers had simply blocked the doors. Far from being "techno-gangsters" or "cyber-terrorists," the denial-of-service hackers were really just common vandals who broke some virtual windows. Mafiaboy turned out, as expected, to be no one more threatening than a spotted Canadian high-schooler.

In fact, a Forrester Research security analyst, Charles Rutstein, pointed out that not only are denial-of-service attacks — frustrating though they may be — the equivalent of high-technology vandalism, but, like vandalism in the real world, there's not much anyone can do about it except clean up the mess and try to chase down the vandals. Because these attacks actually occur at the point where the enterprise network meets the wide-open Internet — in effect, on the sidewalk in front of your store — they're beyond the reach of even the most sophisticated network security technologies. "Denial of service is clearly an important security issue," Rutstein observed. "But, to put it bluntly, it's not something that anyone can do a whole lot about."

However, a whole lot can be done about the other kinds of security problems — the ones that penetrate your network and expose your business processes, your central operation, your customers, and your partners to peril. What the hype-storm around the February 2000 denial-of-service attacks did was to underline just how vulnerable e-business can be to hacker attacks. Though the real threats are far subtler and more intrusive, the brute force denial-of-service attacks did get everyone's attention.

SECURITY IS JOB ONE?

Ask any corporate executive to name his top electronic commerce priorities and the odds are good that security won't be far from the top of the list. That isn't surprising; along with the vast opportunities, economies, and efficiencies promised by electronic commerce have come a whole host of new, potentially disastrous security issues.

Back in the days of the trading post and the neighborhood general store, business security was a simple matter of putting your till in a safe and a stout lock on the front door. You trusted your best customers with credit and everyone else paid cash. Then along came purchase orders, procurement contracts, supply chains, credit cards, debit cards, and the Internet. The speed and scale of business have grown exponentially, while electronic commerce and on-line transactions have become the sine qua non of business success. In the ever-changing, ever-fluid world of e-business, a Citadel lock just doesn't cut it anymore.

It's the consciousness of that reality that makes electronic commerce executives talk the security talk — at least when they talk to nosey business reporters. Whether it's a question of taking casual orders through e-mail for Rolling Stones tickets, selling audio CDs on a self-serve Web site, or maintaining a sophisticated supply chain relationship with dozens of Fortune 500 partners, electronic commerce boils down to asking your customers and clients to trust you with their money, their personal and corporate information, and the keys to their back office. It's an immense responsibility, and no one wants to be seen to take it lightly.

Network security products and services are big bucks. A study released by *Information Security* magazine in the fall of 2000 found that the number of companies spending more than $1 million on network security products and services had increased 188 percent over the previous two years. "Put another way, in 1998, only 8 percent of companies had security budgets topping $1 million; today, it's nearly one-quarter of companies."[1] Forrester Research projects that the U.S. security market will grow to $19.4 billion annually by 2004, and according to IDC Research, the world market for enterprise network security services alone will reach $17.2 billion in the same year, with U.S. companies doing half the spending.

Looking at the tools, technology, and services, then, it seems that companies are venturing into electronic commerce loaded for bear. The problem is that there is a gulf between appearances and reality. Though security is one of electronic commerce's few motherhood issues — everyone believes it's important, even vital — there's a surprising lack of urgency in corporate boardrooms. The attitude is downright lackadaisical. A study prepared for the Information Systems Audit and Control

Foundation and released early in 2000 found that the risks posed by exposing business processes to the Internet barely registered in corporate managers' minds. After all, they had experienced no serious security breaches up until then, and the overwhelming perception appeared to be that they had taken the appropriate measures to secure their companies' electronic commerce processes.

None of that is particularly shocking until you look at the difference of opinion between corporate managers and executives and their IT departments. While managers are generally overwhelmingly confident that their electronic commerce processes and systems are secure — or at least that Internet security poses a relatively low risk — their security personnel and auditors aren't quite so sure. "I'm beginning to think it's complacency," said the report's author, Steven Ross, a director with the E-Business Technology and Security practice at Deloitte & Touche LLP. in New York. "There's a distinct difference between the reactions of people speaking for themselves and management. And there's a feeling among the security people themselves that management doesn't understand the issues like they do."

Whether this is because the people responsible for security tend to paint a rosy picture when they report to their bosses, or because they understand the issues better, Ross wouldn't say. But it's clear that corporate decision-makers seem to be suffering from a false sense of security. It's one thing to say that security is important, but it's another thing to do something about it.

Yet, as the February 2000 denial-of-service attacks showed, anyone may be vulnerable to attack on the Internet. Despite the fact that Mafiaboy never succeeded in penetrating any company's security — indeed, he never tried — security does get compromised. Fully 25 percent of the respondents to the 2000 Computer Crime and Security Survey, conducted by the San Francisco–based Computer Security Institute with the participation of the FBI, said their systems had been penetrated from outside during the previous year. Twenty-seven percent had detected denial-of-service attacks.

The bad news is that every company with a connection to the Internet is potentially vulnerable. Even mighty Microsoft Corp. — the company that makes most of the software most companies rely on to do business on the Internet — got stung when a Russian hacker penetrated its defenses to steal the source code of the Windows operating system. To make matters worse, electronic commerce is an inherently risky business when you expose your company on the Internet. An on-line transaction, whether it is between a bookstore and a consumer, or a manufacturer and its suppliers, is an enormously complex interaction between strangers in an inherently insecure medium. There are no signed paper documents on the Internet, no face-to-face meetings, and even if you are doing business with long-time partners, it's not inconceivable that someone might try to impersonate them to malicious ends.

The good news is that technologies do exist to protect companies' electronic assets, or at least to minimize the dangers of the electronic frontier.

Focus on Security

Robert Thibadeau: Building trust

Your doors are locked, the night watchmen who guard your warehouse are insured and bonded, petty cash is carefully controlled, and you don't keep your operating budget lying loose in a pile of tens and twenties on the floor. Security isn't rocket science, and it's not a new idea. But electronic commerce is new, and it has taken time for the idea of electronic commerce security to sink in. "Generally speaking, everyone is operating in a sphere of severe compromise," said Robert Thibadeau of Carnegie Mellon University's eCommerce Institute. "What's going on is that, if we didn't have the Internet, we'd know what to do. We could close off the corporate environment and use dedicated network connections and VPNs between corporations and suppliers. We would pretty much know what to do. The problem has happened because the Internet largely opens the holes."

Those holes are, to some extent, inevitable. Doing business on the Internet means exposing your vulnerabilities to your trusted partners and, more often than not, to a wild and often hostile Internet. The hard part is minimizing those vulnerabilities, while remaining open for business. "The network guys recognize that all these holes are getting opened up, and they're trying to figure out how to allow people to have what they want while, at the same time, trying to maintain as good a security as they can, given the fact that they've just left the door open," Thibadeau said. "That's where the trick is. That's where it's hard. I don't think it's that the IT guys don't know what's going on, it's that they don't know clearly what to do, because I don't think anybody really clearly knows what to do. This is not a minor problem ... it's a big problem."

It's not that the technology isn't up to the task. The problem is more complex, Thibadeau said, and in many ways, more subtle. "The technology — the cryptography and the authorization and authorization tools — is good," he said. "At that level, when the big question is can you put together an entire security system, the answer is that we know how to put together the system. If we have the integrity, privacy, authentication, authorization, and auditing dealt with, we can create a totally secure computer system. And we have perfectly sufficient cryptography tools available, so we don't need more of that."

The real issue is adapting corporate policies to the open world of electronic commerce. However, managers don't have their IT workers' intimate understanding of network operations. Not only are they all-too-often unequipped to set security policies, they often suffer from a false and dangerous sense of security. "The problem isn't the IT people," Thibadeau said. "They have a fairly decent sense of just how bad this problem is — in fact, I think a lot of people have a fairly decent sense of it, though I don't think it's the majority of people by any stretch of the imagination. Management is different. Some managers get it, but I've met so many managers that don't get it that I can't say that most even understand what's going on. However, if you take the time to show them what's going on, or you give them tools that they understand to find out what's going on, it doesn't take long before they get nervous."

Moreover, the interests of security and the benefits of being open to the Internet are frequently at odds. "There was an action that really illustrates the push-me–pull-you atmosphere around this," Thibadeau continued. "In the federal government, there was an executive order to stop all mobile code, like Java and Javascript, at the firewall. But the plug was pulled on that idea. The decision was that they weren't going to do that. The reasoning was that, if they stopped all mobile code, they'd create such a lousy network work environment that the government would lose all its good employees. So that's the push-me–pull-you. The problem isn't that the IT guys don't understand; it's that they don't know what to do because the problem doesn't have a technical solution. It's a combination of a technical and a policy problem."

So what has to be done? Thibadeau isn't sure. One answer might be to build a system of automated agreements and contracts into every transaction. That, he believes, would help set the stage for a true e-commerce boom. "We could take an Internet that's doing $100 billion in revenue and turn it into a $1-trillion vehicle if we could solve this one problem," Thibadeau said. "This is what's keeping people from talking to each other on the Internet. You can build automated negotiation mechanisms for what amount to standard agreements, so I can permit my partners into my site if they agree to certain things, and I'll agree to certain things in exchange to protect them."

Nevertheless, vulnerability is as much a part of doing business on the Internet as it is a part of falling in love. An implicit part of electronic commerce is the exchange of data — product and catalog information, purchase orders, and money — across the firewall. As soon as it crosses that line, it's out of your hands and out of your control. Trust and technology only go so far, in Thibadeau's view. At some point, security must be ensured, or at least protected, by law. "That I think, is the core of the problem that we have today — which is that we don't clearly understand that technology is not the answer," Thibadeau said. "Everyone concedes that point, but the lawmakers don't know where to draw the line. The issue, in the end, is part technology, part law, and it involves sociological maturity. It's a question of our understanding what's going on on the Internet at the same level of understanding that people in the 18th century understood publishing or public speaking."

PRYING EYES

Secrets have long been the currency of statecraft, war, and commerce. For as long as there have been written messages, there have been techniques, tools, and technologies to conceal them. The Egyptians were probably the first cryptographers, enciphering temple mysteries and Pharaonic confidences in layers of hieroglyphs. The ancient Spartans enciphered battlefield messages by tightly wrapping a strip of parchment around a staff called a *skytale*. A message would be written on the parchment along the length of the staff and then unwrapped, making it illegible to anyone without an appropriately-sized *skytale*.

As a military leader and ruler of the known world — not to mention a wealthy landowner and businessman — Julius Caesar had plenty of secrets. To keep them, he devised an ingenious code familiar to any kid who has ever passed encrypted messages in class. The Roman historian Suetonius notes in *The Twelve Caesars* that Caesar coded dispatches to the Senate and his generals and enciphered letters to his friend Cicero. "To understand their apparently incomprehensible meaning, one must number the letters of the alphabet from 1 to 22, and then replace each of the letters that Caesar has used with the one which occurs four numbers lower — for instance, D stands for A."[2]

Using this so-called *monoalphabetic substitution cipher* — that is, a code based on substituting one letter for another — and the modern English alphabet, the name Cleopatra would be rendered as Gpistexve … well, sort of. What Suetonius didn't mention is that Caesar, no mere schoolboy, added an extra layer of complexity to the code by substituting Greek letters for the original Latin.

Anyone with a knowledge of Latin and Greek and a little time on his hands could conceivably decode the Caesar cipher without too much trouble. With the development of *polyalphabetic substitution encryption* by Leon Battista Alberti in the 15th century, the science of cryptography took a major step forward. Alberti proposed a system that would assign one of multiple possible ciphertext characters (the encrypted text) to any given plain-text character, depending on the position of concentric cipher disks. The resulting code could be deciphered only if the recipient knew the order of the characters on each disk, and each disk's relative position.

That was the principle behind Nazi Germany's Enigma machine. During the early days of World War II, Enigma gave the German war machine an immense advantage over the Allies. The device, which resembled a cross between an Underwood typewriter and an antique gramophone, was equipped with five metal rotors, each engraved with the 26 characters of the Latin alphabet in a different sequence. Each day, the German high command informed its cipher clerks at the front, at air bases, in submarines, and at headquarters which three of the five rotors they would install in the Enigma machine, in which order, and with which starting positions. Any character the clerk punched in could be one of 30 trillion permutations, making Enigma-encoded messages utterly incomprehensible to everyone except the select few who knew the machine's daily settings.

The story of how Allied cryptanalysts at the signals intelligence facility at Bletchley Park decoded Enigma is one of the greatest intellectual adventures of the last century; it is also the story of the birth of the digital computer. In order to crunch the numbers necessary to break the German code, the cryptanalysts developed the concepts and hardware that lie at the foundation of modern information technology. It wasn't much of a stretch, then, to apply the tools devised to break codes to creating increasingly unbreakable codes.

Using computers, cryptographers are able to build codes on complex mathematical formulas, or algorithms, that make Enigma's trillions of permutations look like child's play, but the basic principle hasn't changed since the days of ancient Greece. Every encryption code has a key. For the Spartans, it was the *skytale;* for Caesar, it was the number of offset letters in the alphabet; for German cipher clerks during World War II, it was the order and position of the Enigma machine's rotors. In each case, and equally so in the case of digital encryption, the message recipients only needed to know that value to turn the ciphertext into legible text. What makes digital encryption so powerful is that computers allow cryptographers to use algorithms of immense complexity to convert text into a heap of incomprehensible digital slag. These formulas can be solved only with a missing variable, and that variable is an encryption key that can be hundreds or even thousands of characters long.

How long a key actually has to be in order to provide adequate security depends on the complexity of the encryption algorithm. There's no hard and fast rule, but when it comes to the **bit-length** of encryption keys, longer is better — but only when you're talking about the same encryption techniques. It is theoretically possible for someone with enough computing power to break any key, whatever the length, by brute force. However, the longer the key, or the more complex the encryption algorithm, the more computing power that takes. A good rule of thumb is that if it costs more for someone to invest in the technology needed to get at your data than the data is actually worth, you're probably secure.

Nevertheless, computing power increases exponentially. A computer that can perform one billion floating-point calculations per second (a gigaflop) used to be known as a supercomputer. Not too long ago, they cost hundreds of thousands of dollars, putting them out of reach of all but the biggest corporations and institutions. Today, you can order one from a mail-order catalog for a few thousand dollars. On the other hand, as computers become more powerful, it becomes easier and more practical to use increasingly longer keys. In effect, encryption strength is a moving target, but it is possible to make unauthorized decryption far more trouble than it's worth.

Symmetrical key encryption technologies — systems in which the coder and de-coder use the same key — do have an inherent flaw. You only need the key, whatever its length, to decipher the code, and there's no guarantee that the key won't fall into the wrong hands. You can expose yourself simply by using an insecure communication medium to inform your intended recipient of the key. You have to share a secret, and shared secrets are the most difficult ones to keep. After all, you can't encrypt the message containing the key if you need the key to decode the message! If you have secrets to keep that could be a big problem.

The potential for intrigue in lost encryption keys has been used in the plots of more than a few spy novels and movies. So it shouldn't be a surprise that the problem was solved by the most secret of Her Majesty's secret services, the Communications Electronics Security Group. In the late 1960s, a CESG cryptanalyst named James Ellis proposed an encryption technique that used different keys at either end of the process — **asymmetrical key encryption.** However, Ellis's system was a Cold War secret, and it was only when the American cryptographers Martin Hellman and Whitfield Diffie independently re-invented the technique that it moved out of the shadows of international espionage.

Public key encryption is both ingenious and elegant. The sender and the recipient each have two keys — one that's private and carefully guarded on his computer, and another that he makes publicly available for anyone to use. In fact, the sender might even append his **public key** along with the encrypted message. Both keys are essential parts of the encryption and decryption process. A message that is encrypted using the recipient's public key and the sender's **private key** can only be decrypted using the recipient's private key and the sender's public key. Not only does the technique ensure that messages are read only by their intended recipients, avoiding the possible exposure of a single-key system, but the recipient can be sure that the sender is who he purports to be. A message that can be decrypted using someone's public key must have been encrypted using his private key.

Public key cryptography is a natural for a medium like the public Internet, where you have no control over the routes your messages take and who might intercept them along the way. Privacy advocate Phil Zimmermann, who developed PGP, by far the most popular personal encryption tool used on the Internet, likes to remind people that most of us don't write personal or sensitive business information on the back of postcards and consign them to the mailbox. We use envelopes to keep that information safe and secure. We wrap an extra piece of paper around checks, or use opaque envelopes, and businesses use tamper-proof carbons to send sensitive data to customers. Encryption is the opaque envelope for digital communications.

THE SECURED TRANSACTION

When the messages moving back and forth across the Net are a financial transaction between two businesses, or even between a business and a consumer, the security envelope has to be particularly opaque. Billions of dollars change hands in electronic commerce; purchase orders, requisitions, and sensitive corporate information are in constant movement through the datastream. The first security consideration in electronic commerce is ensuring that these millions upon millions of transactions are completed securely. If the transactions aren't secure, then nothing is.

When Netscape Communications Corp. began developing the **Secure Sockets Layer,** or SSL, protocol in 1995, the Internet was still widely seen as a toy for geeks and techno-weenies. The potential requirements of Internet-based security were far from anyone's mind. At the time, the Internet — created and nurtured in the open environment of academic collaboration — was inherently insecure. The Internet was for sharing information after all, and the profit motive seemed utterly at odds with the prevailing values of the on-line world. The explosive growth in Internet use among the general public and with it the advent of electronic commerce in the mid-1990s made basic transactional security an industry priority. The challenge was to develop a security technology that didn't require users to buy special software or learn all kinds of abstruse technical details.

Netscape Communications Corp., at the time the dominant player in both Internet server software and client software like the Navigator browser, was in a position to make that happen. Not only was Netscape the only company that could make its own solution a de facto standard, but the solution itself, the SSL protocol, was the right technology for the job. SSL was quickly adopted as the foundation for secure Internet transactions, and it soon became an official, recognized standard. Today, almost every secure Web-based transaction is protected by SSL. It's still possible to use a browser or merchant server that doesn't support it, but it's something you have to work at.

Every SSL transaction is a complex dance between client and server software using both public and single-key encryption to identify and authenticate the client and confirm the integrity of the transaction. Every SSL-capable client — like Netscape Communicator or Microsoft Internet Explorer — has its own unique private and public keys. When a user initiates a secure connection to an SSL server, the client transmits its public key. In order to make sure the client is who it purports to be, the server sends a random message that the client encrypts using its private key and sends back. The server automatically decrypts the message using the client's public key and compares it to the original file. If they match, the server knows the client that initiated the transaction is who it purports to be.

Once this authentication pas de deux is complete, the server generates a unique key that the client will use to encrypt its end of the transaction. This ensures that the data sent from the client to the server — a customer's Visa number, or a corporate procurement number — is encrypted. Even though this part of the transaction is protected by symmetrical key encryption, rather than more secure asymmetrical techniques, it has proved to be more than sufficient to protect Web-based transactions. Not only is the entire transaction encrypted, but the key is generated for a single use, and once it is used, it will never be used again. In order to crack the transaction, a cyberthief would have to intercept one transaction among the millions of Internet interactions happening each minute between geographically remote computers, and then decipher a message encrypted with a one-time-only key.

The beauty of SSL is that it operates just above the basic protocols of the Internet itself. That means that SSL functionality can conceivably be integrated into any kind of networked application requiring client authentication and transaction encryption. Thus, the protocol has found its niche on the Web. Though developed by Netscape, it is an open, de facto standard, and it has been adopted by all browser vendors and most developers of electronic commerce server software. Netscape has submitted SSL to the World Wide Web Consortium for recognition as an official standard. In 1999, the Internet Engineering Task Force, the body that oversees the establishment of Internet standards, published a draft standard called Transport Layer Security that is largely based on SSL.

It all adds up to a level of security second only to a formal, notarized transfer of funds overseen by a reputable financial institution and completed on its premises. In fact, SSL provides far more protection than most of us are accustomed to in the real world.

"No one encrypts my credit card when I hand it to a waiter at a restaurant," observed Nick Jones, then business development manager and electronic commerce evangelist for Chapters Online, the on-line version of Chapter's Bookstores. "Who knows what happens when my card is out of sight, or when it's swiped in a reader? Anything can happen. There's a lot of worry about transaction security on the Internet, but the truth is that the Internet makes commerce more secure, not less." SSL transactions are theoretically breakable, of course. Nothing is perfect.

No one should ever make the mistake of believing that any method of encryption is fool-proof. Given enough time and resources, and assuming it's all worth the investment in time and resources, anything can be cracked. Moreover, because it authenticates only the client and not the server, SSL is vulnerable to an attack called hyperlink spoofing, where a digital con man sets up a site that impersonates a legitimate electronic business to take bogus credit card orders.

The value of the volume of transactions between companies is far greater than anything you'd put on your credit card. Moreover, a great deal of business-to-business electronic commerce, whether it's automated procurement or automated warehouse management, happens without human intervention or supervision. One of electronic commerce's main values is the efficiency that can be realized by fully automated, networked, and computerized business processes. Moreover, while SSL identifies and authenticates the client, it doesn't authenticate the server, so it doesn't obviate the need to validate your business partners before you do business with them. As with everything else in electronic commerce, technology is no substitute for good business sense.

CONTROLLED ACCESS

In the best of all possible worlds you would be able to open your network up to the riches of the Internet with no worries. In the worst of all possible worlds, you would simply bar the doors and keep the big bad Internet outside your network. In the real world, no one has the option of closing up his or her business to the Internet — at least not if he or she wants to stay in business — and no one should venture onto the Internet without protection. When a hacker pilfered customer credit card information from CD Universe in January 2000, he didn't attack the transaction system and he didn't intercept messages in transit. What he did was far more dangerous — he entered CD Universe's corporate network and scooped the numbers out of accounting. It was as if someone had walked through the front door and rifled a few desks and filing cabinets without anything stopping him.

While transaction security technologies like SSL protect electronic commerce transactions from being intercepted between buyer and seller and encryption ensures that those communications that are intercepted cannot be read, they're only part of the story. Even more important is the question of access — who and what can get into your company network or intranet. If you think of the Internet as a busy commercial boulevard, then your company's Web site is like a front office. Anyone can walk in off the street to make enquiries, place an order, or apply for a job. That's what front offices are for, after all. However, no company would ever permit someone who just came in off the street to traipse past the front desk and through the door to its inner sanctum. Every company carefully controls access to the heart of its business operations in the off-line world using combination locks, security guards, and — late at night — trained guard dogs. On the Internet, you do it with a **firewall.**

In its strictest sense, a network firewall is the software that resides on a system, at the very edge of an internal enterprise network, and ensures that only a small, manageable gateway opens the company network to the public Internet. In its broadest sense, however, the term "firewall" has come to mean the software itself, the server it resides on, and even network equipment and appliances like routers and access gateways with built-in access control functions. In every case, the firewall does two things. It blocks outside traffic to the internal network, but permits traffic that meets a very narrow set of criteria. In effect, a firewall ensures that the front door remains locked, except in exceptional circumstances.

While this may sound like unnecessarily rigid security, it really isn't all that different from the way most companies keep their inner doors locked except for the employees and rare partner who has been issued a key. Indeed, the first rule of network access should be "Keep everyone out." Once you've done that, you can permit access to those individuals and organizations that absolutely must be able to get inside so that

Figure 9-1: A sample firewall

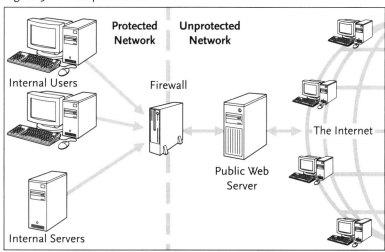

your business can continue. None of this means that you should close up shop to the Internet, only that a firewall lets you select which functions are accessible to the public. Typically, your Web server would be located outside the firewall to inform the public and take SSL-secured orders. It would then be the only computer permitted to cross over the firewall to access your customer database and accounting system.

Firewalls are the essential component in securing the boundary layer between the internal network and the Internet, between the intranet and the extranet. However, as essential a tool as it may be, the firewall has two inherent shortcomings. First of all, it is only a physical implementation of an enterprise's security policy. The most expensive firewall hardware and software in the world will amount to nothing if you simply decide to leave the virtual door open and give everyone access. Electronic commerce is a fluid business, and that means firewalls cannot be a "fire and forget" tool. They have to be constantly monitored, tweaked, and updated to ensure maximum security. Moreover, firewalls are only really useful when you have a clear distinction between us and them, between the inside and the outside of your network. If your business processes extend across several locations or enterprises, then you have to secure the external and not just the internal network. "Do SSL and firewalls and all of that make it safe to get into the electronic commerce forest?" asked Deloitte & Touche's Ross. "Will it be good enough for broad-based consumer transactions? Yes. Is it enough for all of the things we plan to use the Net and electronic commerce for? No."

For electronic commerce to realize its full potential in enabling an automated, seamless supply chain, it isn't always enough to ensure security at the starting point and end point of a transaction — there are times when the whole network has to be secure. In the days before words like electronic commerce and e-business entered the commercial lexicon, that was relatively easy to do, and early electronic business processes like EDI habitually flowed through secured network connections. In the dawn of electronic commerce, before the Internet became a medium for business, secured networks were the rule, rather than the exception, for one simple reason. There was no information highway as we now know it; if you were doing business over a network, you probably owned the network from one end to another. That was a costly proposition. The whole advantage of electronic commerce, of course, is that it makes business faster, cheaper, and more efficient, and one of the key technologies that makes that possible is the *virtual* **private network.** The VPN has allowed companies that once managed their own costly private network, or that relied on expensive access to secure value-added networks (VANs) maintained by telecommunications and computer companies, to migrate en masse to the Internet. Now that almost every company in the industrialized world is connected at least casually — and usually quite thoroughly — to the Internet, the cost-benefit analysis of VPNs couldn't be more clear-cut. With an IP network connection, a VPN can be set up in a matter of minutes, and the cost of an additional connection like a new partner can be minimal.

When you add a new connection to a VPN, you're not actually laying new cable. Instead, a VPN wide-area networking device like a router or a gateway encrypts traffic before it gets sent out over the Internet and decrypts traffic coming in. Because each VPN has its own encryption key, it can route data in any direction without having it intercepted along the way. In effect, a VPN creates a private lane on the information highway, extending a secured network to remote users and systems. Though the network performance isn't usually any better than using unsecured communications over the Internet, the VPN does guarantee private communications across the public Net, no matter what kind of communications they are.

While an increasing number of e-business-hungry enterprises are moving toward SSL-secured Web-based commerce, VPNs offer a different kind of security. The technology is inappropriate in situations where millions of customers come and go, day in and day out — such as an on-line bookseller. Because the VPN has to be installed at both ends of a network connection, the sheer number of connections, and the fact that a bookseller probably doesn't have on-going business relationships with the vast majority of its customers, it would be exorbitantly costly and impractical. Besides, when faced with the prospect of installing a piece of hardware at their premises in order to buy a few books, most consumers would just shop elsewhere. However, the technology does become practical when you have on-going relationships with fewer than, say, 10,000 customers.

What the VPN allows you to do, unlike SSL, is secure both ends of the network transaction, and that, in large part, is the VPN's big sell. Technologies like EDI, direct-to-database interfaces, and advanced supply chain integration — in effect, any application that might expose the enterprise core and open business processes to the Internet — often require a greater level of trust than you can get from the Web. Networking equipment vendor Cisco Systems Corp. uses a VPN (running on its own hardware, of course) to connect its resellers to its contract manufacturers, like Celestica. When a reseller orders a Cisco router, the order goes through Cisco's Oracle database system, which is in constant communication with the manufacturer, automatically updating orders and managing the supply chain. The actual hardware will often be shipped directly to the reseller from the manufacturer, using customer information from Cisco's databases but without ever going through Cisco's offices. That kind of integration requires very tight security. Should it be compromised at any step along the way, Cisco could have a major disaster on its hands. However, with a VPN, the whole process moves from secured gateway to secured gateway.

In fact, it's pointless to compare VPNs to the Web. While the latter is essentially an application interface, VPNs are an infrastructure technology that can support a wide range of applications from remote access and voice-over-IP to corporate intranets and extranets based on the Web itself. The big advantage is that you can leverage a VPN for multiple applications.

That's a compelling advantage, and VPNs have all but supplanted private networks and the value-added networks once rented out by companies like IBM for mission-critical, secure network operations.

While the private network and VAN market has been steadily contracting since the business world discovered it could do its commerce on the Internet, the VPN hardware market grew to $445 million in 1999, and is likely to reach $3.2 billion in 2003, growing 46 percent this year alone, said Laurie Gooding, senior wide-area networking analyst for Cahners In-Stat Group.

While the traditional corporate users of private networks and VANs have been migrating to VPNs in droves, smaller-scale users are adopting the technology from the other end. Small and medium-sized enterprises can benefit just as well from the efficiencies of electronic commerce, and many are participating in supply chain partnerships that require secured networks. However, traditional VPNs can be expensive, even when a carrier or an access provider offers it as a service. According to Gooding, a one-year commitment with one of the leading U.S. service providers for VPN-based remote access costs between $380,000 and $880,000. Whether that's an acceptable price tag depends on a lot of factors, including the size of your company and how important VPN technology is to your business processes. Of course, it's much easier to justify the cost if you can take advantage of a wide range of networked applications, like remote access, video-conferencing, and IP telephony. Because it's an infrastructure technology, VPN doesn't care what kind of traffic it carries.

It's also easier to justify the cost of a VPN if you do it yourself, but the hardware can be expensive. A bare-bones VPN router typically costs between $1,500 and $2,000. Multiply that by the number of premises, branch offices, and partners that you need to connect in a secure network, and you have a hefty bill. Software VPNs are a partial solution. After all, a router is just a single-purpose computer that directs network traffic and, in one sense, the VPN is just the encryption software that runs on top of it. Smaller enterprises that can't afford a router or a VPN gateway, or who aren't prepared to shell out hundreds of thousands of dollars for VPN services, can install a program on a run-of-the-mill PC that emulates the functions of a hardware VPN router in software. Ideally, it would be the same system that hosts the network firewall software residing at the edge of your internal network. Indeed, VPN functions are often included in the premium firewall software packages. Most of the VPN software on the market conforms to the IPSec secure networking standard, which means it can operate with any other standards-based VPN software or hardware. It won't have all the bells and whistles of a full-fledged, dedicated VPN router, but it does permit small and medium-sized enterprises to participate in a VPN-based supply chain.

Unfortunately, software VPNs have two main drawbacks. The first problem is that they are slower than dedicated networking devices. Every time data passes through a VPN it must be either encrypted (if it's on the way out) or decrypted (if it's on the way in). That takes time, and hardware devices like routers and gateways almost typically offload the encryption duties to special circuitry used for just that purpose. That keeps the whole networking process humming along without interruption. However everything slows down when, as in the case of a software VPN, the same processor that routes traffic and manages the firewall rules also handles the encryption and decryption duties. And, in a networked economy, degraded network performance can cost bucks. It depends on what you can, or what you're willing to, give up in performance. If it's not a mission-critical transaction, it can afford to move relatively slowly. But that leads to the question — if it's not a mission-critical transaction, what's the point of going to all the trouble of securing the network?

The second problem is that someone has to configure your VPN. If you buy a VPN from a value-added reseller or a system integrator — the usual channels for such a purchase — you're usually also paying for someone who knows security to come to your office and set it up. If you buy VPN services from a telecommunications carrier or an Internet service provider, you can call on their expertise to make sure everything works. But when you pick up a shrink-wrapped box of VPN software at your favorite computer store, you're pretty much on your own, and that can be a problem for smaller enterprises. According to the research of Cahners

In-Stat Group, inadequate security is the biggest concern when it comes to companies deploying their own VPNs, whether they are hardware or software. And when the tool is software, those concerns increase. "At the end of the day, if I'm a small enterprise, I probably don't want to have to devote the resources needed to make a do-it-yourself solution work," Gooding said. "I don't want to have to support the thing myself."

Software VPN vendors like to say that their products are just another security option in a spectrum that ranges from top-end carrier-class solutions to quickly deployed, easily managed software, and in a sense they're right. To a large extent, it depends on your security requirements. You might not want to rely on a software VPN if you're handling hundreds of simultaneous connections, but the server that manages a small enterprise's firewall is probably adequate to handle encryption for occasional use. Moreover, it might be difficult to justify even a $2,000 expense when your secured network needs are intermittent at best. A software solution permits the inversion of the typical hardware VPN usage. Instead of tunneling multiple applications and processes, the software lets the user employ the VPN — with its resulting performance degradation — only for those applications that must be carried over a secured connection.

Who's That Knocking at My Door?

For all of the impressive encryption and security tools available to the e-business person, knowing who you're doing e-business with and knowing who has access to what are still the most critical parts of doing e-business at all. In a traditional business, you see your employees. They sign off on memos, and if they want access to certain information, they have to walk up to a filing cabinet or the company safe, both of which are protected by stout locks and stern-faced office managers and security guards. In a store, you see your customer and you get a signature on the transaction. When you deal with suppliers and partners, you hear their voices on the telephone and you see their signatures on memos and purchase orders. However, on the Internet, you're dealing totally out of sight.

The same automated efficiencies that make electronic commerce so attractive can be its biggest security holes. Because e-business processes occur largely out of sight, with everyone at their own keyboards, in their own cubicles, or in their own offices dozens, hundreds, even thousands of miles away, it can be difficult to keep track of who is doing what, when. Yet, unless you know just that, all the security you may have acquired in the form of firewalls, gateways, and VPNs may be a fool's illusion.

Most of the time, the real security threat doesn't come from the anarchic wilds of the public Internet at all. According to the 2000 CSI/FBI survey, most network security problems — more than 75 percent — originate within the enterprise; in 1999, they amounted to over $200 million in losses. Writing in *Network Computing,* Greg Shipley attributed that appalling statistic to "hardened perimeters with mushy innards. It's usually much easier to infiltrate a company from the inside because most organizations place a huge emphasis on defending the perimeter but do little to detect, much less protect against, hostile internal activity."[3]

It's not hackers like Mafiaboy or Kevin Mitnick or the Legion of Doom that you have to worry about, but the guy in marketing who has been having a bad week, or the disgruntled supply chain partner who thinks he's been getting a bad deal, but who happens to have the keys to your virtual back door. The hacker is wildly over-glorified in the media. He may know how to get into a company's network, but he probably doesn't know how that company works and where it keeps its really valuable data. But someone who knows where to look can cause a lot of damage if he has free access to the most sensitive parts of your network.

Cynical as it may sound, business is based on trust, but there are limits to how far that trust should go, and the best way to set those limits is with a technology called **public key infrastructure** or PKI. As the name suggests, it's based on the same encryption technology that secures much of the sensitive data that flies through the digital ether, but PKI takes asymmetrical key encryption a step farther. The idea is brilliant in its simplicity: Why not use everyone's cryptographic key pair as identity tokens in a security infrastructure? Such an infrastructure could benefit from the same rigorous security that public key cryptography provides for encrypted communication. Instead of access passwords, users are identified by a certificate signed with their private key and verified against their public keys by a certificate authority server. The certificates can contain additional information like a digital signature — a cryptographic hash created by the user's private key — and information on which applications he or she can use and which parts of the network he or she is entitled to access.

It's just that kind of control that makes PKI so compelling. The three main points to PKI are identification, authentication, and authorization — the key concerns of network security. However, the authorization mechanism can be applied across a wide range of applications and even across enterprises. At sales of $500 million in 1999, the growth of PKI was held back somewhat by concerns over the dreaded millennium bug. IT departments were hesitant to commit to wide-scale security technology deployments until they were sure their systems would survive Y2K, and the expense of compliance-testing and conversion drained IT budgets of a great deal of capital. However, analysts are confident that PKI is about to take off as e-business security's killer app.

Indeed, both Netscape Communicator and Microsoft Internet Explorer have built-in certificate support, and there has been a big, though ultimately ineffective, push from the consumer credit industry to standardize a kind of PKI for credit card–based consumer transactions on the Internet. In addition to providing strong encryption protection for credit card transactions, the **secure electronic transactions (SET)** standard, published in 1997, provides for a system of certificates that authenticates both the client and the server before the credit card company will authorize the transaction.

Although SET provides a far greater level of security than SSL, it never really caught on with consumers or consumer-oriented Internet merchants. SET is caught in a kind of catch-22. Merchants have been hesitant to adopt the standard until consumers jump on the SET bandwagon, and consumers have shown little interest in acquiring either the software or the digital certificates — in some cases, they even need to get a new credit card — when the existing SSL-based transactions seem to be safe enough. Visa and MasterCard, the main sponsors of the SET initiative, only reinforced that impression through marketing efforts designed to encourage consumers to use their credit cards on-line, SET or no SET. And the major browser vendors have shown little interest in integrating SET wallets (or client software) in their products until there is a demand for it from consumers … And that doesn't seem likely to happen any time soon.

Though SET remains moribund in consumer commerce applications, it has experienced a revival in business-to-business commerce, where the demand for user authentication and the potential for loss is significantly greater. SET implementations have experienced modest growth since 1997, although the protocol remains far less ubiquitous than its sponsors had originally hoped. Some vendors, notably Hewlett-Packard and its subsidiary Verifone, have endeavored to include SET features in their product offerings, despite the browser vendors' continued indifference.

Nevertheless, SET was originally conceived as a consumer-based technology for electronic commerce across the whole expanse of the public Internet. The needs of business-to-business commerce — establishing trust in a finite environment both between and within enterprises — don't quite match SET's specification. The real need is for PKI solutions that are both on a smaller scale and more flexible than SET's globe-spanning vision. However, PKI vendors have had to overcome two major hurdles to make the technology a compelling sell.

For one thing, until recently, there was little agreement on standards that would allow different companies' PKIs to interoperate. All PKIs, including SET, implement the ITU's X.509 digital certificate specification, so they can, in theory, read each other's certificate information, and the Lightweight Directory Access Protocol, or LDAP, allows enterprises to share digital certificates between certificate authorities. The problem has been to settle on common standards for how those certificates are managed so that PKIs from different vendors use the same method for requesting and delivering certificates and for granting access privileges. This isn't a trivial matter; in fact, it goes to the heart of what electronic commerce is all about. Without standards, there would be no way to integrate your company and its partners in one seamless and transparent security infrastructure unless everyone used the same vendor's PKI.

And standards have been long coming. The Internet Engineering Task Force's Public-Key Infrastructure working group has been preparing the PKIX protocol, which is needed to support interoperability between PKIs, since 1995. In 1999, the protocol was upgraded from a proposed, to a draft standard, and the working group began developing additional standards for PKI interoperability. The security industry has shown a great deal of interest in standards development and, early in 2000, some of the lead players in PKI development, including Ottawa's Entrust Technologies, RSA Security, and IBM, announced the creation of the PKI Forum. Though the forum's chief aim is to promote the technology's adoption in e-business, its members made a commitment to interoperability by establishing a mechanism for standards and interoperability testing.

The other main obstacle to the widespread adoption of PKI has also begun to disappear. Just having a PKI isn't quite enough, but until recently, although PKI could secure a network, there was no easy way to integrate the technology with e-business and electronic commerce applications. In effect, you could control who went where on your network, you just couldn't control what they did because few applications were PKI-aware. The challenge was to have transaction, accounting, and ERP applications that can actually take advantage of the trustworthy business environments that PKIs promise to create. "The truth is that PKI has no value if nothing uses it," Jones said. "More and more products use it at the server side, and it's easy to add functionality to browsers with plug-ins."

Indeed, security in general is moving rapidly from the network layer to the application layer, and the question of when we will have truly PKI-enabled applications is quickly being answered. Most of the leading electronic commerce application vendors, including Oracle Corp., IBM, SAP, and PeopleSoft, have begun to integrate PKI hooks into their products. The process has been somewhat simplified by the way the major PKI vendors are aggressively promoting PKI developers' toolkits that let software vendors create those hooks in their products and allow network managers to retrofit their existing back-end systems. With the emergence of generic PKI toolkits that can integrate any standards-based PKI with almost any application, PKI appears set to take off. Of course, the security industry has been naming every year since 1995 the Year of PKI, so it remains to be seen if the big surge will happen this year, next year, or the year after.

As with many technologies, the big final barrier to the widespread adoption of PKI isn't technological, but financial. A full PKI deployment can be very costly, ranging from hundreds of thousands to millions of dollars, depending on the size of your company and the breadth of your needs. That price tag seems likely to keep the technology out of the hands of smaller e-businesses for some time. What it all boils down to, of course, is the old cost-benefit analysis — unless your company is very large, does a very high-volume, high-value business, or has extremely sensitive secrets, it may not be worth the expense, at least for now. This is particularly true when you consider that the most important part of electronic commerce security has little to do with technology at all, and everything to do with policy and procedure. And unless that part of the equation adds up, even the best new technology is nothing more than locking the barn door after the horse has fled.

THE HUMAN FACTOR

If the rash of on-line credit card thefts at the beginning of 2000 are any indication, sometimes it's a whole herd of horses, not to mention cattle, sheep, goats, and chickens that flee. Within a few months, CD Universe, SalesGate.com, and RealNames were all penetrated by hackers seeking customer credit card numbers. In each case, the thieves profited from human errors and lax policies to work their way around the technological security barriers. In June 2000, employees at America Online, the world's largest Internet service provider, infected several hundred subscriber e-mail accounts with a virus when they opened suspicious e-mail attachments. What makes the AOL incident so pathetic is the fact that an epidemic of e-mail viruses that year had brought the dangers of suspect attachments to newspaper front pages everywhere. AOL had even warned its subscribers to be careful. Evidently, the provider's careless employees didn't read newspapers and had never seen the warnings.

The most dramatic example of security sloppiness, however, occurred in Canada. Early in 2000, a Canadian software engineer named Terry Hamilton announced to any journalist who would listen — and they were all listening — that he had access to the personal and account information for between 30,000 and 50,000 applicants to Air Miles, a Canadian loyalty reward program. Though the information did not contain details on purchases, it did include phone numbers, addresses, and personal credit history information. It was the kind of mother lode that hackers dream of striking, but Hamilton wasn't some highly skilled computer miscreant who used his wiles to break through Air Miles' tough network security and attack its accounting system. No, all the data was open for anyone's perusal on an insecure directory on the company's public Web site, outside its network firewall. Air Miles hadn't secured the information at all.

It was the kind of careless security snafu that can cost a company its credibility and a whole lot more. According to Datamonitor, a London-based technology research firm, security breaches cost companies around the world $15 billion every year. Few companies are likely to publicize their security problems because they are rarely the result of malicious or larcenous intent, but rather simple old-fashioned carelessness and sloppiness. The problem is that many businesses put too much reliance on the technology, and while that can be dangerous, it means big business to the people normally hired to clean up the mess. "It's like buying a steel, triple-reinforced door but neglecting to lock it, and it's a pattern I've seen over the years," said network security specialist Eric Packman. "A company buys a firewall and feels secure. But it's only a tool, and if you don't know how to use it — or you haven't worked it into your business processes — you'll be getting a false sense of security."

Though most companies will tolerate a certain level of risk, and even though security can never be completely perfect in the real world, no one should accept the kind of complacency and sloppiness exemplified by the Air Miles debacle. The fundamental point for anyone doing electronic commerce is that you must know how secure you are, and how your security works. Even more important than firewalls and PKIs is a clear, effective security policy. Not only does that make good security sense, it makes good sense with regard to ROI and the bottom line. "At the end of the day, a lot of people buy a lot of security that they don't use," said Forrester's Rutstein. "There's little point in investing in technology if you don't have policies and procedures to use it."

That much seems like preaching to the choir. It's just common sense that any company that wants to protect its digital assets would take the time to create an explicit security policy. But, as Albert Einstein once observed, the problem with common knowledge is that it's not very common. Only a third of the respondents to the Deloitte & Touche study had a thorough, formal security policy. While another third had, at least, an incomplete policy, the rest had no policy at all. It may be, as Rutstein observed, that rather than putting the effort into a security plan, many are simply hoping their insurance will cover their potential losses. There's a certain logic to that. If your security has never been seriously compromised, and security technologies cost more than the data you would protect is worth, then it can be hard to justify the expense and the bother. But good luck collecting on the insurance.

"The first thing we look at is the surety policy," said Jennifer Soper, a principal at insurance giant St. Paul International. "There's the whole idea of the 'moral hazard' here. Any client that looks at insurance as its principal protection, without being proactive, and without establishing a coherent security policy, wouldn't be viewed very favorably." Anyone doing business on the Internet has to know what their security procedures are, where their weaknesses may be, what can go wrong, and what can be done when they do go wrong. You can't know any of that unless you examine your security with a fine-toothed comb.

The Great Houdini is reputed to have said that you can never know whether a jail cell is escape-proof until you try to escape from it. By the same token, you can never know how secure your network is from intrusion until you try to break in. Regular audits of security procedures and intrusion testing are the bedrock on which any serious security policy must be based. Not that that's news. As long ago as 1995 (the dark ages in the history of electronic commerce), no less a personage than SATAN drove home the benefits of intrusion testing. The Security Analysis Tool for Auditing Networks (SATAN) was developed by Dan Farmer, formerly of Silicon Graphics of Mountain View, California, and Wietse Venema of the University of Eindhoven in the Netherlands. The idea behind the program was to provide administrators of systems on the Internet with a powerful and easy-to-use tool for probing their computers' security.

In order to underline the need for better on-line security, Farmer and Venema released SATAN to the general public, creating an unprecedented panic among system administrators and the embryonic electronic commerce community. It didn't help matters that star hacker Kevin Mitnick had been arrested just weeks before, priming the media, the business world, and the general public for a big Net security scare. The great fear was that the program would fall into the hands of malicious hackers as well as the computer-security experts for whom it was intended. That was the point all along. As the U.S. government's Computer Incident Advisory Capability (CIAC) announced at the time: "SATAN is being promoted as a security tool for system administrators, not an attack tool for crackers. Unfortunately, it can be utilized in either manner. It is up to system administrators to decide what its impact will be. The safety of any particular system is dependent on who utilizes SATAN first."

Apparently the good guys used it first and there were no reported unauthorized intrusions using SATAN. There were, however, many unconfirmed reports — it's not the kind of thing that companies like to confirm — that legitimate SATAN users all over North America had discovered all sorts of security holes, which they proceeded to plug. Despite the panic, or perhaps because of it, SATAN emphasized the first unbreakable rule of security management: Test your systems. "In the short run, SATAN will inevitably cause some problems," said CIAC security analyst John Fisher at the time. "But in the long run, it will certainly help to create an awareness of computer security, and that's something that's really needed." SATAN was particularly effective thanks to its ominous name and because the Internet had not yet become something that both businesses and the general public take for granted, like the phone system.

With that in mind, it's not even enough to take your partners' security precautions for granted. Due to the very nature of electronic commerce, everyone in a supply chain is interconnected, and the security of that chain is only as good as its weakest link. Though the Deloitte & Touche study found that most companies either do or plan to test their own security, they don't plan to test their partners' security. That, said Ross, is simply foolhardy. "When it comes to business-to-business trading partners, the attitude is often 'it's not my problem,'" he said. "It's a sense that the hole's not in my end of the boat. The problem, of course, is that, when you're connected like you are in e-business, it doesn't really matter where the hole is — you're going to sink."

To some extent, that reflects attitudes deeply ingrained in the business culture. After all, we're all told from an early age that we should mind our own business, and when someone comes snooping around your most sensitive secrets — and how a company's network security works certainly fits that description — the normal reaction is to clam up. And that reaction is almost guaranteed to subvert the benefits of the electronic commerce value chain. The whole point of electronic commerce and e-business is to seamlessly extend the enterprise through partnerships and network-enabled collaboration. As Bernard Burnes and Barrie Dale of the Manchester School of Management observed in their book *Working in Partnership,* "The partnership process is ongoing, aimed at building up an effective business relationship based on openness — a relationship which demands greater and quicker exchange of information between both parties."[4] There can be nothing of more importance for an open exchange of information than the security of the electronic commerce process upon which you and all your partners depend.

Key Terms

bit-length
symmetrical key encryption
asymmetrical key encryption
public key
private key
secure sockets layer (SSL)
firewall
virtual private network (VPN)
public key infrastructure (PKI)
secure electronic transactions (SET)

E-Business Law
and Policy

If you're going to play the electronic commerce game, you have to know the rules. The governments and courts in most of the industrialized world have taken a special interest in business on the Internet. Washington has identified electronic commerce and the national information infrastructure as a major national priority. However, electronic commerce is, almost by definition, global business, and with much of the rest of the world pulling ahead of the United States with policies and legislation tailored to the new economy, most of the rules of the game are still up in the air.

The New Frontier

In September 1993, before most Americans had even heard of the Internet, let alone electronic commerce, Washington placed the burgeoning new medium at the top of the national public policy agenda. In presenting Washington's Information Infrastructure Task Force report, Vice President Al Gore symbolically opened the information highway to business and set the foundation for all of the Clinton administration's subsequent

Internet-related policy initiatives. Gore's vision was of an information infrastructure open to everyone, where business — particularly American business — would thrive and build the new information economy. Washington, he said, would lead the development of policies that would make the vision possible. "We are in the midst of a global transformation," Gore wrote a few months later, "one as profound as those caused by the invention of the printing press and the steam engine."[1]

It was all heady stuff at a time when the Internet appeared as a vast, open frontier of possibilities. The "Information Highway" was on everyone's lips, and anything related to the Internet became above-the-fold front-page news. The information revolution was off to a fine start ... but more than a few observers were skeptical. "Yet most newsworthy is the report's silence on the policy battles that are most intensely debated within the industry and which affect billions of dollars in investment," wrote Edmund L. Andrews in *The New York Times*. "In many ways, the report provides evidence that the Administration is still groping for its role, while industry and technology race ahead of Washington."[2]

That, in a nutshell, has defined the challenge facing government and lawmakers in the United States and around the world ever since. How do they promote the growth of the Internet and electronic commerce, cultivate a business environment where innovators and entrepreneurs may build the new economy, while at the same time ensuring that they observe the authority of the law and the conventions of fair play? How can government assert its legitimate interests without stifling competition and innovation?

If the state of e-business law and policy is any indication, the answer remains elusive. Though Washington got right to work putting its own e-commerce house in order with a framework for automated government procurement and the Paperwork Reduction Act, issues such as its role in electronic commerce generally, how existing laws will apply to e-business, and the question of whether the medium requires new legislation have all remained far from clear. Much of the time, lawmakers have appeared to be playing catch-up with the players in electronic commerce and the ever-evolving technologies that make it possible. When Clinton administration advisor Ira Magaziner presented the government's Framework for Global Electronic Commerce, which opposed new taxes and new regulations on Internet-based business, he seemed to simply be acknowledging that the way e-business was *already* being conducted was the way it would continue to be done.

However, Washington isn't the only government wrestling with how to assert its laws in a business environment evolving at light speed; neither is it the most confused. The European Union succeeded in creating an electronic commerce jurisdiction nightmare by implementing contradictory legislation; lawmakers in Canada — the United States' largest trading partner — spent most of 1999 wrangling over electronic commerce legislation that was never more than a compromise solution. Moreover, because electronic commerce is, almost by definition, a global activity, the still-unsettled relationship *between* national laws continues to have serious ramifications for e-business.

Washington got it right, however, when it observed in the Framework for Global Electronic Commerce that one of the most important policy challenges for government and business in the 21st century will be the establishment of agreements on common legal standards for electronic commerce. The new economy is global, and no country can hope to participate in it without recognizing the need for common standards in the world market. The problem is that the rules of the game are still largely up in the air.

YOUR LAW OR MINE?

You may have the hottest and sharpest legal department in the country, but when it comes to doing e-business, they might not be enough. The odds are pretty good that you'll be doing business — maybe a lot of business — with people and companies outside of the United States. The very nature of the Internet and electronic commerce almost guarantees it. So here's the nut of the problem: Whose laws are going to govern business-to-business electronic commerce? While it's true companies that use the Internet to connect to their partners and suppliers usually have legal departments to draw up papers to ensure their interests are protected, even those legal departments are subject to the law and to government regulation. But which government, and whose laws? That was easy enough in traditional commerce. A transaction was subject to the laws of the jurisdiction where it occurred, and that is usually defined as the place of origin of the product or service being purchased — not a problem when the buyer is based in the area. Unfortunately, the Internet adds a considerable wrinkle.

Most companies that sell over the Internet would prefer to deal with customers under their own laws, according to the rule of origin, of course. The prospect of having to observe the legal minutiae of every jurisdiction from which their partners can buy their products and services is unappealing to business, to say the least, daunting to say the most. On the other hand, if you are buying over the Internet, the rule of origin can be a problem. If your procurement process reaches from your head office in Seattle to a vendor in Schenectady, then New York State law applies. That's not normally a problem, but if you're importing widgets from a partner in Albania, you're subject to Albanian law, and if you get stiffed, you'll need a plane ticket to Tirana to sort it out.

The American Bar Association Global Cyberspace Jurisdiction Project, an international task force of more than 100 lawyers, has tried to clear it all up. In July 2000, the group released a report called *Achieving Legal and Business Order in Cyberspace.* The 200-page draft recognized the difficulties created by commercial activity on the Internet and acknowledged that governments are unable to change the laws fast enough to meet the technology.

One of its proposals was to empanel a group called the Global Online Standards Commission (GOSA) to study jurisdictional issues and develop uniform principles and global protocol standards.[3] The report's recommendations went further, including proposals that governments develop voluntary industrial councils and "cybertribunals" to resolve e-commerce disputes, that buyers and sellers should identify the jurisdiction or state where they reside, that intelligent electronic agents be employed to communicate rules and information pertaining to jurisdiction, and that the international community continue to develop safe harbor agreements.

Nevertheless, these are recommendations, not laws. In the absence of any international harmonization of laws and standards, the question of jurisdiction remains unsettled. Indeed, Estella S. Gold, chair of the e-commerce and high technology practice group at Philadelphia-based White and Williams LLP, doesn't mince words. Jurisdictional laws are "a mess," she said. "There is no other way to describe it. Companies who never did business in foreign jurisdictions are now doing it, and it's very chaotic."

In the best of all possible legal worlds, both buyers and sellers would have equal protection and claim to jurisdiction. Suffice it to say, the legal world of electronic commerce is far from the best possible. Some solutions have been proposed, including harmonization of international law and fair business practices. Unfortunately, that's all much easier said than done. International legal harmonization can involve the laws of not only several countries, but of several levels of government. In order to work out the issue of jurisdiction, jurists have to ask which jurisdiction. Legal confusion is suicide for commerce, as the European community found.

The European Directive on Electronic Commerce, which is supposed to encourage European companies to get on-line, bases jurisdiction on country of origin. The directive was approved by the European Parliament in May of 2000. Under the directive, which applies to both business-to-business and business-to-consumer commerce, a vendor legally entitled to sell on the Web in one European Union country is allowed to sell in all of them. In most cases, the law of the country of origin prevails. However, until the directive was passed, no one was entirely sure if it would be the law of the Net or of the pending Brussels Convention, which has it the other way around — observing the law of the country of destination. "If you want to kill electronic commerce in Europe, then that's the way to do it," said Michael Pullen, EU public affairs and regulatory counsel for DLA Upstream in Brussels, at the time. "What's worse is that the Brussels Convention completely contradicts the European Union's proposed electronic commerce directive. You have to wonder if they've thought it through."

The Brussels Regulation was signed into law on November 30, 2000, updating the 1968 Brussels Convention. When it goes into effect in March 2001, it will mean that European e-commerce companies will have to comply with the local laws of any EU country where they do business; it will also mean that European consumers who buy goods and services from a non-EU business over the Internet may sue the vendor in their own national courts of the consumer. Some EU business leaders fear that forcing companies to comply with 15 sets of local laws will drive them away from e-commerce and limit the influx of venture capital. Wim Mijs, vice president of EU affairs at the Dutch bank ABN Amro, expressed his concern for the smaller businesses. "The consequences of what the European parliament agreed would hurt small and medium-sized businesses looking to take advantage of the Internet," said Mijs. "[It] could actually hinder e-commerce in Europe."[4] The E-Commerce Directive is due to be transposed into the laws of the 15 member states by June 2001.

Achieving harmonization on a global scale will be a good deal more difficult than passing contradictory laws. Harmonization can be a loaded term. It often merely means lowest common denominator, and that doesn't usually sit well with countries with more rigorous standards. However, establishing minimum standards means forcing someone else to play by foreign, often more rigorous rules. It can take years to iron out which way harmonization should go.

That doesn't mean the courts haven't tried. American courts have been willing in the past to assert jurisdiction even when their link to the case is tenuous. *Bochan v. La Fontaine,* a libel case heard in a Virginia court, may well be a clue to the future. The details — a tiff between JFK conspiracy buffs — aren't very important. Neither is the fact that the court decided in favor of the defendant. What is significant is that the court decided that it had jurisdiction in the case despite the fact that at least one of the parties to the case has absolutely no ties to the state of Virginia. Except for one thing: His Internet service is America Online, which happens to be headquartered in Reston, Virginia.

It's not entirely unusual for a court to exert extraterritorial jurisdiction, but it is rare. It usually happens when all parties have some sort of connection to the court's jurisdiction, even if the offence occurred somewhere else. "Unlike most jurisdictional cases, which involve an analysis of the underlying activity to determine whether it is active or passive, this case suggests that the location of the ISP can be a determining factor in finding jurisdiction," said Michael Geist, an Internet law expert at the University of Ottawa in Canada. "This becomes particularly significant given AOL's market share."

The same logic could equally apply to the users of any other Internet service — say UUNet, based in the Washington, D.C. suburbs south of the Potomac — or even users of a Web hosting service. It's an argument that could appeal to a lot of lawyers and a lot of governments. Sites could be subject to the peculiar laws of wherever the server happens to be located, and with the rapid internationalization of hosting services — any given Web site can be anywhere from El Salvador to Croatia — that could be a problem.

It's also the $64,000 question for American courts, like whether a Web site constitutes enough of the presence required for personal jurisdiction and possible liability under a state's laws. In a 1997 Pennsylvania case, *Zippo Manufacturing Co. v. Zippo Dot Com, Inc.,* the manufacturer of Zippo lighters, Zippo Manufacturing Co., sued an Internet news service, which had registered the domain names "zippo.com," "zippo.net," and "zippo-news.com." Following that case, most courts have judged the interactivity of Web sites on a "sliding scale"; at one end are passive Web sites that are merely used to post information, and not business. At the other end are active Web sites used for conducting business. Most state courts won't assert jurisdiction over passive sites, but "interactive" sites that fall somewhere between the two categories and may not be used for active commerce are still problematic. In those cases, courts will examine the level of interactivity and the nature of the information exchanged.[5] One of the recommendations of the ABA draft report was that passivity of a Web site not be the sole criterion for determining personal or prescriptive jurisdiction.

Until the world's courts and lawmakers sort the mess out, any company doing business on the Internet is best advised to familiarize itself with any applicable laws in countries where they may be doing business. "Don't take risks beyond what you can afford," said Gold. "Don't do business in unfriendly jurisdictions if you're worried about being sued there, and by all means insure yourself. For intellectual property clients, I recommend insurance." Gold also suggested that companies should include jurisdictional clauses on their Web sites, with a highly visible tab where users can click and find all pertinent legal disclaimers and jurisdictional clauses. "It's also good to have an opt-out button; if they don't press 'I accept' then you turn off the Web site. While self-help in making a contract on jurisdiction is not foolproof (since the contract could be preempted by statute in some jurisdictions), the on-line agreement is some measure of protection in the constantly evolving environment of changing case law."

Focus on Law and Policy

Sunny Handa: Making the law make sense

If you're looking for a grand vision of the future for electronic commerce and the law, you just won't find it, in the opinion of Sunny Handa, an Internet law specialist with Faksen Martineau Dumoulin LLP in Montreal and co-author of the book *Cyberlaw*. "There is no grand vision that anyone has put his or her finger on yet. The governments are playing catch-up with business, but spin it so that it looks like they're charting the course of e-commerce and all the e-commerce strategies. But all they're doing is taking the laissez-faire approach."

Change in electronic commerce is driven by business and technology; law and policy are always one step behind. That's just the way things are, said Handa, and that's the way it should be. "Law has always played catch-up and probably should — you don't want law coming out that isn't going in the right direction," he commented. "A lot of what's being done in Canada [in law and policy] is really there to patch up what needs to be patched up so that business moves forward."

In effect, business and technology progress until they run into a legal obstacle, and government and policymakers fashion a solution that allows business to continue moving forward. U.S. e-commerce policy has so far left it up to the business community to motivate the solutions.

While lawmakers have been more proactive in protecting the interests of consumers than in setting the ground rules for business-to-business commerce, Handa believes that's just good sense. Consumers need the direct intervention of government to keep them safe and secure in electronic commerce; companies are big enough to look after themselves.

That doesn't mean business-to-business commerce exists in a legal gray area — far from it, Handa said. However, the legal and legislative landscape is still a work in progress, and e-businesses have to be savvy enough to navigate it on their own. Companies are wrestling with the issue of how to fashion on-line contracts and how to enforce them, especially when doing business with other countries. In business-to-business electronic commerce, both parties are considered to be sophisticated and can fashion a solution by contract, suggested Handa, but on-line contracts are still a problem. In order to avoid potential problems with on-line contracts, Handa advises that both companies simply be as reasonable on-line as they would be when negotiating a contract off-line. "If there is some outrageous clause buried in the contract and someone pushed the 'I agree' button, the courts will say, 'Look, you should have read it but it was so outrageous we'll give you the benefit of the doubt.' It's hard to tell if you read an on-line contract, but the courts will be rigorous."

One solution is to meet at the outset with your company and decide on an on-line contract. And also have a written version drawn up. "If you're doing a lot of business at a high volume I suggest that over and above the on-line contract ... you have a written contract," Handa said.

Electronic commerce also necessarily implies global commerce, which means dealing with companies in other jurisdictions. Although jurisdiction is not a problem with a contractual situation, doing business with other countries means specifying the choice of laws by which you conduct business. "With B2B you will set up your choice of law in your contract, which governs all transactions," Handa said. "With a Web site the company who owns the Web site will set up the contract. They will say where jurisdiction will be heard and where to seek recourse if necessary."

The problem with on-line contracts is that you can't just sign one with a pen and ink. However, the law is gradually catching up to the reality of electronic contracts to the point of recognizing the validity of electronic signatures. "It has been determined in most of the cases heard that electronic contracts are enforceable," Handa said. "They have to be, if we're going to move forward and allow companies to fashion the allocation of risk with their counterpart ... It's an area where the law did need to react ... rather than having legislation coming out. It's a sensible thing that allows B2B to move forward."

However, law and policy continue to lag behind business — dangerously behind — on the question of digital signatures. With no public key infrastructure (PKI) in place, there are unresolved legal questions on the validity of electronic signatures. "PKI was the classic area where, at first, business realities and legal realities seemed to be out of sync with what business was demanding and technologies were demanding," pointed out Handa, adding that, even though many governments have studied the issue, they did not accurately foresee the need for PKI. "They guessed wrong — business and commerce didn't develop the way they projected, and PKI was not deployed in a society-wide context."

Sign on the Dotted Line

It's one thing to know which law applies to electronic commerce transactions, but it's another to know how it applies to electronic commerce contracts. While it is a simple matter to include a jurisdiction clause in a written, hard-copy contract, the real-time demands of much electronic commerce often make such paperwork either impossible or, at the very least, impractical. A statement specifying jurisdiction as a condition of a transaction on your Web site may stand up under some legal systems, but since there is no way to affix a traditional pen-and-ink signature to a Web site, it may be thrown out of other courts. And leaving a contract's jurisdiction up to the courts only opens the question to greater uncertainty.

Typically, courts will decide on whether they have jurisdiction based on the balancing interests of the two parties involved, or the offeror and offeree. Because cyberspace connects parties from different jurisdictions there will be varying expectations in the event of a breach of contract. Another challenge lies in making sure that companies have equal bargaining power in cross-jurisdictional contracts. A contract between two businesses in different jurisdictions should include a clause selecting the choice of law. If a smaller company is dealing with a larger company in a business-to-business transaction, such a clause will give them equal bargaining power.

However, there have been moves to regularize on-line contracts and define their legal framework. In order for that to happen, however, lawmakers have to settle on a practical system of electronic or digital signatures. After all, for on-line contracts to be binding, you have to be able to sign on the dotted line. In the broadest sense, a digital signature can be any mark indicating endorsement that can be infallibly traced back to the signer. That, unfortunately, is somewhat easier said than done, since the Internet makes it relatively easy to appropriate — or *spoof* — someone else's identity. There is nothing stopping someone from listing a public key linked to a bogus identity on a public registry. The only sure way to make a digital signature worth the bytes it's printed with is to link it to a trusted certificate authority.

The legislative framework is being built, and there are moves toward standardizing the e-commerce environment. In 1995, Utah became the first state to enact a law on the use of digital signatures, the Digital Signatures Act, which applied mainly to commercial transactions. Forty other states enacted similar legislation regulating digital or electronic signatures, but there remained a wide variety of approaches to the law, as well as to the definition of electronic signatures and specifications for encryption technologies and their applications. The legal and business communities began to reflect on the inconsistencies in electronic signature legislation and how they would affect businesses conducting electronic commerce.

"Uniform laws regulating the use and legal recognition of digital signatures are necessary because Internet transactions are often interstate," wrote Richard Raysman and Peter Brown in *The New York Law Journal* in 1999.[6] They're not only necessary for interstate transactions, but international deals as well. Other countries, including Malaysia, Canada, South Korea, and Singapore, had already enacted digital signature legislation. On January 19, 2000, the European Union's directive on electronic signatures went into force, and 15 member states had until July 19, 2001, to sign it; most were expected to sign by the end of 2001. If the United States wanted to conduct secure electronic commerce globally, they needed a legal and technological framework to bring it up to speed with legislation in other countries.

In the spring of 1999, Rep. Thomas Bliley introduced in the House the Electronic Signature in Global and National Commerce or E-sign Act, HR 1714, which was signed into law in June 30, 2000, by President Clinton. The E-sign law would create a legal framework for interstate electronic commerce, by giving electronic signatures the same legal validity as handwritten signatures, and would eliminate much of the interstate disputes over electronic commerce. As it stands now, the E-sign law, which went into effect on October 1, 2000, updated federal statutes to include electronic transactions with the federal government and interstate transactions.

With E-sign, consumers will be able to use electronic versions of mortgages, financial agreements, and insurance policies and sign them digitally — and it will be considered as legally binding as paper documents. Customers have to consent to receiving on-line documents and can opt out of the electronic document if they want paper only. Some documents, however, are still required to be issued and retained on paper: wills, family law documents, eviction notices, and some legal documents such as court orders.

As the law went into effect, consumers as well as the law and business communities debated its effectiveness and impact on business and electronic commerce. Some consumer groups maintained that the law was too technologically vague. The term "digital signatures" never actually appears in the law but is defined as "an electronic sound, symbol, or process attached to or logically associated with a contract." It does not specify technologies companies must use to create and authenticate digital signatures; in essence, it is technologically neutral. This means that clicking on an "I accept" button or a hyperlink on a Web page could be considered to be an electronic signature. The vagueness and technological neutrality has consumer advocates concerned that once consumers press the "I accept" button, they may be charged fees for transactions even if they back out at the last minute.

Although electronic signatures will be recognized in a court of law, E-sign also doesn't address "identification authentication." You could possibly receive a document that is not authentic or authorized because there is no way to ascertain that the person sending you the document is the right person and not, say, the night watchman fooling around with the computers. "On one hand, the law promotes the universal acceptance of electronic signatures," wrote Benjamin Weinstock and David P. Leno, in the *National Law Journal.* "On the other hand, the authenticity of those signatures is open to investigation and [they] are ultimately susceptible to rejection based on the available technology and circumstances of the transactions."[7]

There are still uncertainties on how the new E-sign law will play out. White and Williams' Gold said the key would be important transactions such as banking, securities, and large contracts. "The law must ensure the vendor of services that the signature is authenticated and authorized," she said. "The customer has to be sure that the contract he or she signed is the authenticated contract. If you consent to buy 1,000 shares of IBM on-line you want to know it's 1,000 not 10,000, and that the price you pay is the price at the time of submission."

E-signatures are a two-sided deal — authorization and authentication — where both sides have to be certain. "We have the technology to accomplish both those tasks," Gold said, "to take a snapshot and to give a person proof of contract and proof that the contract was what they thought it was, and the person signing it was the person qualified to enter into the agreement."

Companies will also have to measure risk against profit. Loading down your system with security may make it slower or clumsier. For some industries such as securities, which rely on swift transactions, this may present a dilemma. Some companies are going to have to balance the risk against the need for speed. "Companies with a high degree of risk are hopefully going to be very careful in planning, designing, and implementing their security systems," Gold said. "Those who don't are going to be caught. I think for a while to come there will be hard-copy paper backup." For those who don't trust e-signatures and want to conduct their business on paper, the law requires that companies provide their customer the choice of opting out — choosing paper documents, for which vendors can request a fee. They must, however, inform the customer what that fee will be beforehand. This could be a complication for companies that are solely Net-based, such as dot-coms, who outsource most of their functions and may not have the staff to handle paper.

Weinstock and Leno expressed doubts on the eve of E-sign becoming law about the law's effectiveness. "The speed with which the states and the marketplace adopt uniform standards for authenticating electronic signatures will be more significant as this technology will be the keystone to the expansion of e-commerce … E-sign is not a strong enough initiative to accomplish effectively the desired expansion of e-commerce."[8]

Eventually, how the E-sign law is interpreted will be up to each state. Each can adopt its own version of the law, which could lead to 51 versions of the law. However, if any part of the state law conflicts with the federal law, federal law will override invalid portions of state law and strike it down. While not as consistent and technologically specific as the EU law on electronic signatures, the E-sign law will bring some measure of consistency nonetheless, Gold believes. "Businesses want to make money and do business with other states," she said. "Everyone will be anxious to comply and be consistent. The e-signature law is good for business. It allows you to operate efficiently, it's faster, it allows for a faster income stream, and it has a lot going for it."

The technologically neutral aspect of the E-sign Act does give businesses the flexibility to select the technology that gives them the greatest sense of security; it also means that the law won't have to be rewritten as technology advances. Off-the-shelf products like VeriSign are sufficient for most businesses, said Gold, but they might not be enough for high-security transactions. Moreover, electronic signature technologies are gradually becoming more uniform and interoperable. "If you want communication, by transmitting electronic signatures from one system to another, we'll see some uniformity because it's practical for business," Gold said, but pointed out that the E-sign law is only an enabler. "It doesn't tell you *how* to do it, but enables you do to it — it's up to the business and individual to see how they get the job done."

NET AND TAXES

The main difference between death and taxes is that you only die once. Taxes, on the other hand, hit you where you live almost all the time. You dutifully pay them every spring, usually waiting for the last moment in case a deductible receipt turns up that can get you out of the tax-debt doghouse. You pay them at that cozy lunch counter a block from the office; you pay them when you pick up a toner cartridge for your laser printer; you pay them when the network wiring guys send you their invoice; you pay them when you gas up on the way home. You pay them when you buy a half-ton of rubber O-rings to use in your product. And it doesn't matter if you're part of an electronic commerce supply chain; if money changes hands, and products are shipped, there's tax to pay. There was no way governments could ignore electronic commerce for long. Unfortunately, the status of electronic commerce taxation remains, if anything, even more unsettled than jurisdiction.

In November 1996, the Treasury Department's office of tax policy issued a policy statement called Selected Tax Policy Implications of Global Electronic Commerce. The department stated that new communications technologies should be allowed to develop on a global basis, and that "in order to ensure that these new technologies not be impeded, the development of substantive tax policy and administration in this area should be guided by the principle of neutrality. Neutrality rejects the imposition of new or additional taxes on electronic transactions, and instead simply requires that the tax system treat similar income equally …"[9]

In effect, the Treasury Department recommended that Washington steer clear of new Internet-specific taxes. Businesses conducting electronic commerce were off the hook, at least temporarily. In 1998, Congress passed the Internet Tax Freedom Act, which imposed a three-year moratorium on any new discriminatory taxes on Internet sales, effective until October 2001. The law also set up the Advisory Commission on Electronic Commerce to study Internet taxation and report back to Congress with its recommendations. In its April 2000 report, the committee recommended extending the moratorium and making the ban on Internet access tax permanent.

The Internet Tax Freedom Act bars states and localities from taxing Internet access or transactions and prohibits the imposition of "Internet-specific" taxes. Nevertheless, a grandfather clause in the Act allows states that *were* taxing Internet access when the ban was imposed to continue to do so. The moratorium covers a number of taxes, so a single transaction cannot be taxed simultaneously by multiple jurisdictions. It also bans any new discriminatory taxes, which means that states cannot tax e-commerce more onerously than they tax other forms of commerce. It can be taxed at the same rate, but not punished by a higher rate.

What does the moratorium really mean for electronic commerce? "Symbolically, the moratorium does have import," said Jeffery Friedman, partner at KPMG's e-tax solutions practice. "It sends the message that Congress is watching e-commerce and sees it as important, and that states ought to move in a way that is viewed as being fair to e-commerce. But in terms of its application, actual substance — it doesn't have much teeth. It doesn't prevent tax on e-commerce."

Electronic transactions are still subject to sales and use taxes by states and localities, and each determines which Internet sales they can tax or exempt. "There's this notion that the Internet Tax Freedom Act takes care of everything and there is this notion that the Internet is tax free," said Jeremy Sharrard, tax and policy analyst with Forrester Research. "Any change means a politician can be branded as trying to tax the Internet, and nobody wants that label." However, little has changed in the tax structure that would apply directly to electronic commerce or the Internet. Interstate commerce is governed by a 1992 Supreme Court decision, *Quill Corp v. North Dakota,* which ruled that businesses must have physical presence, or nexus, within a state in order to collect sales taxes from customers in that state.

Electronic commerce has complicated the picture, and businesses are now conducting electronic commerce under a tax regime that dates back 70 years or more. Taxpayers and governments are struggling to apply existing laws to electronic business, where transactions cross jurisdictional and commercial boundaries, where the buyer and seller are in different states, and where the goods sold can be digital rather than tangible. Businesses are now expanding their tax exposure by selling to jurisdictions where they may or may not know the tax laws and rates, including overseas tax jurisdictions. A single electronic transaction may take place in up to 15 different locations, from the buyer to the final delivery, according to a 1999 report by Ryan & Company, a Dallas-based tax-consulting firm. Any transaction can involve several different locations, all of which can have different sales tax laws and rates.

There is general agreement in taxation circles that, as with out-of-jurisdiction procurement and mail order, consumption taxes like value-added tax should be paid by the buyer to his or her government. If you had to pay taxes only in the seller's jurisdiction, there'd be an e-commerce boom in places where there is no consumption tax while electronic commerce outfits bailed out of more highly taxed jurisdictions. One of the big questions, of course, is who's responsible to see that the tax is paid, the buyer or the seller? It's beginning to look like the responsibility will fall to the seller. However, CommerceNet's public policy director, Kaye Caldwell, has pointed out that, under existing U.S. law, a state has the right to impose a collection obligation on out-of-state companies that sell to its citizens. That means that a Chicago-based vendor could be in a position where it would have to charge a customer in Mississippi that state's sales tax and then send the funds down to Jackson ... and that could be a problem. "There are about ten thousand jurisdictions in the United States alone that are empowered to collect taxes," Caldwell said. "The administrative burden would be a true nightmare." You have to wonder how many companies would stay in business, collecting and paying taxes in thousands of jurisdictions.

The borderless nature of e-commerce makes the navigation tricky — sales and use taxes depend on the location where the products are sold and used, and any business, large or small, has to understand the siting of electronic commerce activities. "Businesses today need to be tax sophisticated," KPMG's Friedman advised. "They have to be cognizant of where they have physical presence. Where are you present and how much physical presence is required to trigger that tax collection obligation? Businesses are struggling with that if they're doing B2B or B2C. The key is to be proactive and decrease your tax liabilities."

Things are complicated enough stateside, but electronic commerce crosses international borders as easily as state lines. In a global market, American businesses will be subject to the laws and policies of Japan, Canada — and Europe, where lawyers and trade experts are trying to weld together 15 distinct national traditions. Their efforts may be a clue to how the thorny issue of tax jurisdiction may eventually be worked out on a global scale. At the center of the controversy are the member nations' unique but similar value-added taxes.

Europe's VATs are very broad and can cover nearly everything, including digitized products that never physically cross European borders. EU finance ministers are still discussing how to deal with exactly that situation. As Jeffery Friedman pointed out, this can lead to problems with enforcement. "Suppose I'm in the Bahamas and sell software online to France and then decide I don't want to pay the VAT. How do they enforce it? In most cases, when the country doesn't like a seller, they can seize the goods — it's kind of hard to do that when they're digitized." Jeremy Sharrard, of Forrester Research, said that the VAT would eventually show up on the radar screens of policymakers. "Once they get it figured out domestically, the international issue will heat up. They'll realize that the international tax issue is as big or bigger."

The European Commission, the executive branch of the European Union, has drafted a formula that it believes will allow non-EU companies to do business in Europe, while obliging them to pay European VATs. Under the proposal, companies doing electronic commerce in the EU will simply pay the VAT in their countries of origin. "The VAT in Europe used to be based on the country-of-destination principle," said DLA Upstream's Michael Pullen. "That doesn't work for electronic commerce, so there's been this move to country of origin. What they want to do for companies that are non-resident in the EU is apply the rules that apply to telecommunications companies." That means foreign companies with annual sales in Europe exceeding 100,000 Euros will be obliged to register as residents of a EU member state for tax purposes, even if they have no actual physical presence in Europe.

In one sense, nothing could be simpler. The proposal allows foreign companies to buy and sell in Europe without having to pay VAT 15 times, to 15 different governments — that would be a surefire barrier to Europe's participation in the global electronic commerce market. And the model likewise provides a formula for the EU to collect taxes from companies operating in its territory from virtual space. Like the ship registration regulations of the maritime law that appear to be its inspiration, the formula could well become the basis of a new international electronic commerce tax regime. However, according to Pullen, it shares one inescapable consequence with the law of the seas. "It's the flag of convenience," he said. "It simply means that all the foreign companies that want to do business in Europe will just register in Luxembourg because they have the cheapest VAT rate."

Clearly, taxation — and tax jurisdiction — is an issue that will have to be worked out at an international level. Most governments in the industrialized world have responded to the growth in international electronic commerce by re-examining their tax systems and trying to find ways to retool them for the new economy. In fact, that was one focus of the summit of the group of eight industrialized nations in Japan in July 2000. In their report to their heads of state, the G8 finance ministers identified electronic commerce taxation as a priority and endorsed the efforts of the Organization for Economic Cooperation and Development's Committee on Fiscal Affairs. That was hardly surprising, but endorsement did give the OECD a much higher level of prominence. There is little doubt now that the taxation guidelines of the international economic cooperation forum will figure prominently in whatever solution emerges in the next few years.

In March of 2000, the OECD created a definition for a physical establishment on the Internet. The model attempts to resolve the issues of what constitutes a place of business in a virtual commerce environment. To some extent, it's a lot of legal hair-splitting, but that may be the only way to resolve the issue. For example, the OECD has determined that a Web site hosted by an ISP is not itself a place of business, because it doesn't involve tangible property at a physical location. Consequently, it does not constitute a physical establishment. On the other hand, a server established at a fixed location of the business that operates it is a physical establishment. Moreover, the location of the equipment at the core operations of a business also defines physical location establishment.

Picayune hair-splitting it may be, but it is all an essential step in determining who can tax what and where. Under international treaties, for example, the U.S. government can tax the U.S.-source income of a non-resident business only if that business has a physical establishment in the United States. The same kind of issue impedes the resolution of jurisdiction for contracts and torts, but unless physicality can be defined in a virtual world, it could be extremely difficult to collect taxes from companies active in the United States but whose headquarters are located offshore.

The OECD also plans to address the question of what can be taxed and how, with a series of suggested classifications. For example, tax on a physical product ordered on-line — like a book from Amazon.com — delivered by a postal carrier or Federal Express, should be paid by the customer and collected by the seller. That would be fine if all products had to be delivered physically. However, everything from media content like movies and MP3s to downloadable software can be sold on the Internet, and the Committee on Fiscal Affairs hasn't quite resolved how to deal with that issue. Indeed, with so many issues yet to be resolved, there is growing concern that the OECD's guidelines may be too restrictive to deal adequately with the realities of electronic commerce — particularly between businesses. Businesses may sometimes make purchases *as* consumers. EDI may have defined specific relations between customer and vendor, but the Internet has created different relationships.

For one thing, with the rise of ASPs and the increasing popularity of outsourced operations, the business-to-business tax picture has become somewhat more complicated than a question of applying consumption taxes to imported and exported goods and services. Supply chains may stretch through several tax jurisdictions, and often overseas. Despite the promises of automated commerce, many companies will still want people on the ground; and that could create problems. "If you outsource various steps of production it can get complicated," KPMG's Friedman said. "There is the desire on the part of companies to centralize their functions. The problem is it's hard to do when you're primarily in Canada or the U.S. and open offices overseas; it also means you have to have employees in multiple taxing jurisdictions. So you have to hire local tax talent or outsource, so it's another expense."

The OECD guidelines indicate that if a country has a tax treaty, the physical establishment concept applies: if a seller not located in your country creates a physical establishment in your country, income attributable to that physical establishment can be taxed by you. However, the definition of a physical establishment is being rethought even now, creating additional burdens on businesses conducting B2B overseas. "There is a struggle with how you attribute income to a physical establishment," said Friedman, giving the example of an ASP. "Where is income earned in that activity? Is it where the customers are? Where ASP servers are? Where it's being transmitted across? Should we attribute it to multiple points? It places these businesses in the position of having to sort through it — by struggling with evolving business principles and applying ancient and archaic tax rules."

Keeping abreast of tax rules and trying to determine what is the best solution in a complicated tax environment is a frustrating business at best and seemingly futile at worst. The best approach is to be forewarned and forearmed and to be prepared to react quickly to change. Friedman counsels that businesses proceed with caution and do everything they can to learn everything about all the taxes they may be expected to pay. "If you're selling overseas, know what you're selling and what jurisdictions are taxing. Do they impose tax, or not? You have to know if they're going to impose sales tax on you. And they aren't beholden by the U.S. constitution, and they might say you don't need a physical presence in their jurisdiction to be taxed."

Converting to a new delivery mechanism can make a difference in how something is taxed, and companies now sell digitized goods as well as hard goods on-line. These businesses now have to face compliance with different tax structures in other countries or jurisdictions. "Businesses are dealing with the compliance burden in multiple jurisdictions and the regularity hurdles placed on them," said Friedman. "They are also frustrated with the slow movement of governments toward changing the burdensome tax-compliance system."

The labyrinthine issue of how international tax regulations and jurisdictions will ultimately apply to electronic commerce won't be completely settled for some time to come. It took more than a century for the world's commercial powers to work out all the details of international maritime law, and the changes to each country's tax laws are happening no more quickly. Internet tax issues continue to be contentiously negotiated both domestically and abroad and seem to move along at the rate of a micron each year. For the foreseeable future it will be up to companies themselves to assess each situation and be fully aware of all tax obligations. "We have a facts and circumstances system right now," Friedman said. "You have to try to take the best guess, because the issue hasn't been directly addressed."

PERSONAL PRIVACY

With the continued growth of electronic commerce, the issue of data privacy remains front and center for business, lawmakers, and policy makers. Although most of the concerns regarding data privacy are consumer oriented, B2B commerce companies exchange personal information — about their employees, and about consumers — with corporate business partners every day. Both business and consumers are becoming savvier as to what kind of data is being collected and exchanged, and fears about their own privacy can impede the growth of electronic commerce.

Internationally, the concerns about data privacy have motivated other countries to enact privacy legislation of their own. The European Union Data Privacy directive, which went into effect on October 25, 1998, applies to data collected both electronically and manually (files, paper documents) in all 15 EU countries. Under the directive, any information relating to an identifiable person is defined as personal data and any company that collects personal data (including data collected on Web sites) must tell their customers what data is being collected, what it will be used for, and with whom it will be shared. The directive lays out specific principles on the manner in which data can be used, processed, or collected: data must be processed in a confidential manner; the subject or client must have the right to access all data, correct any errors or inaccuracies, and register objections or complaints. Additionally, the directive bans the transfer of personal data on European citizens to any country that does not have adequate privacy protection.

That was enough of a concern for the Canadian government to bring its own privacy legislation in line with that of the EU. The Canadian government's electronic commerce policy, launched in 1998, aimed to make Canada a world leader in electronic commerce; part of the strategy was to introduce privacy legislation that would safeguard consumers and bring Canada in line with the EU. The federal government passed Bill C-6, the Personal Information Protection and Electronic Documents Act, which received royal assent in April of 2000. Since it came into effect in January 2001, the privacy law covers federally regulated firms such as banks, airlines, telephone companies, broadcasters, and railways. It requires a company to obtain a consumer's informed consent before it can collect or disclose personal information in any medium. As with the EU directive, consumers have legally guaranteed access to the information collected about them. Though the law focuses on electronic commerce, it also applies to off-line transactions where information is stored electronically, like ATM machines and credit card companies.

While other countries, including Australia, India, and Argentina, continue to introduce and enact privacy bills and legislation, the United States remains without any federal privacy law comparable to that of the EU directive or Canada's C-6. Instead, the legal landscape for data privacy in the United States can be described as a mixed bag of various laws, each with its own scope. The Gramm-Leach-Bliley Act, which became effective on November 13, 2000, and which will be fully implemented in July 2001, governs financial institutions and requires they disclose their privacy policies to customers once a year. COPPA, the Child Online Privacy Protection Act, is aimed at restricting the collection of data from Web sites aimed at children under 13. The Health Insurance Portability and Accountability Act of 1996 (HIPAA) regulates the sharing and collection of medical data by health-care professionals.

However, the current legislation does have shortcomings and limitations. The Gramm-Leach-Bliley Act does not solely apply to financial institutions like banks; it relates to any business engaging in financial activities and can include any institution that issues a credit card — the American Association of Retired Persons (AARP), for example. HIPAA, the health care privacy act, bars only the sharing of electronic, not written data.

The FTC's regulations, which prohibit deceptive acts or practices in commerce (Section 5 of the FTC act), are the closest the United States has to a blanket policy on privacy. Although this law dates back to World War I, it is broad enough to continue to be applied to 21st-century electronic commerce and vague enough to leave the working details to regulators. Under the FTC act, a company with a stated privacy policy, on a Web site or elsewhere, could face legal action if it fails to safeguard the data as promised. The FTC provides guidelines for businesses with privacy policies, requiring them to announce on their Web site what their privacy policy is and to announce any changes; however, there are no guidelines for what a privacy policy *should* be, and a company is not legally obliged to have a privacy policy.

"The baseline reality is that there is very little privacy legislation, and you can do whatever you want with personal data, unless you are part of a specific area that has regulations that apply to it," said Jay Stanley, law and policy analyst with Forrester Research. "If you don't have a privacy policy, you can do what you want with customer data."

That leaves it up to e-businesses to wend their way through a maze of sectoral privacy laws, including a number of varying state laws — with more being proposed — that can mean having to be aware of constant changes not only internationally, but in 50 states. "The strains on e-businesses are just beginning to be felt now," said Jay Stanley. "Companies need to expend resources on following regulations — how they apply, hiring lawyers, on training sessions and overseeing implementation," Stanley said. "Even with a broad privacy law you'd still have to worry about implementation, but at least everyone would know the ground rules."

For many companies, privacy is neither an issue nor a priority. According to the Cutter Consortium's 2000 study, *E-Business Trends, Strategies and Technologies,* only 53 percent of the 134 companies surveyed had privacy policies. The ones who do, however, take their policies seriously, with 73 percent of them using data for internal purposes only. Another 9 percent said they shared data with carefully screened parties. However, consumers as well as companies doing business-to-business electronic commerce may be concerned with the remaining 47 percent who have no stated privacy policies at all.

The absence of privacy laws or company privacy policies could spell trouble for American businesses seeking to do e-commerce with countries that have their own comprehensive national privacy laws. For example, the European Union's Data Privacy Directive prohibits the transfer of personal data to countries not meeting the EU standards for privacy protection, including the United States. According to the Department of Commerce, that could add up to the potential disruption of billions of dollars in Europe-U.S. trade. After protracted negotiations, Europe and America reached a compromise — a "safe harbor" agreement, which went into effect November 1, 2000. Under the agreement, American companies that receive data from EU countries must comply with the EU directive; they are then certified to be "safe harbors" for data transfer. Compliance with the agreement is, however, totally voluntary. "Companies with brand names will be ones more likely to voluntarily comply," Stanley said. "Big brand names who have reputations to protect will be the least likely to jeopardize that. Companies like American Express would be in serious trouble if they couldn't export their data."

So far, American companies appear to be cautious about the safe harbor arrangement. In December 2000, *Computerworld* reported that only three U.S. entities had signed up for the agreement.[10] However, some American companies are already beginning to examine how to comply with the Canadian privacy law. American Express began its move to compliance long ago by adopting the Canadian Standards Association's model code of privacy, on which C-6 is based. "A lot of businesses who want to comply with privacy laws like C-6 will be forced to impose policies that reflect the highest common denominator," Stanley said. "Some will probably keep their data segregated, but for those for whom data is not the core of their profit model, they will impose a blanket privacy policy that will satisfy C-6. That may eventually decrease corporate opposition to a broader privacy law."

Until that happens, e-businesses will have to be vigilant — as with taxes and jurisdictional laws, the onus is on them to navigate through a number of policies, agreements, and international treaties. Estella S. Gold advises her clients that honesty — or at least full disclosure — is the best policy. "A good start is a privacy notice on your Web site," she said. "Decide if you are collecting data or not, and if you are, say so. Disclose what you are collecting and who you are giving it to."

Gold stressed that being upfront is also the ideal way to avoid legal entanglements over data privacy, especially when doing business outside the United States. "If you collect data, be forthright and let them know what you're doing with data and that you are collecting it," she said. "If it's in the EU and they're offended, having a notice on your Web site is a good start — it lets them know to turn off the Web site." For smaller companies without lawyers, Gold admitted it can be troublesome. "Make that part of your privacy policy and put it on your Web site: 'We collect data in the U.S. only.' When you make promises on the Web, keep those promises."

But Wait!
There's More...

Change happens. And in the world of electronic commerce, change can happen very quickly. The challenge is to be able to adapt to change and maintain a competitive edge. Unfortunately, that may be easier said than done, and the science of change management has become an on-going necessity. Picking technological winners can be even more difficult, until, that is, you separate the hype from reality.

The Future Is Now

It almost goes without saying that a technological prophet with an un-failing vision of the future of electronic commerce would be both immensely rich and immeasurably powerful. He would know which technologies will succeed and which ones are doomed to failure. He would be able to chart a safe course through the swift currents and complex eddies of technological innovation. That person does not exist; no one can guess the future when it's just 30 seconds away.

That, in a nutshell, is the conundrum facing every enterprise hoping to make it big — or make it at all — in electronic commerce. How do you stay competitive if competitiveness means taking advantage of the latest technologies, and the "latest" technologies keep changing? How do you pick a technology winner from among the dozens of likely contenders battling for market dominance and survival? How do you understand technologies that are in constant flux? It's simple; you don't. "Like anything else in today's market, there are very few forecasts that are reliable, or even close to reliable," said Thomas Nolle, president of CIMI Corp., a Voorhees, N.J.–based telecommunications and networking consultancy. "It's important to remember that most forecasts are made for manipulative reasons [more] than for any desire to reflect reality."

One of the dominant myths of electronic commerce — perpetuated in equal measure by vendors and the business media — is that the technological tools of the trade will make or break your e-business. That's only partly true, however; the tools you use are important, but what is more important is how you use them. In the high-tech, high-speed, global, and plugged-in world of electronic commerce, the tools you use are only as significant as the processes they enable, improve, and streamline. You won't be competing on technology. "That's why companies should focus on optimizing their processes," advised Al Lounsbury, a technology strategist at EDS Corp. in Canada. "They should take the time to understand the total business process and look at how they can streamline it with technology. Doing it the other way is an invitation to disaster."

How much of a disaster? Nothing underlines the fundamental flaw in trying to fit processes to technology better than the debacles attending the widespread deployment of ERP solutions in 1998 and 1999. Though ERP promised — and often delivered — greater enterprise efficiency through integration, that came at a cost. Lounsbury believes that not only was the price too high, but that it was often unnecessary. "If you looked at the process at the time, you would have seen that it was doomed," he said. "ERP is all about changing your processes to fit the technology. But what if your processes work? What if you've been in business successfully for decades? There's no business sense in re-engineering something that works just so you can deploy the latest tech! Better to choose the tools that help you do business the way you do business."

Of course, that all comes back to the original problem. Obsolescence is a way of life in our high-tech world. Vendors always have something new up their sleeves, and users feel a constant pressure to keep up or risk being left behind. In the summer of 2000, for example, only eight or nine months after it had released its Office 2000 business application suite, Microsoft began demonstrating its next version. Netscape Communications Corp. released Communicator 6.0, without even stopping to consider a version 5.0. The one thing that doesn't change seems to be the pace of change itself.

Yet so many technologies, tipped as the killer app of the Internet, or of electronic commerce, or of life in general, fail to live up to their advance billing. It is utterly impossible to forecast technological change more than a few months in the future and that has some managers scratching their heads or pulling out their hair. "I don't know about this Internet thing," said one anonymous business executive at a computer and software industry trade show in 1997. "I'm going to wait and see how it all turns out." Though that may not seem like sensible advice a few years later (it's worth wondering if the executive still has his corner office), things never turn out the way you expect them to.

Some technologies fail miserably, only to be re-born a few years later as startling successes. Apple Computer's Newton handheld computer, for example, died a miserable death in the face of a widespread lack of interest on the part of the technology-buying public shortly after its 1995 debut. The handwriting recognition software was dodgy at the best of times, it was pretty pricey, and no one could think of a reason to carry around a handheld computer ... until US Robotics launched the PalmPilot a few years later. Essentially a slimmed-down Newton with basically the same level of functionality, the PalmPilot — now just the Palm — became the essential high-tech accessory in boardrooms and airport departure lounges everywhere.

The network computer, or NC, seemed to be an idea whose time had come when, in January 1996, Oracle Corp. CEO Larry Ellison unveiled a sexy black box that looked like a prop from Star Trek. "The network is the computer," he intoned and promised a brave new world of computing, freed from the confining shackles of the desktop and Microsoft Corp.'s desktop OS domination. The idea was that, with the growth of the Internet, low-power, low-cost appliances like NCs could simply use networked resources for their storage and processing requirements. Great idea, but nobody bought it. After all, it sounded so much like the discredited dumb terminals of the mainframe era. And with the plunging cost of full-blown computers, who needed it? Yet the NC is one of those ideas that refused to disappear, and Sun Microsystems' Sun Ray network appliance has begun to appear in trials in educational and business environments. Who would have guessed that?

And that's just the point. Who would have guessed? Who could have imagined that EDI would remain an essential part of electronic commerce into the 21st century; who would have foreseen the importance of XML; who would have guessed that SET, widely promoted and pushed by the credit card industry, would have faded into insignificance just when electronic commerce really started to take off? And then there's the problem of knowing how to invest in the right technologies to optimize your processes if you don't even know which technologies are going to be important. No company has the resources to keep throwing money at technologies, hoping one of them will turn out to be a winner.

Unfortunately, there's no simple answer to the problem of technological change. What it takes to stay ahead of the curve, or even stay current, will vary from one enterprise to the next, but there is one imperative they all share — the need for constant, consistent change management. The idea that companies need to plan for the integration of technological change, and that they need to have formal processes for assessing its impact on the bottom line, isn't exactly new. However, the pace of technological change and the ever-increasing pressure to move into electronic commerce have given the idea particularly deep resonance. Because the only thing that doesn't change in the hyper-accelerated world of electronic commerce is change, change management is no longer an ad hoc effort, thrown together as the situation requires. The situation requires that it become an on-going management process.

The key component of successfully managed technological change, whether it's a new tool or a new channel, is understanding how the technology fits your enterprise. Emma Grieg was writing of call centers in *The British Journal of Administrative Management,* but she could have been referring to any new e-business tool: "The need for management to respond to the refinements of new technology roles and environments is absolutely paramount. If businesses fail to identify the changing characteristics of both the call centre employee and the e-centre employee ... the very premise on which new technology has flourished — increased efficiency — will become the very premise on which e-commerce will flounder."[1]

Nevertheless, there's always the danger that change management can turn into an anal-retentive exercise in micromanagement. By sweating the details, managers simply divert resources and effort from the really important change issues. You need to learn to prioritize. "Not every information technology project requires formal change management techniques," wrote Leslie Goff in *Computerworld.* "Upgrading from Windows NT 4.0 to Windows 2000 or switching to a new voice-mail system isn't likely to create tremendous angst among users. But new applications that fundamentally alter the way a group of people operate, both as individuals and as a whole, and the way they relate to suppliers, customers, and one another will create a lot of anxiety."[2]

The big question is whether the expertise to make those assessments exists within your company. For smaller enterprises just starting down the electronic commerce road, the answer is usually fairly simple, and they are most likely to seek the services of a consultant. It may sound like a cop-out, but there are some situations that require a hired gun, for example, "to obtain expertise and access to leading-edge technology," advised Thomas Landers in *Modern Materials Handling.* "Seek consultants who can help empower employees, explain concepts, recommend sound design principles, and provide enabling tools and technologies."[3]

Even large enterprises can take advantage of the insight and fresh vision of an outsider. Indeed, Lounsbury said, the whole idea of integrating new technologies means, implicitly, that your enterprise may not have the expertise to manage the change within itself. "Once you've identified which processes you want to change, then — and only then — you can start looking for technology," he said. "The big mistake most managers make, however, is they try to do that part of it all by themselves, or they just ask the boys in the IT department. But managers, almost by definition, aren't technology experts, and your IT people don't usually know what's going on outside their own department. What every company needs to do is get a good technology advisor on board, and finding one of those is probably the hardest part of the process."

Until that happens, it's important to take a cautious approach to technological change. The evolutionary tree of technology has a lot in common with the evolution of biological organisms. Mutations and changes happen all the time as nature or developers experiment with new ideas and new ways of doing things. However, almost every branch on the tree is a dead end. Real evolutionary success in technology, as in biology, is very rare.

WHERE THERE'S HYPE, THERE'S VAPOR

What's the Next Big Thing in business-to-business electronic commerce? Is it something flashy, sexy, and exciting? Will it change everything? Should you follow the hype? They're all relevant questions, and inescapable ones in the face of the high-tech media saturation concerning anything to do with the Internet. Every new technology, or minute variation on an old technology, is trumpeted by marketers and the trade and business press as the Next Big Thing. Yet it's also worth asking, "If no one can predict where technology will lead, how can you know whether something will be the Next Big Thing?"

There's a word that people in the high-tech world use to describe a product that has been announced and hyped to within an inch of its life but that turns out to be either a non-product — announced but never released — or something that leaves everyone scratching their heads, wondering what all the fuss was about. That word is "vaporware," and it has been leaving its contrails all over electronic commerce for the last few years.

Take the SET protocol proposed, developed, and hyped by the credit card industry in 1997 or, more specifically, the SET-enabled browser that was supposed to change the way consumers purchased products on-line. In order for consumers to buy into the technology, it had to come bundled with Web browsers, but the browser vendors — Microsoft and Netscape — showed little interest in doing that until merchants deployed SET storefronts. And the merchants? They didn't want to go to the bother until consumers asked for it. Look at digital cash stored-value cards like Mondex. The Mondex card's sponsors were sure that it would be a big part of consumer commerce both on-line and off, and let everyone know it. But, after pilot projects in the United States and Canada demonstrated that consumers couldn't get excited about a complex system that, in fact, offered no greater convenience than a bank debit card, it finally began to fade away.

Where there's hype, there's vapor. And there are no technologies more hyped today than **IP telephony,** or **VoIP (Voice over IP)** and mobile electronic commerce.

IP PHONE HOME

The idea behind IP telephony is actually pretty straightforward. Why not route the voice traffic normally carried over the public switched telephone network (PSTN) over the Internet? The value proposition is that companies can use more cost-efficient IP networks to integrate the telephone services of remote locations and satellite offices in a central PBX and save on long-distance charges when calling overseas. The promise for electronic commerce is that Web-based call centers will revolutionize sales, marketing, and customer service by giving users access, through the Web, to both the Internet and a telephony channel. Ideally, a customer will click on a button on a company's commerce Web site to initiate a voice connection to the call center. Using advanced computer-telephony integration technologies, a service representative will be able to talk to the customer while simultaneously watching him or her navigate the Web site.

IP telephony has been a hot, hyped technology since about 1997. Large networking equipment vendors like Cisco Systems, Lucent, and Nortel now offer IP products with voice functions as a matter of course. In fact, there's a strong feeling in some technology circles that the convergence of voice and data technologies is as inevitable as January snow in Vermont. "The network market is coalescing around data," said Dan McLean, an analyst with IDC Research. "I think there's an understanding that the vast majority of traffic is going to come from the data side, and everything else will ride along with it. It doesn't make sense to maintain different networks for different network services when there is a way to carry it on a single infrastructure."

The problem is that, for all of the products, all of the efforts, and all of the work on VoIP networking standards, IP telephony call quality still falls far short of PSTN standards. Make no mistake; placing a call over the Internet is easier than it ever has been. The quality, which was execrable in 1997, is merely bad now — a little like placing a call on a cellphone in a moving car going under an overpass on an expressway — and at the back end of many of the big carriers' networks, traffic is routinely routed between traditional and IP telephony.

But the sound quality, with its noise, jitter, and delays is still too poor for any kind of meaningful communication. It would alienate rather than empower your customers. Moreover, the regulatory tariff-arbitrage advantage that made carrier-replacement so promising all those years ago has effectively disappeared, and with plunging long-distance rates, it's hard to make the commodity case for IP telephony. "There has never been a topic that has fixated the telecommunications market so thoroughly and that has been so utterly irrelevant as VoIP," CIMI's Nolle ventured. "Telephony and public networking services are not developed on the basis of technology, but on the basis of revenue. The question is not *can* we build an IP voice infrastructure, but *why* build it at all?"

IP telephony was kept out of the telecommunications mainstream by a number of factors. For one thing, in order for there to be carrier-level IP telephony in any meaningful sense, carriers would have had to install VoIP-enabled equipment at the local exchange level. The regional Bell carriers were vital to the success of IP telephony as a carrier medium, and they would only install VoIP — cannibalizing their traditional PSTN business — if there was market advantage. Once the FCC ruled that they had to provide wholesale access to voice services to competitive local exchange carriers, however, any financial advantage in deploying VoIP services effectively evaporated. Unable to grasp any market share in the carrier space, VoIP equipment vendors were particularly badly hit by the stock market's high-tech massacre in 2000.

Nevertheless, IP telephony still has a play in the premises networking market. There, the promise of consolidating enterprise network traffic between and within geographically disparate locations over an inexpensive IP infrastructure remains compelling. For vendors, though, it's little more than a consolation prize. "The premises market is a better market because there's actually a value proposition there," Nolle said. "It's worse because the price pressure is phenomenal. There are about 800,000 locations in the U.S. that are prospects for premises VoIP, but they're very small. They don't have the carriers' deep pockets."

Premises VoIP opens up the prospect of talk-while-you-surf on-line help desks and customer support. One of the technology's earliest proposed applications was the fully integrated on-line call center. In theory, at least, the idea of having your customers interact with sales and support representatives in the same medium that they buy products and services — an on-line consolidation of the electronic commerce channel — could be a killer app. The problem is that, with the exception of a few hobbyists, computers and network appliances are not users' tools of choice for basic voice communications, and it doesn't look like they will be any time soon. "When used for certain applications, IP desktop devices tend to foster the idea that the PC is a primary means of communication," Nolle said. "The thing is that we're just not there yet. What we've got here is that we've proved that it's probably not reasonable to deploy VoIP when most of the instruments that you'd want to connect to it are not naturally IP instruments."

None of that will stop the IP telephony hype, though. With some justification, Nolle characterizes the VoIP as a movement — a crusade to find a useful application for cool technology. The only reason why the hype is still there is that the technology still seems like such a new, radical departure from mundane telephone service. "All of the discussions about VoIP fall into a category of over-generalization," he said. "The problem is that, because we're so news-driven, when something like VoIP happens, the first instances are news. Then, to justify this news, the spin doctors construct an attractive combination of conditions to justify the media's continued coverage. It eventually burns itself out, but sometimes it takes time."

WHO PUT THE "M" IN M-COMMERCE?

The business-to-business promises of **m-commerce** — electronic commerce services delivered to mobile wireless devices like Palm computers and cellular phones — are, if possible, even more tenuous. It's not that it's such a bad idea, and there's something strangely compelling about being able to whip out your cellphone and make a deal over the Internet, but there's no way for any idea, now matter how good, to live up to the m-commerce hype.

A key m-commerce pitch is that it will be a significant part of the future of business-to-business electronic commerce. Sixty-seven percent of respondents to a March 2000 poll by Britain's *Computer Weekly* said they expected m-commerce would be as important to business-to-business commerce as the Internet has been for the last five. Indeed, wireless Internet technologies like the still-new Wireless Application Protocol, and iMode succeed admirably in connecting mobile devices to the Internet, and throughout 1999 and 2000, companies as diverse as Europe's Vodaphone and Digital Insight of Silicon Valley lined up to offer business-to-business applications. It certainly looks like the hype wave is being translated into something real.

"If the enthusiasts are even partially correct, in the near future many of us will be doing business on the go and by hand — that is, via cell-phone and other personal devices, such as digital organizers," wrote Richard Shaffer in the July 2000 issue of *Fortune*. "Now that electronic commerce is here to stay, we're about to move on to mobile commerce, or m-commerce, which supposedly will enable us to buy everything from anywhere over the Internet without the use of a personal computer."[4]

The market is growing; the devices in question are the hottest hot-ticket techno-toys for the people with the most money to spend. Some industry analysts see that as an unbeatable combination for electronic commerce. It's clear that wireless networking is poised to get really big really fast, said Ken Orr, president of the Ken Orr Institute in Topeka, Kansas and a fellow at the Boston-based Cutter Research Group. "My opinion is that the wireless Internet will be bigger and will happen faster than the traditional Internet," he said. "In fact, everything is already in place."

Wireless communication devices are proliferating at an astounding rate. By some estimates, there will be as many as one billion mobile phones — that's just phones and not hand-held computers, mind you — by 2003, compared to 420 million in 2000. In some places, such as the developing world and parts of Europe, where the landline telecom-munications infrastructure is barely adequate where it exists at all, the wireless communications penetration rate is expected to be even more dramatic. Mobile communication devices are ubiquitous, convenient, and relatively cheap. Every businessperson has a cell phone, and hand-held computers are as common in some boardrooms as silk ties and double-breasted suits.

Internet-ready mobile devices are flying off of dealers' shelves, and software vendors are falling over each other to OEM their microbrowsers — Web-browsing software designed to display in small screens and run on the new Wireless Application Protocol. WAP is the hot acronym on every mobile Net jockey's lips. It's easy to see where the hype has come from. "But hype machines tend to sputter sooner or later, and some of those influential analysts, though not questioning the projections for phone proliferation, are skeptical that the boom in voice services will translate into m-commerce for the masses all that soon," observed Jeffrey Kutler in *Institutional Investor*.[5]

It just isn't clear what role WAP is going to play in that future. Sure, it lets vendors create mobile devices capable of browsing the Web, but there are other, less hyped technologies like iMode that do it more simply, though with less flash. And while some wireless Internet developers are charging ahead with ambitious, mobile micro-browser technologies that build on the WAP foundation, they may be premature. For one thing, the limitations of m-commerce technology are daunting. It may be a cool trick to browse a Web page on your cellphone, but very few phones, or even handheld computers, are equipped with a display that would make it much more than a trick. Moreover, while many planned wireless Internet applications require substantial bandwidth — as much as two million bits per second — the actual bandwidth available is usually much closer to 9,600 bits per second. That may be enough to transmit some of the more popular consumer-oriented applications available now and planned for the immediate future, like jokes and basic text-based content, but the demands of business-to-business users are somewhat more complex.

A more serious question is whether handheld, mobile wireless devices like cell phones and personal digital assistants are even particularly well suited to on-line browsing. You can't build much of a display into a mobile phone without seriously compromising its portability, and unlike computers, most mobile devices are designed to be operated with one hand. By the summer of 2000, no one had even yet proposed an XML m-commerce application.

If the recent history of the Internet is any indication, however, the technological barriers can be and probably eventually will be overcome. The main problem with the m-commerce hype is that its play in the business-to-business space is more than a little bit of a stretch. Wireless Internet certainly has a strong appeal for consumers and for businesses wishing to plug their employees into the company network without tying them down to costly infrastructure. But does it have a future for business-critical commerce applications? Lounsbury doubts it. "It's a great application for day traders — I'd live to see that — and it makes sense for the UPS guys, but the commerce application is much less than convincing," he said. "It's great for e-mail and most people would say e-mail is a business-critical application, I'll give it that. Wireless is hot — but m-commerce isn't."

The main proposed business-to-business uses of m-commerce — things like stock updates, advertising, and marketing information — are only tenuously commercial. Wireless devices may be ideal sales force automation tools, just as laptops were in the 1990s, and they certainly have great utility as communications devices within the enterprise. However, wireless devices are almost by definition personal devices, and while that might make them the ideal appliances for personal commerce, the main trend in electronic commerce today is toward greater integration between systems, without the sidestep to human intervention. Wireless may, as Lounsbury said, be hot technology, but business-to-business m-commerce will remain, for the foreseeable future, vapor.

Focus on Change Management

Marco Argenti: Keeping up

It's no secret that there's a business boom on the Internet. It's on the front pages of every newspaper business section and it dominates the financial news on television. The volume of American business-to-business electronic commerce transactions was $700 million in 1999 —more than twice that of the rest of the world. It's getting to the point that commerce is electronic commerce, and it's also no secret that everyone who's in business will be in e-business sooner rather than later. "It's not hard to convince companies to go to electronic commerce today," said Marco Argenti, CTO of Microforum, a Toronto-based electronic commerce solutions provider. "It's a must-have sort of thing; the case for e-business is very compelling. A company without a Web site, or commerce site to complement it, is really going down the path of losing market share."

It's also clear, however, that any company that dives into electronic commerce without a clear idea of what it's doing is in for a nasty shock. Change management has become an imperative. Electronic commerce may be commerce, but it's a whole new way of doing things, and companies have to prepare for the change. "There are so many points of change, but the most obvious ones are on the customer's side," Argenti said. "On the Web, you're dealing with customers in a much more direct channel. For most companies, that's a whole new way of doing business. It's a matter of marketing or branding, a matter of customer engagement, a different level of customer support. Companies have to learn a whole new set of skills."

And the changes go far beyond the way you deal with customers, Argenti added. "There's also a transformation from an operational standpoint. Everything is faster, or it has to be done much more efficiently, with the maximum possible efficiency. You can't skip a step in the supply chain, so companies have to get used to operating at a more detailed level."

It's a lot more complicated than registering a domain name, setting up a Web site, and hoping buyers will drop by for a look. Not only does it require an investment in software and systems, success in electronic commerce is very much dependent on process integration and developing a new level of expertise throughout the entire enterprise. It is a complex transformation and in order to make it successful, Argenti believes the best strategy is to move ahead incrementally, in baby steps. "It's a network of highly interdependent systems," said Argenti. "And the complexity goes up with every new element you add. You have to shoot for minimal risk at first deployment. This means careful planning, controlled and phased deployment — not adding too many new elements but building on top of what you've already done."

It's a never-ending process. The pace of technological innovation on the Internet and in electronic commerce virtually guarantees that, by the time you've deployed one tool, its successor will already be on the market. One of change management's main focuses today is future proofing — making sure that the technology and strategy decisions you make now don't come back to haunt you later. The big question is how do you do it? "There's really no formula," Argenti said. "The best thing you can do is stay informed. You have to watch changes in customer behavior, and new demands or trends in dealing with your partners. It's important to look carefully at areas where changes are happening, and try to understand why they are changing and how they can operate more efficiently."

At the end of the day, however, it adds up to much more than staying ahead of the technological curve. It's about leveraging knowledge and information across the enterprise and out across the supply chain and that, Argenti said, requires a much greater kind of change — a new way of thinking. "There's a change of management thinking," he said. "The Internet extends your reach beyond where and how you normally do business. There's more information from more customers in a greater range of locations and industries. Managers have to be open-minded enough to take that all in and to be able to accept and initiate change within their organizations."

THE WINNER IS...

With all the hot air surrounding the latest candidates for the Next Big Thing, it might seem sensible, on balance, to follow the lead of the cautious executive who wanted to see how it would all turn out. After all, if all the latest, greatest technologies are turkeys, there doesn't seem to be a whole lot of profit in pushing the technology envelope. The problem is that there is at least one new tool, electronic bill presentment and payment (EBPP) that, despite the hype surrounding it, promises to be one of the killer apps of the next stage in electronic commerce.

Look at the stack of bills on your desk. Bills are as old as commerce and as inevitable as Monday morning, but electronic commerce is about to change the way we send, receive, and pay them. The concept of giving customers a site where they can view and pay their bills in one easy step on the Internet — without the cost and aggravation of paper — is catching on in a big way in e-business. The idea has actually been tossed around for a few years. In fact, it was two financial-service technology mega-deals in 1997 that put the technology on the map in the first place. In the fall of that year, Microsoft Corp., still smarting from the regulatory kibosh on its planned acquisition of Intuit Corp., inked a deal with First Data Corp. to offer on-line bill presentment services. MSFDC, as the joint venture was dubbed, emerged at almost the exact moment that Integrion Financial Network, the electronic commerce provider of choice to most of the United States' biggest banks, announced a 10-year alliance with CheckFree Corp. and acquired Visa Interactive Inc., Visa International's EBPP pioneer. The deals put the idea of on-line billing and payment on the map.

Though the evolution of EBPP has been relatively slow — in electronic commerce terms — over the last few years, it is one of those rare technology ideas that just keeps looking better year after year. Now, it looks like a shoo-in for the Next Big Thing. E-billing seems to be on everyone's lips, Web sites, and computer screens. All the conditions seem right for it to finally take off. "A lot of key components were still missing three years ago — not the least of which was acceptance by the billers themselves," said IDC analyst Albert Pang. "With Y2K, a lot of them had other things on their minds. E-billing was put on hold. But that's all changed, and billers are starting to see a very compelling value proposition in the technology."

The idea behind EBPP is that, instead of sending paper bills to customers, companies will be able to present them on a Web site — usually after an e-mail notification — where the customer can examine the charges and invoke a direct payment from his or her bank. For products and services delivered over the Internet, nothing could be simpler, and nothing could be more important. "It definitely has an important place in some applications," said Kneko Burney of Cahners In-Stat Group. "I can see electronic bill presentment being particularly important for service providers — from ISPs and telcos to ASPs."

From the provider's point of view, EBPP spells one big cost saving. According to the research firm Killen & Associates, the average cost of printing up and mailing a hard-copy statement and processing a bill can be as much as $2.75 per bill. In contrast, EBPP billing costs only 50 cents. Multiply that a few thousand or — in the case of a telecommunications carrier — a million times, and the potential economy is staggering. It's not much of a surprise, then, that some of the biggest early adopters of this still-young technology are the telcos. A carrier like Verizon Communications Corp. sends out some 60 million bills annually. You need only multiply the cost of paper bills by that number — that's $165,000,000 — to see why telcos are so eager to deploy EBPP services.

However, there's more to it than that. Paper bills have to be handled; if subscribers send checks, they have to be sorted; the biller doesn't get paid right away; and when it does, it has to reconcile manual billing processes with its own electronic financial back end. "The major benefit for us is that e-billing eliminates the paper bill," said Keith Gill, Verizon's senior e-business executive for channel integration and implementation. "A big part of it is being able to move to electronic processing of payment. It eliminates check float and it greatly reduces the overhead in some of our processes."

Yet for all of the consumer-oriented EBPP offerings — the U.S. Postal Service formed an alliance with CheckFree in 1999 to get its own E-billing service off the ground — it has yet to really penetrate that market. Although EBPP can represent great efficiencies and cost savings for the people who actually send bills, its value proposition for consumers is not quite as clear. Not so in the business-to-business realm. "The rewards go even further in the B2B segment," wrote Jim Carr in *E-Commerce Business*. "Both the biller and the payee stand to gain in automating a wide variety of bill-related business practices, such as delivering and authorizing purchase orders and handling disputes on-line."[6]

Those advantages can range from consolidating a company's enterprise-wide charges in a single itemized account that a manager can simply load into his or her own spreadsheet, to automated invoice-and-payment processes using XML. In effect, EBPP is the poor man's EFT. Smaller companies that participate in the electronic commerce supply chain but don't have either the volume or inclination to use EFT can simply have their traditional billing moved, part and parcel, to the Internet. For a company like the Burlington Northern and Santa Fe Railway Co., EBPP is a particularly attractive way of doing business with the little guys. BNSF deployed E-Pay, its Web-based, freight billing and payment application in the fall of 2000 with just those customers in mind.

"The traditional reconciliation process is laborious, paper heavy," said Kathleen Regan, BNSF's vice president of e-business development. "E-Pay expedites the settlement process and matches the exact goods to each shipment making sure we have the right shipment. It's a kind of one-stop shopping service for all your freight bills, and it's really successful for smaller customers who don't have big EDI pipes. A lot of them are still mailing in orders. This lets them do it electronically for the first time, and we've really had great success with smaller customers like lumber companies, small grain shuttle, and perishable commodities."

Electronic bills also have a strong appeal to business-to-business marketers. By providing billing information on your Web site, you give your customers a reason to drop by for a visit. "That's a big deal," Burney said. "It's a great way to attract people to a location where you can give them access to personalized services like on-line provisioning. It also provides an important customer management touch-point. You can offer a lot to your customers along with a bill. In that sense, it's like all that literature that comes with a traditional phone bill."

It's also like having a customer representative on hand to answer your questions when you actually get around to paying. The ability to manage the customer relationship using automated processes rather than call center agents who get paid and take vacations is particularly attractive to Verizon. "Our initial strategy is to put a full set of billing out there," Gill said. "That's a common draw, and while the subscriber is at our site, we can promote products and services that fill their needs. Our higher-level goal is to have the whole set of core capabilities there, so they don't have to make a call to our call center."

What *has* been holding the technology up for all these years isn't a lack of acceptance — that's almost assured — but the difficulty of deployment. Enterprises weary from the successive dislocations of ERP and eSCM implementations may be willing to take their time on electronic billing. Indeed, getting an EBPP system up and running can be a daunting prospect. "Companies must redesign bills so they are readable on-line," observed Carolyn Gruske in *The Globe and Mail*. "They must provide outside access to their accounts payable systems and, either directly or through a third-party service provider, must hook into a financial institution's funds-transferring system."[7]

In fact, it's that last step to the bank that is most responsible for the slow deployment of business-to-business electronic commerce's real Next Big Thing. Despite the early maneuvers of 1997, the banks — essential players in anyone's EBPP system — still have a lot of catching up to do. "It's still a very complex thing for them to pull off," Burney said. "It requires a whole lot of system integration. And the banks, in particular, have an awful lot of legacy data and systems at the back end. It's not a canned solution, and that's why we haven't seen it reach a mass business market."

Upgrading your back-end and integrating systems so they can send bills and receive them electronically is an uphill struggle for most companies, whether they're tied to legacy systems like banks, or whether they're high-tech powerhouses like Verizon. "I won't trivialize it," Gill admitted. "It's a huge effort, but we're working through it. We're spending a lot of time and resources in this area, and we've done a lot of the work to get it going … but there certainly is work still to be done."

Nevertheless, Burney notes that the technological barriers are beginning to fall as billers and financial institutions update and improve their systems. It's inevitable, she said, because there's so much to be gained and very little to lose. "Make no mistake, there's an opportunity here," Burney said. "They want a part of that."

Key Terms

IP telephony
VoIP
m-commerce

ENDNOTES

INTRODUCTION

1. A.T. Kearney, Inc., *Strategic Information Technology and the CEO Agenda* (Chicago: Information Technology Monograph, 2000), 16.

CHAPTER 1

1. Patricia B. Seybold, "Just say 'yes' to the Internet," *Computerworld,* March 28, 1994.
2. Ibid.
3. Brendan P. Kehoe, *Zen and the Art of the Internet* (Englewood Cliffs, New Jersey: Prentice Hall, 1992). http://www.cs.indiana.edu/docproject/zen/zen-1.0_6.html, January 1992.
4. *U.S. International Trade in Goods and Services — Annual Revision for 1999* (Washington: Bureau of the Census and Bureau of Economic Analysis, Department of Commerce). *Note:* These figures represent the total for the categories of semiconductors, telecommunications equipment, computer accessories, computers, business machines and equipment.
5. Obie G. Whichard, *United States Statistics on Trade in Services* (Washington: Bureau of Economic Analysis, Department of Commerce, August 2000), 7.

CHAPTER 2

1. It's a system that RAND Corporation researcher Paul Baran called "distributed adaptive message block switching." Both Baran and British researcher Donald Davies conceived of packet switching at about the same time as Kleinrock.

CHAPTER 3

1. Katherine Jones, "SCM's missing link," *Manufacturing Systems* 18 (April 2000): 4, 38.
2. Don Tapscott, *The Digital Economy: Promise and Peril in the Age of Networked Intelligence* (New York: McGraw Hill, 1995), 63.
3. Adapted from a sample EDI message in Margaret A. Emmelhainz, *EDI: A Total Management Guide,* 2nd ed. (New York: Van Nostrand Reinhold, 1993), 77.
4. Mark Vigoroso, "Fate of OBI standard uncertain," *Purchasing* 126 (March 25, 1999): 4, 73.
5. Chris Pickering, *E-Business: Trends, Strategies and Technologies* (Arlington: The Cutter Consortium, 2000), 149.

CHAPTER 4

1. Heather Green, "A New Year's Resolution for E-tailers: Let's Fix the Logistics," *Business Week,* January 31, 2000.
2. Ibid.

CHAPTER 5

1. Hiroyuki Tezuka, "Success as the source of failure? Competition and cooperation in the Japanese economy," *Sloan Management Review* 38 (Winter 1997): 2, 83–93.
2. Donna Fenn, "Sleeping with the enemy," *Inc.* 19 (November 1997): 16, 78.
3. Don Tapscott, *The Digital Economy,* 10.
4. Howard Rheingold, *The Virtual Community: Homesteading on the Electronic Frontier* (New York: HarperPerennial, 1994), 110.
5. Jeff Sabatini, "ANX: The anti-nerd explanation," *Automotive Manufacturing & Production* 111 (July 1999): 7, 45.
6. Clinton Wilder, "Slow revolution in e-commerce," *Information Week* 720 (February 1999), 18.
7. The Burgess Shale is a fossil field in Alberta, Canada, containing evidence of the first explosion of multi-cellular life on Earth. Though

there are fossilized remains of hundreds of bizarre species, most of their evolutionary lines soon died out.

CHAPTER 6

1. August-Wilhelm Scheer and Frank Habermann, "Making ERP a Success," *Communications of the ACM* 43:4, 57.

CHAPTER 7

1. Wayne W. Eckerson, *Marrying E-Commerce and Customer Intelligence* (Boston: Patricia Seybold Group, 1999), 1.
2. Francis Buttle, *The CRM Value Chain* (Manchester: Manchester Business School, 2000), 6.
3. Tom Hennings, "Overcome Your B2B Challenge," *e-Business Advisor,* April 2000, 22.
4. Ibid.
5. Ted Gannon, "A business solution: EIP," *DM Review,* June 2000.
6. Steve Konicki, "Powerful portals: A new wave of software has helped the concept of in-house portals evolve into something essential," *Information Week,* May 1, 2000.
7. A terabyte is one thousand gigabytes. A three-terabyte data warehouse would be the equivalent of the contents of 5,000 CD-ROMs.

CHAPTER 8

1. Andy Grove, *Only the Paranoid Survive* (New York: Currency Doubleday, 1996), 153.
2. Denise Pappalardo, "Users not flocking to converged services," *Network World,* October 23, 2000.

CHAPTER 9

1. Andy Briney, "Security Focused," *Information Security* (September 2000), 42.
2. Suetonius, *The Twelve Caesars* (Harmondworth: Penguin Classics, 1957), 38.

3. Greg Shipley, "How Secure Is Your Network?" *Network Computing,* November 27, 2000.

4. Bernard Burnes and Barrie Dale, *Working in Partnership* (Brookfield: Gower, 1998), 157.

CHAPTER 10

1. Al Gore, "The Role of Networking — Better Communication Has Always Led to Greater Democracy and Greater Economic Growth. That Is Our Challenge," *InternetWeek,* January 3, 1994.

2. Edmund L. Andrews, "Policy Blueprint Ready for Data Superhighway," *The New York Times,* September 15, 1993.

3. American Bar Association Global Cyberspace Jurisdiction Project, *Achieving Legal and Business Order in Cyberspace: A Report on Global Jurisdiction Issues Created by the Internet,* American Bar Association, Washington, 2000.

4. Paul Meller, "Brussels: Critics Rap E-commerce Legislation; Say EU Rules Would Kill Online Sales," *Ad Age Global,* October 1, 2000.

5. Ron N. Dreben and Johanna L. Werbach, "Senators versus Governors: State and Federal Regulation of E-Commerce," *The Computer Lawyer,* June 2000.

6. Richard Raysman and Peter Brown, "Legislation on Digital Signatures," *New York Law Journal,* April 13, 1999.

7. Benjamin Weinstock and David P. Leno, "Impact on B2B, B2C, B2G," *National Law Journal,* September 25, 2000.

8. Ibid.

9. Office of Tax Policy, *Selected Tax Policy Implications of Global Electronic Commerce,* Department of the Treasury, Washington, 1996.

10. Patrick Thibodeau, "Few takers for European safe harbor agreement," *Computerworld,* December 4, 2000.

CHAPTER II

1. Emma Greig, "From Call Centre to 'E-centre' Managing Change in the New Technology Centres," *The British Journal of Administrative Management* 20 (May-June 2000): 17.

2. Leslie Goff, "Change Management," *Computerworld,* February 14, 2000, 7, 54.

3. Thomas L. Landers, "When to Hire a Consultant," *Modern Materials Handling* 53 (June 1998): 7, 26.

4. Richard A. Schaffer, "M-commerce: Online Selling's Wireless Future," *Fortune,* July 10, 2000, 2, 262.

5. Jeffrey Kutler, "Institutional Wireless: Mobile Commerce Without the Hype," *Institutional Investor,* London, May 2000, 20.

6. Jim Carr, "The check's in the (e)mail," *E-commerce Business,* July 29, 2000.

7. Carolyn Gruske, "Electronic Bills Just One Step Toward 'On-line Customer Care'," *The Globe and Mail,* Toronto, May 26, 2000, C-10.

GLOSSARY

"One thing's for sure," said John Lawler, an assistant professor of linguistics at the University of Michigan in Ann Arbor, and one of North America's leading authorities on technical jargon, "geeks are news. As a society, we're paying more attention to technology, and we're buying into technology companies. What we're seeing is a special in-group way of talking that has rarely made its way out of that group suddenly leaking into the outside world." There are times when the jargon gets so thick on the ground that it loses its tenuous grip on meaning. When the good old boys in the IT department start talking about *sequel,* do they mean the next installment of the *Star Wars* series, or SQL? Knowing computer guys, it could be either, but if you have to get a presentation out to a partner that explains the virtues of database integration, you sort of have to be sure.

Jargon exists principally for two reasons, Lawler said. Jargon is a kind of verbal shorthand that scientists and technicians use to communicate quickly and precisely among themselves. Jargon can seem obscure to outsiders because it has a context-specific utility. Of course, Lawler said, it can also be used to exclude the hoi polloi. "You can dazzle people with jargon and leave them gasping for air," he said. "I would hesitate to say that was the dominant purpose of jargon, but it does happen. It depends on who you want to exclude and why."

Bridging the gap between the specialized community and the rest of the real world is, to say the least, a challenge. A specialized language all itself, jargon is often so context-sensitive and self-referential that it defies translation. You'll probably never have to know about "dense wave division multiplexing," and that's just as well, because the term only really makes sense to someone who knows *how* dense and *which* waves, not to mention what multiplexing is. "It's practically impossible to translate jargon," Lawler said. "It's a self-defeating task. If you're writing a document, or you're communicating a technical concept, you don't usually know what your audience already understands — you have to pick a starting point, and even that's fraught with difficulties."

The only way to master jargon is to forget that it exists. It's just language, after all, and in the normal course of things the really important words — the ones you need to know — will soon just be part of the vernacular, anyway. We talk about *leeway* and *flying colors,* and we swap *scuttlebutt* about deals in the offing every day without stopping to consider that all of these terms were part of the specialized language of sailing and navigation — the revolutionary technology of the time — a few centuries ago. "The truth is that you don't have to understand the jargon itself," Lawler said. "You have to be prepared to ask, 'Why are they using these funny words?' If you can understand that, then you can translate the metaphor into another set of metaphors. What does a jargon term like 'interface' mean but 'meeting face-to-face'? Once you have that worked out, it becomes clear."

THE B2B GLOSSARY

Agent A small program that performs specific processes, particularly information classification and preparation, on behalf of another software program. Intelligent agents are automated programs, capable of performing these tasks with minimal user direction.

Application server A system that provides remote applications to clients over a network.

ARPAnet The direct ancestor of the Internet. ARPAnet was created by the Pentagon's Defense Advanced Research Projects Agency in 1969 to prove the viability of a distributed, packet-switched data communications network and to share computing resources between DARPA-funded research sites at universities across the United States.

Artificial intelligence A discipline of computer science concerned with modeling certain aspects of human cognitive processes and intelligence in digital computer systems. The stated goals of AI research are not so much to replicate human intelligence in a machine as to create systems capable of complex analysis and symbolic inference. Specific applications of AI are fuzzy logic, expert systems, natural language processing, and pattern recognition.

ASP Application service provider. A company that provides outsourced IT, network- and electronic-commerce-related services like enterprise resource planning and merchant server hosting on a subscription basis. Typically, ASPs simply provide subscribers with access to remote applications.

Asymmetrical key encryption See Public key cryptography.

Bandwidth Network capacity. Bandwidth is a measure of how much data can be transmitted through a network connection in a given time period. Networks with higher bandwidth can transmit data more quickly than networks with lower bandwidth. Often confused with speed — as in "high-speed networking" — network bandwidth is usually measured in a multiple of bits-per-second.

Beta A pre-release version of a computer software or hardware product. Betas are usually free and are used to test the product for potential problems and bugs, most of which will hopefully be corrected in the final release version.

Bit length The length and complexity of the keys used in a cryptographic system. Cryptographic tools that use longer and more complex keys are typically more secure than systems that use less complex keys.

Boolean logic Strictly, Boolean logic is a subset of conventional logic which reduces all values to "true" or "false." Applied to database search techniques, this permits the formulation of complex queries using Boolean operators like "and," "or," and "not," enabling complex database searches. Most Web-based search tools employ Boolean logic in their searches.

Brochure-ware A Web site with no interactive content that simply provides product information and glossy graphics.

Bundling The vendor practice of including additional products — usually software — with a shipping product. Examples of bundling include a copy of an office application suite that comes with a new computer, and network backup software included with a mass storage device.

Bursty A characteristic of data communications in which traffic is not transmitted in a continuous stream, but in short, intermittent bursts.

CAD Computer-aided design. Software and systems that permit designers and engineers to design physical products using computers. Modern CAD systems provide 3-D solid modeling functionality and permit complete digital prototyping.

CAD/CAM Software and systems using computers to create products and control production. Modern CAD/CAM systems permit products to be manufactured directly from digital prototypes, with limited human intervention on the assembly line.

CAM Computer-aided manufacturing. Automated manufacturing processes controlled or directed by computers.

Carrier class Describes a high-volume, extremely reliable networking product, usually equipment, which is appropriate for use in a major telecommunications carrier's network. Networking devices that can handle hundreds or thousands of simultaneous connections are typically referred to as "carrier-class."

Certificate authority An organization, institution, company, or other "trusted third party" that issues and oversees digital certificates in a public key infrastructure. The CA verifies and confirms the identity of the individual using a digital certificate. CAs are an essential component in public key–based authentication.

Circuit-switching A communications model where a dedicated network connection is established between two points and maintained for the duration of a transmission. Traditional telephone networks are circuit-switched, making them inefficient for data communications, which are typically bursty and intermittent.

Client A computer system or application that requests data or services over the network from a server. A Web browser that displays content from a Web server is an example of a client application.

Client-server A network computing architecture model based on distributed computing assets. In a client-server system, each user's workstation employs its own application logic to process data resident on common servers.

CNC Computer numerical control. The use of computers to direct and control precision manufacturing instruments.

Cookie An information token sent by a Web server to a Web browser when the latter first accesses a page. The token is then sent back to the server on every subsequent visit. Cookies, which are stored in a text file on the user's computer, can be used, among other things, to identify a user or store configurations and authentication information like passwords so the user doesn't have to log in every time he or she visits a page. They can also be used to tag a user for customer tracking and to match on-line behavior with identification information entered in an on-line form.

CTI Computer-telephony integration. Software and computer systems that match in-coming and out-going telephone communication to business and customer information in centralized corporate databases. CTI, which is most commonly employed in call-centers, routes data to the appropriate call-center representative in real time.

Data mining A type of database application that searches for patterns, trends, and anomalies in a given data set without a pre-defined context for the data. Data-mining systems can be used to track buying and customer-behavior trends in data collected by a customer-tracking system on a commerce Web site. Such trends can be used as the basis for business intelligence forecasting and planning.

Data warehouse A centralized database containing all of the diverse information and files collected, generated, and used by an enterprise. Data warehouses are typically aggregated from numerous departmental and special-use databases as part of an ERP deployment.

Digital certificate A software token that identifies a user in a security system like a public key infrastructure. In a PKI, a digital certificate typically contains the user's identification information, public key, and digital signature, and can be verified by a third-party certificate authority. The most common certificate standard is the International Telecommunications Union's X.509.

Digital prototype A complete product design, described down to the finest detail and modeled in a CAD system. Digital prototypes are typically used to create and test complex products like aircraft and computer circuit-board designs virtually before production.

DTD Document type definition. A file that explains the meaning and context of XML meta-tags.

E-fulfillment The use of electronic commerce technologies to manage logistics and customer fulfillment processes.

EBPP Electronic bill presentment and payment. The practice of presenting bills and accepting payment over the Internet. Typically, a buyer will read his bill on a supplier's Web site and invoke a direct payment from his bank. Also called e-billing.

EDI Electronic data interchange. The electronic exchange of information and documents over networks like the Internet and VANs, using standardized message formats called "transaction sets." EDI was developed in the 1970s to facilitate the exchange of supply chain data between companies and is governed by the ANSI X12 and UN/EDIFACT standards.

EFT Electronic funds transfer. The computerized movement of funds between financial institutions or from one account to another.

Enterprise information portal An application that provides a Web-based interface to enterprise documents and other networked content. EIPs typically aggregate information in a hierarchical directory structure and provide access to networked search tools and applications.

eSCM The use of electronic commerce technologies to manage industrial and commercial supply chains.

ESP E-business service provider, or enterprise service provider. An ASP specializing in electronic commerce applications.

Expert system An artificial intelligence system or application that employs a knowledge base of human expertise to solve complex problems that would normally be solved by a human expert. Expert systems have been employed to predict stock market fluctuations, model business strategies based on varied contingencies, and play chess.

Extranet A private corporate network accessible to a company's employees, partners, suppliers, customers, and other authorized users through the public Internet. Access to an extranet is usually controlled by access control software or a firewall.

Firewall Software, and the system or network appliance on which it runs, that screens traffic entering an internal network and blocks unauthorized or unwanted traffic. Firewalls typically operate at the packet level and are designed to admit traffic only from known IP addresses.

Gateway The generic term for a networking device or system that connects one network to another, often converting between network protocols. An enterprise intranet is typically connected to the Internet through a gateway.

Glass room The centralized IT department. Glass room typically refers to an enterprise computing model where application and information assets are concentrated in few — or even one — systems, typically a mainframe or large server. In the days before personal computers became common, valuable computing assets like mainframes were typically housed in centralized locations, separated from the rest of the company by a glass divider, where access and the physical environment could be carefully controlled.

Groupware A type of software that allows a group of users to work collaboratively on a project over a network, and often in real time.

GUI Graphical user interface. A software interface that represents application and operating system processes and documents as icons and lets the user interact by clicking on buttons, icons, and menus using a pointing device like a mouse. Once referred to as the window-icon-mouse program, or WIMP interface.

Heuristic logic A subset of artificial intelligence that employs common-sense rules to solve problems. Heuristic logic systems can find approximations and are capable of self-learning. Most expert systems employ heuristic logic.

Heuristic search A search employing heuristic logic. Such a search technique can learn from example, increasing the precision of each subsequent search.

HTML Hypertext markup language. The authoring language used to create World Wide Web pages and sites. A Web browser interprets special text tags to define the format of text and graphics on the page.

Information management The management, classification, and control of an enterprise's information resources.

Intranet Any internal TCP/IP-based enterprise network. An intranet may be — but is not necessarily — connected to the Internet. An intranet allows enterprise users to share information resources and services like printing. Even when it is connected to the Internet, an intranet is not usually accessible from outside the enterprise.

IP Internet Protocol. See TCP/IP.

IP address The unique numerical identifier of a computer on a TCP/IP network. The IP address is a series of four groups of numbers, from 1 to 255, separated by periods (e.g., 192.168.22.34).

IP telephony The use of IP networks as a carrier medium for voice and other telephonic communication.

IS Information services. See IT.

ISP Internet service provider. A company that provides subscribers with Internet access and connectivity services. Many ISPs offer additional related services, like Web hosting and IP telephony.

IT Strictly, information technology. In the enterprise context, IT is the management of computer, information processing, and network systems and assets. For example, the IT department is responsible for the maintenance and operation of a company's computers.

Kereitsu The Japanese term for a vast, horizontally integrated corporate network. A *kereitsu* is typically a self-contained industrial federation anchored by a mega-corporation that manufactures everything from automobile exhaust manifolds to computer games and which, by virtue of its integration, can be totally self-reliant in all manufacturing, distribution, and commercial operations.

Killer app An application or product which, by virtue of its innovative nature and utility, dominates its class and defines all subsequent products. The Mosaic browser was the original killer app of the World Wide Web.

Knowledge management Similar to information management, KM is the application of an enterprise's information and data processing resources to produce actionable intelligence.

Knowledge worker Anyone who works in any discipline concerned with the accumulation, organization, or dissemination of information and intelligence. A company's researchers, librarians, and corporate communications representatives are all knowledge workers.

LAN Local area network. An internal network at a single location like an office or campus providing users with access to shared services like file and print sharing. Unlike an intranet, a LAN is not necessarily a TCP/IP-based network. All intranets are LANs, but not all LANs are intranets.

LDAP Lightweight Directory Access Protocol. The protocol that permits the sharing of PKI digital certificates between certificate authorities and between enterprises.

Legacy system An older computer system, typically a mainframe, that runs mission-critical applications or hosts mission-critical data and which, consequently, has not been replaced, despite its age.

Logistics The organized movement of material in the supply chain. In electronic commerce, logistics is concerned with all products, assets, and resources that cannot be transmitted electronically over a network.

M-commerce Electronic commerce services delivered to wireless mobile devices like cellular telephones and handheld computers.

Mainframe A powerful, centralized computer system capable of running applications for multiple simultaneous users. Mainframes are designed to be extremely robust and secure.

Merchant server World Wide Web server software with electronic commerce features, like transaction processing functions, security and authentication, catalogs, etc.

Metadata Literally "data about data," metadata describes the content of a message or document.

Natural language search A search performed by phrasing a query in a normal human language like English or French. A database or search engine with natural language capability is able to provide meaningful search results to queries like "Who is our biggest competitor in the Canadian market?"

NC Network computer. A stripped-down computer system with limited or no local storage, designed to access IP networks like the Internet and run server-hosted applications.

OBI Open buying on the Internet. A standard for low-cost, high-volume, catalog-based procurement over the Internet.

ODBC Open database connectivity. An interface standard for accessing database information in other applications. An ODBC-compliant CRM system, for example, is able to make direct queries to an ODBC-compliant database.

OLAP On-line analytical processing. A category of software that lets users perform complex, multidimensional analyses on diverse data sets. OLAP software can be used to find trends and patterns in immense data warehouses.

OS Operating system. The software that controls a computer's basic processes and permits it to run application software.

Packet-switching A communications model in which transmissions are divided into smaller pieces (packets) and then individually routed along the most expedient network route at the time. Packet-switching only uses network capacity for short bursts, making it ideal for data communications. Moreover, because packet-switched communications select the most expedient network route as needed, it can adapt to changes in network topology and outages.

PBX Private branch exchange. An organization's or enterprise's private, local telephone network.

Peer-to-peer A network architecture model where each system on the network is equal and may be a client or server to any other system on the network, as required.

PGP Pretty good privacy. The public key cryptography software developed by Richard Zimmermann. "Pretty Good Privacy" is available as both open source and proprietary commercial software.

PIP Partner interface process. The basic transaction definitions in the RosettaNet XML framework.

Plug-in An auxiliary program that adds more functionality to a Web browser, like Netscape Communicator and Microsoft Internet Explorer, or to a server.

POTS Plain-old telephone service. Network services carried on the PSTN.

PSTN Public switched telephone network. The network that carries basic voice telephone traffic.

Public key cryptography An encryption method that uses two keys — one publicly known and one private — to encrypt a message. A sender uses his private key and his recipient's public key to encipher the message, which can only then be decoded using the intended recipient's private key and the sender's public key. Public key cryptography is the strongest encryption system in common use.

Public key infrastructure A system that uses public key cryptography and digital certificates to verify and authenticate users and control their access to information or parts of a network.

Push A technology that broadcasts Web-type content, applications, and data to a large number of subscribers over a network simultaneously.

Router A system or network device that connects one network (e.g., a LAN) with another (e.g., the Internet). See Gateway.

Schema The vocabulary of meta-tags for an application of XML. Each industry vertical implementation of XML has its own schema.

Screen scraping A technology that presents the character-based interface of legacy mainframe systems in a browser window.

Server Computer software, and the system that runs it, that provides a service to other computers over a network.

Server farm A company that provides outsourced Web hosting services to a large number of business clients.

SET Secure Electronic Transactions. A PKI security protocol developed under the aegis of MasterCard Corp. and Visa International. SET provides for encrypted credit card transactions and the authentication of both buyer and seller. The SET 1.0 specification was published in 1997, but it has yet to see wide deployment.

Smart card A plastic card, similar in appearance to a credit card, with an embedded microchip and memory. Smart cards can store digital certificates to be used as network and physical access tokens.

Sneakernet Computer slang for physically transporting digital data on a removable medium like a floppy diskette from one location to another.

SOHO Small office/home office. A small, typically one-person, business operated from a home office.

Spider A program that automatically retrieves Web pages and all the Web pages it links to. Spiders are used to create database catalogs for on-line search engines.

SQL Structured query language. A query language used to search databases.

SSL Secure Sockets Layer. A transaction security protocol developed by Netscape Communications Corp. for Web-based electronic commerce. SSL uses both public and private key cryptography to authenticate an electronic commerce client and to encrypt the transfer of the client's transaction information.

Symmetrical key encryption An encryption technique in which a single cryptographic key is used to encrypt and decrypt data. See public key cryptography.

TCP/IP Transmission control protocol/Internet protocol. The basic technological rules according to which data travel on the Internet and related networks.

TCP/IP provides a common format for data "packets" and allows for the inter-connection — the "internetworking" — of disparate networks.

Telco A telecommunications company. Carriers like Bell Canada and AT&T are telcos.

Trunk line A dedicated communications connection between two points.

VAN Value-added network. A private, secure network maintained and operated by a telecommunications carrier or network services provider that can be accessed only by subscribers.

Vaporware A product or technology loudly promoted and hyped by a vendor and/or the press that is either never released or turns out to be a massive disappointment. Digital cash is an example of vaporware.

VoIP Voice over IP. See IP telephony.

VPN Virtual private network. A security technology that encrypts outgoing transmissions and decrypts incoming data to provide a secure connection through an otherwise insecure network like the Internet. VPNs are typically much less expensive to maintain than traditional private networks.

Wa Literally "harmony," *wa* is the Japanese conception of a mutually supporting commercial community. Often equated with *inhwa* in Korea and *guanxi* in China, it does not normally carry the latter's suggestion of cronyism.

WAN Wide-area network. An enterprise network that extends beyond the immediate enterprise premises. A WAN will usually consist of a number of LANs in geographically diverse locations, connected over the public Internet.

WAP Wireless application protocol. A networking protocol that allows hand-held wireless devices like mobile telephones and palmtop computers to receive Web content.

XML Extensible markup language. A language, similar to HTML, which permits the creation of self-describing electronic documents. Unlike EDI, a message in an XML-based transaction does not have to be formatted in a specific structure because it contains metatext that describes the content and explains how it should be interpreted.

RESOURCES

FEDERAL GOVERNMENT
Bureau of Economic Analysis
The Department of Commerce's research arm, the BEA provides on-line access to some — though by no means all — of its reports and analyses.
www.bea.doc.gov

Federal Trade Commission
Information of use for electronic commerce, regarding policy on privacy, legal issues, consumer protection, news of formal actions, studies, and policy papers.
www.ftc.gov

FedWorld Information Network
A portal to federal government sites and information, featuring a searchable index and browsable directory.
www.fedworld.gov

Department of Commerce Export Portal
Contains information on doing business outside the United States, in particular the new Safe Harbor agreement between the United States and EU regarding data privacy. Explains how to apply for Safe Harbor certification, which can be done directly on the Web site.
www.export.gov/safeharbor

United States Government E-Commerce Policy
Everything you need to know about the federal e-commerce policy — documents, policy papers, links, statements, press releases.
www.ecommerce.gov

INDUSTRY ASSOCIATIONS AND CONSORTIA

Better Business Bureau

The BBB's Web site is aimed at informing businesses about privacy, including its own on-line privacy program and reliability program. Businesses can apply on-line and receive the certification if they meet the BBB criteria.

www.bbbonline.org

CommerceNet

Based in Silicon Valley, founded in 1994. A nonprofit association of companies seeking to promote electronic commerce and involved in a number of projects on interoperability. The Web site contains news, research, and links. Some of the research reports are for members only.

www.commerce.net

Computer and Communications Industry Association (CCIA)

An international nonprofit organization of communications firms, based in Washington, D.C. The Web site has valuable information on electronic commerce and public policy, including reports which can be downloaded for free.

www.ccianet.org

Council of Logistics Management

For logistics professionals, aimed at helping improve logistics management skills, with workshops, educational incentives, training programs, and scholarships.

www.CLM1.org

Global Business Dialogue on Electronic Commerce

The GBDe is made up of CEOs from 60 member corporations worldwide. The objective is to provide a working dialogue that will lead to the standardization and harmonization of international electronic commerce.

www.gbc.org

National Association of Purchasing Management

Founded in 1915, the NAPM's mandate is to educate and advance the purchasing and supply chain professional. The Web site contains information on membership, as well as publications and educational materials.

www.napm.org

Supply Chain Council

Formed in 1996, the Supply Chain Council provides members with opportunities to improve supply chain efficiency, with workshops, conferences, and executive retreats. Chapters in both the United States and overseas.

www.supply-chain.org

INFORMATION PORTALS

ASCET Project (Achieving Supply Chain excellence through technology)

Information portal with library of research and articles on all aspects of supply chain management in the e-commerce age. White papers by industry gurus, academics, end users, as well as case studies.

www.ascet.com/ascet2

B2B Now

A search engine/portal/business directory focusing on B2B. Business directory, news, articles, white papers, and company profiles.

www.b2bnow.com

B2BiNetwork

A portal for small enterprises involved in, or interested in, business-to-business electronic commerce. The site includes news, business and financial services, and a directory of small e-businesses.

www.b2binetwork.com

B2Business.net

Portal aimed at B2B professionals. A comprehensive site with resources on e-marketplaces, company research, startups, and infrastructure.

www.b2business.net

BRINT

An information portal for business, knowledge management, and IT. News, articles, search engine, free e-mail subscriptions. A comprehensive site with vast amounts of information on business, technology, and e-commerce.

www.brint.com

CRM Daily.com

On-line news portal for CRM professionals. Comprehensive and constantly updated with headline news on technology, back office integration, and e-tailing.

www.crmdaily.com

Crypto.com

An information and news page about security, privacy, and cryptography, with papers, articles, research, and news.

www.crypto.com

E-Commerce Info Centre

An e-commerce portal with resources on technologies, products, government, and international issues, B2B, and small business. A search engine will call up dozens of articles.

www.ecominfocentre.com

E-Commerce Times

Comprehensive on-line news portal with headline news on all aspects of e-commerce, privacy, technology, research, international e-commerce, special reports, and small business news.

www.ecommercetimes.com

eMarketer

Information portal specializing in Internet and e-commerce statistics. Content is updated almost daily, with news on all aspects of Internet commerce. Research reports can be ordered on-line, and there are free newsletters available by e-mail. Excellent site for statistics.

www.emarketer.com

GInfo B2B Global 1000 directory

Directory and search engine for global e-business. Comprehensive, with listings also available by country.

www.ginfo.net/indexg.asp

Individual.com

On-line news service where you can personalize your topics and read new stories every weekday. Topics include IT management, e-commerce, analyst reports, industry news, marketing news. Subscription and registration required but free.

www.individual.com

International Business Guide

An on-line guide to the Web's most important business sites. The International Business Guide categorizes information providers, portals, and vendor sites, providing incisive commentary on the value and content of each.

web.idirect.com/~tiger/supersit.htm

Internet.com

News portal with articles and headlines on Internet commerce, technology, marketing, investing, and Web development. Updated constantly.

www.internet.com

netmarketmakers.com

A magazine and information portal for e-marketplace builders, netmarket-makers.com offers a wide range of information services, including newsletters, technology tutorials and a searchable database of 4,000 e-marketplace providers, vendors, and consultants.

www.netmarketmakers.com

Markets and Exchanges

A marketplace of marketplaces. Marketplaces and Exchanges is a portal for e-business people looking for a community to trade in, or for information on how to set up their own exchange. The site features searchable databases, newsletters, and original editorial content on a wide range of e-business issues.

www.marketsandexchanges.com

ZDNet E-commerce

Part of ZD Net's publication portal. News, articles, research, downloads, advice, case studies, and reports. Specialized newsletters are available for free by e-mail.

www.zdnet.com/enterprise/e-business

INTERNATIONAL ORGANIZATIONS

Organization for Economic Cooperation and Development (OECD)

An organization of 29 member countries, based in Paris. International forum with committees on law and policy, e-commerce, trade, and development among others, including electronic commerce. The Web site contains news, publications, and papers, statistics. The documentation library is extensive.

www.oecd.org

United Nations Centre for Trade Facilitation and Electronic Business

UN/CEFACT's goal is "to improve the ability of business, trade and administrative organizations, from developed, developing, and transitional economies, to exchange products and relevant services effectively — and so contribute to the growth of global commerce." The body's working groups make recommendations to the International Standards Organization and other UN organizations. In addition to supporting initiatives in EDI harmonization and XML development, UN/CEFACT provides a searchable database of international trade documents and standards.

www.unece.org/cefact

Legal Information

ABA Business Law: Committee on Cyberspace Law

The American Bar Association (ABA) provides valuable legal information on business law — privacy, taxation, jurisdiction, encryption, and digital signatures. The site contains articles, studies, and surveys, as well as a listserv.

www.abanet.org/buslaw/cyber/home.html

Professional Associations

Computing Technology Industry Association (COMPTIA)

With offices in the United States, Canada, Europe, Asia, and South Africa, COMPTIA represents nearly 8,000 companies. Its mandate is to provide vendor-neutral standards and guidelines for e-commerce, certification, work-force development, and customer service.

www.comptia.org

Institute for Operations Research and the Management Sciences

Serving the needs of operations research and management science researchers, educators, and managers, INFORMS provides educational and information services to its 12,000 members, including a searchable database and discussion forums. Though OR/MS is not specifically electronic-commerce-related, INFORMS has begun to focus on the field as it has grown over the years.

www.informs.org

Internet Society

Created in 1992 by some of the Internet's most distinguished pioneers, the society's stated mission is "to assure the open development, evolution, and use of the Internet for the benefit of all people throughout the world." To do this, it provides resources for Internet standards groups like the IETF and IESG, promotes communications and discussion through its annual Inet conferences, fosters international cooperation on high-level Internet issues through chapters in most of the major cities in the world, and provides educational planning and resources to develop networking skills in the developing world. The society also provides a wide range of documentation of the current state and history of the Internet on its Web site.

www.isoc.org

PUBLICATIONS AND NEWS SERVICES

BizReport.com

On-line news service, with daily headlines, research, and features on Internet commerce and e-business.

www.bizreport.com

Business 2.0

Both an on-line and print magazine for professionals who want to be in the know about the new economy. Articles on e-business, investing, technology marketing, as well as research, newsletters, and on-line forums.

www.business2.com

Business Week Ebiz

The on-line counterpart of the venerable business magazine. *Business Week*'s Ebiz section focuses on electronic commerce, technology, news stories, analysis, columns, and features.

www.businessweek.com/ebiz

CIO Magazine

One of the leading magazines for information executives, available on-line and in print. The Web site includes research centers with articles and reports on various aspects of Internet commerce, including CRM, IT staffing, knowledge management, ERP, and so on.

www.cio.com

E-Business Advisor

On-line version of the publication, part of the Advisor.com portal. Features insightful articles on all aspects of electronic commerce. Not all of the print articles are available on the Web site. Subscriptions available.

www.advisor.com

E-Com world

Faulkner and Gray's e-commerce magazine for professionals. Articles on telecom, procurement, and supply chain, among others. Available in print by subscription.

www.ecomworld.com

E-Commerce Management

A free monthly e-zine focusing on electronic commerce management issues. Articles on trends, marketing, strategy, and developments.

www.ecmgt.com

Ebiz Chronicle

On-line e-business magazine. Headline news and articles about e-commerce, both B2B and B2C.

www.ebizchronicle.com

E-Commerce Business Daily

Updated daily, Ecommerce Business Daily is the on-line counterpart of *Ecommerce Business* magazine. The site provides breaking e-business news, access to research and some content from its sister print publication.

www.ecommercebusinessdaily.com

eCompany Now

The Internet equivalent of *eCompany Now* magazine, this site provides all of the content of the print publication with daily electronic commerce news and e-business resources.

www.ecompanynow.com

Infoworld

An on-line daily news service and weekly print magazine. In-depth news on technology aimed at professionals and buyers.

www.infoworld.com

InternetWeek

A general Internet and networking trade magazine, *InternetWeek* covers electronic commerce from a staunchly IT-oriented angle. Its reporting places much more emphasis on technological and technical news and information than on management issues.

www.internetwk.com

Journal of Commerce Online

On-line news service for transportation and business professionals — news on logistics, e-commerce, freight, and transportation, as well as analysis and updated headline news.

www.joc.com

Line56

The on-line sister publication of *Line56* magazine, this site provides access to daily news and selected content from the print version. Its focus is emphatically on business-to-business electronic commerce and offers users access to a directory of business-to-business companies, financial and investment information, and research

www.line56.com

Logistics Management

A monthly publication for supply chain and logistics professionals, on-line and in print. Subscriptions are free to professionals in the United States and Canada.
www.manufacturing.net/magazine/logistic/main.html

netmarketmakers.com

A magazine and information portal for e-marketplace builders, netmarketmakers.com offers a wide range of information services, including newsletters, technology tutorials, and a searchable database of 4,000 e-marketplace providers, vendors, and consultants.
www.netmarketmakers.com

Network World

A networking and Internetworking trade magazine, *Network World's* primary focus is the nuts and bolts of the Internet. Nevertheless, it provides on-going coverage of electronic commerce issues from a technical angle.
www.nwfusion.com

The Standard

The on-line sister publication of *The Industry Standard,* The Standard lives up to its mission of providing "intelligence for the information economy." Daily news articles are supplemented by feature articles, research and metrics, and a truly bewildering array of e-business resources.
www.thestandard.com

RESEARCH CENTERS

Carnegie Mellon Institute for eCommerce

A joint venture of CMU's Graduate School of Industrial Administration and the School of Computer Science, the institute's mission is to be a "focal point" for education and research into electronic commerce at the university.
www.ecom.cmu.edu

Center for eBusiness @MIT
A research center of the MIT Sloan School of Management, the center focuses on multidisciplinary research into electronic commerce.
Ebusiness.mit.edu

Center for Research in Electronic Commerce
Based at the University of Texas in Austin, the center's Web site contains valuable research and links to articles, journals, papers, reports, publications, and books, all relating to electronic commerce.
cism.bus.utexas.edu/main4.html

iXL Center of Electronic Commerce
Established in 1999 at Georgia Institute of Technology's Dupree College of Management, the center sponsors research into electronic commerce.
www.dupree.gatech.edu/centers/centers_ixl.shtml

Supply Chain Management Research Group
Part of the Fisher School of Business at Ohio State University, the Web site has valuable resources, including research articles written by the group. Also includes links to other logistics and supply chain links.
fisher.osu.edu/scmrg

STANDARDS BODIES
American National Standards Institute
Founded in 1918, ANSI administers and coordinates voluntary standardization in the United States and, by extension, in much of the rest of the world. Most importantly for electronic commerce, ANSI administers the X12 EDI standard. In addition to developing and ratifying private sector standards, ANSI provides complete documentation and standards guides.
www.ansi.org

Data Interchange Standards Association

The mother of all EDI user groups in the United States, DISA promotes a free exchange of information and ideas about the deployment, use, development, and evolution of EDI and related technologies through its newsletter, e-mail list, and annual conferences.

www.disa.org

Internet Engineering Task Force

Dating to the earliest days of the Internet, the IETF is the principal Internet standards body. Its membership is open to any interested individual — it has no dues or membership requirements. Technical work is done by working groups subdivided in "areas," and all area directors are members of the Internet Engineering Steering Group. Standards are developed through a rigorous peer review process and are published at each stage as "request for comment" (RFC) papers. The IETF maintains a publicly accessible and searchable database of RFCs that go back to the very beginnings of the Internet.

www.ietf.org

United Nations Trade Data Interchange Directory

The UNTDID is the principal information directory for the UN/EDIFACT EDI standard. In addition to providing directories for each sub-standard of UN/EDIFACT, UNTDID maintains a complete glossary of EDI technical terms.

www.unece.org/trade/untdid

World Wide Web Consortium (W3C)

Founded in 1994, the W3C is a nonprofit organization that promotes Web interoperability by establishing common technological standards and technical specifications. The consortium has over 400 member organizations, including almost every significant Internet and electronic commerce company. The W3C's advisory committee is made up of one representative for each member organization. The W3C's publicly accessible publications include complete specifications for current and pending Web standards.

www.w3.org

INDEX